NOBODY WALKS

Bringing My Brother's Killers to Justice

Dennis M. Walsh

THOMAS DUNNE BOOKS
St. Martin's Press
New York

THOMAS DUNNE BOOKS.
An imprint of St. Martin's Press.

www.thomasdunnebooks.com
www.stmartins.com

ISBN 978-1-250-00548-9 (hardcover)
ISBN 978-1-250-02112-0 (e-book)

First Edition: February 2013

10 9 8 7 6 5 4 3 2 1

This book is dedicated with love and gratitude to my family, especially to my brother Christopher's children, my nephew Shane and niece Ashley, as well as to everyone who has suffered the heartache of having a family member or close friend murdered. Every single life has meaning. No one should be entitled to take a life, for when they do they steal not only all the hopes and dreams of their victim, but also part of the hearts of family and friends. For all of those who bear that unrelenting pain, I cannot offer comfort, only a shared camaraderie.

AUTHOR'S NOTE

This is the true story of my brother's murder and of the apprehension and conviction of those responsible. As recounted, in the course of the murder investigation many witnesses came forward or were identified as having information potentially pertinent to the investigation. And many among the book's colorful cast of characters, whether they were witnesses or not, did have records of past criminal or other questionable activity. But others named in the book were not criminals, and were not witnesses to, or in any way implicated in, the murder. They were simply caught up in the unfolding events or they were associated in some way with me or with my family or friends. In naming all of these persons as a part of my story, it is not my intention to suggest or imply any guilt by association.

NOBODY
WALKS

PROLOGUE

Sometimes life deals a hand you may not be prepared to play. When my younger brother was murdered, it quickly became obvious that many potential witnesses were either afraid to cooperate with the police or didn't want to be considered rats, or both. My brother's murder was not about to become a cold case, not if I could help it. This was a hand I thought I could play. I was better equipped than most people to hit the streets to try to convince the dopers, thieves, prostitutes, porn stars, and jailbirds that populated my brother's world to come forward. My father had been a detective with the Cleveland Police Department, but traded that life for a life of crime. I grew up under his tutelage, exposed to the likes of Julius Petro, Ray Ferritto, Frank "Skinny" Velotta, and Jimmy "the Weasel" Fratianno, among numerous other organized crime figures. Our Irish-Catholic heritage made my four brothers and me no strangers to bare-knuckled brawls. I may have been the lone brother who hadn't done time in jail, but I had no problem slinking into the sordid crystal meth underworld of the San Fernando Valley. I had the street smarts to speak to the denizens of that universe without a trace of fear in my voice, in a tone and in a manner that got results.

To round it out, I was a criminal defense attorney. I knew the law and knew how far I could push the envelope, or so I thought. I did not write this story to promote vigilante law or to encourage crime victims to take the law into their own hands. By getting involved in a criminal investigation, you walk into a minefield. Aside from putting your own life in danger, you also run the distinct risk of jeopardizing the prosecution's case. I had spoken with many witnesses. I would ultimately be put on trial, accused of threatening and intimidating those same witnesses. It's not an easy thing to live with—the fact that something you did or said might lead to freeing the people who murdered your brother. I do not recommend that anyone follow in my footsteps. My story is an isolated instance, where my instincts and particular background allowed me to do what I really had no choice but to do. It could, however, very easily have gone the other way—very easily.

Nobody Walks is the true story of how I avenged the murder of my youngest brother, Christopher. In 2003, he was found shot five times in the head and neck, stuffed headfirst in a trash barrel, and hidden in a storage locker in Van Nuys, California. Staying on the right side of the law to assist law enforcement officials in hunting down his killers and putting them away for life would result in the arrest of over one hundred people and test every commitment I'd ever made, to myself and to my family. This is the story of how it played out.

THE LOSS

1

DO WHAT YOU THINK YOU'RE
BIG ENOUGH TO DO

MY FATHER ONCE TOLD ME, "Do what you think you're big enough to do." Not particularly profound, but certainly practical advice. I don't recall the particular circumstance that warranted this admonition, only that his father had imparted the same bit of wisdom to him after he had forged his birth certificate and enlisted in the navy during World War II at the tender age of fifteen. When I joined the navy in 1972, he told me his father had driven him to the train station in silence, put him on the train, handed him a five-dollar bill and tersely advised him, "Keep your eyes open, your mouth shut, and your dick in your pants." He was not inclined toward much heart-to-heart conversation.

My grandfather had been a boyhood friend of Bob Hope in Cleveland and served as Hope's boxing manager. The famed comedian fought under the name of Packy East, but after getting knocked cold by a fighter out of Cincinnati named Happy Walsh, decided to pursue a career in show business. My grandfather went on to play semi-pro baseball and football in the 1920s and was signed by the Boston Red Sox, but shattered his shoulder playing football in the winter, ending his hopes of playing major league baseball. He returned to Cleveland and became a clerk of the Cuyahoga County Common Pleas Court. He proceeded to drown his sorrow in alcohol with such fervor that my grandmother eventually fled, leaving him with four children. She was never to be heard from again.

My father, Robert Emmett Walsh, survived a kamikaze attack on the USS *Nashville,* returned home after the war, and joined the Cleveland Police Department. Shortly thereafter, he met Kathleen McFaul, a strawberry blonde who was babysitting for her aunt. He and a friend were picking up her cousin and several other girls for an evening at the movies. She had hardly paid him any attention.

As he was leaving, he leaned over and boldly informed her, "Oh, by the way, I'm going to marry you."

She watched from the porch while the others sped away in a 1942 Packard convertible.

Well, now, isn't he full of himself? she thought.

They were married in August 1951. I was born on December 18, 1952. My grandfather died three years later. My father worked his way up in the police department from patrolman to detective. He was making about forty-five hundred dollars a year, roughly "eighty-six bucks and change a week," he would say. Apparently, this was not nearly enough to support a growing family. He left the Cleveland Police Department in early 1957 to pursue what he thought might be a more lucrative venture: a life of crime.

By 1966, our family had grown. I was the oldest of seven children, five boys and two girls. A pretty much typical Irish-Catholic family, or at least we seemed so. As was the custom with second generation Irish-Americans, my parents gave their first six children Irish names: Dennis Michael, Timothy Robert, Kathleen Mary, Daniel Patrick, Laura Kelly, and Robert Emmett, Jr. Then, oddly enough, in September of 1965 they broke tradition and christened the last addition to our family Christopher John, a traditional English name. Being the youngest of five brothers, Christopher came to be called Finnegan, Finny, or Fin—a slang term for "five." I, on the other hand, always referred to him as Christopher. At his baptism at Saint Paschal Baylon Church in Highland Heights, I stood up as his godfather. I'm not sure whether my parents thought me to be particularly responsible at the age of twelve or whether I was the only family member who had a clean suit at the time.

In the meantime, my father's criminal endeavors had steadily increased. He and his crew had been hacking through roofs in the dead of night and blowtorching bank vaults for a few years. They always managed to exit in time, thanks to a police radio supplied by a friend of his still on the Cleveland PD, in exchange for a cut of the score.

I got a hint about my father's line of work at about nine or ten years of age, when I innocently ventured into the garage, where he and his cohorts were busy torching a safe. I'd later learn that they would practice on dummy safes before the real heist, so there's no telling if this was a hot one or not, but I knew enough to follow orders when my father yanked up his welding mask and sharply ordered me to get the hell out of there.

I scooted back into the house, where my mother was preparing dinner. *Supper,* as she called it.

"Hey, hey, don't go out there, your father's working," she cautioned.

This was the first time I realized that my old man wasn't an insurance salesman or anything else of the kind.

Early in 1966, an FBI agent roused one of my father's confederates, Frank "Skinny" Velotta, out of bed and warned him that J. Edgar Hoover himself had sent word that if one more bank got burglarized in northeastern Ohio, Frank, my father, and Ray Ferritto would go down for it, whether they did it or not. The federal agent's threat of recrimination did *not* fall on deaf ears. The next we knew, we were pulling up stakes.

It was the morning of July 5, 1966. My brother Tim and I were ordered to clean out the garage and burn whatever wasn't going with us in a rusted trash barrel in the backyard. In one box, I fished out my father's detective journal and flipped to December 18, 1952, the day I was born. In big bold black letters, his notation read, *8:18 A.M. FIRST SON BORN!!!* I tried to ask the old man if I could keep the journal, but he cut me short.

"Goddamn it. I told you to burn all that shit. Hurry up, we don't have all day."

I tossed the journal into the fire. You didn't argue with the old man.

As flames leaped from the makeshift incinerator, my parents packed themselves and their seven wide-eyed children into a wood-paneled Ford station wagon, hitting the road for sunny Southern California.

My siblings and I had no idea that we had been run out of town. Instead, the old man had been hyping the wonders of California for weeks.

"You loogans can pick oranges and grapefruits off trees in your own front yard out there," he crowed.

My father routinely referred to his brood as loogans or loogan heads. *Loogan* was an Irish slang term for "misfits."

"You loogan heads can swim in the ocean in the morning and then ski in the mountains in the afternoon."

We were nothing less than astonished at the thought. Tim and I nearly wore out our two favorite 45 rpm records, "California Dreamin'" and "California Girls."

The cross-country trip proved to be quite an adventure. Our large family coupled with my father's line of work hadn't allowed for many family vacations. With one hand on the wheel and his right arm draped across the back of the front seat, the old man worked us like a carnival barker, whetting our appetite for the upcoming sights.

"Fifty miles to the Big Muddy, the Mississippi River. Wait till you loogans see the Gateway Arch in Saint Looey.

"Now we're gonna be crossing the Rocky Mountains. You hooligans are gonna see snow in the middle of July.

"Pretty soon we're gonna cross the Bonneville Salt Flats. Any of you loogan heads ever see a whole desert made of salt? Keep your eyes peeled."

We hit all the tourist spots as we zoomed westward on Route 66, "the Mother Road" as Steinbeck had dubbed it. We crammed into two motel rooms each night.

Eventually we crossed the California border and made our way to our destination, the San Fernando Valley. It was a warm, balmy July evening. We marveled at the mountains that ringed the Valley, and the stately palm trees that seemed to have popped out of nowhere. As our packed station wagon motored down Ventura Boulevard, we craned our necks, hoping to spot a movie star.

"Don't worry, they're all over the place," the old man had promised.

We turned north onto Sepulveda Boulevard. After a few blocks, my father eased the station wagon into the parking lot of the 777 Motor Inn in Sherman Oaks. We got two rooms as usual and got ready for bed. My father left and came back shortly with two large boxes loaded with cartons of Chinese food. He took great delight by having each kid read the fortune cookie messages out loud. He read for the younger ones, Laura and Bobby, and teased us about our various fortunes. I don't know that our family was ever as happy together as we were that night.

We had no idea what lay ahead of us in California, but we were all excited to be there.

How were we to know it would all go wrong?

Fast-forward thirty-seven years, to late June 2003. I'm an attorney, a sole practitioner, living about sixty miles north of Los Angeles in a quiet little rural town in the Angeles National Forest. My youngest brother, Christopher, had been missing for maybe seven or eight days. He, his two children, and I were the only family members still living in California. My brother Tim and sister Kathy are living in Vegas. My brother Dan and his wife and kids live in Phoenix, around the corner from my mother and sister Laura. My father and my brother Bobby are doing a stretch in federal prison due to a major cocaine deal that went south in 2000.

All week long, I'd been telling my other brothers not to worry.

"The kid'll show up sooner or later. He's probably on a bender somewhere."

Even though he was thirty-seven years old, I still referred to Christopher as the kid. I hadn't seen or spoken to him for at least a year since he was behind glass in the prisoner lockup at the San Fernando Courthouse, begging me to bail him out on a drug-possession charge. Although it was not that unusual for me to be speaking with family members behind glass, I lit into him, telling him he was a poor excuse for a father.

Christopher remained calm. Probably since I hadn't yet agreed to post his bail. He sighed and leaned toward the glass. "Dennis, don't talk to me like that in front of these guys," he said.

Before I could reply, one burly inmate, a heavily tattooed skinhead, took exception to my comments. "Dude, you don't have to take that shit from this dump truck. You ought to report his ass to the state bar," he said.

I not only resented the inmate butting into our conversation, but also took exception to being referred to as a *dump truck,* jailhouse slang used to describe attorneys who pleaded out cases rather than took them to trial.

"Mind your own fucking business, asshole," I fired back.

Christopher rolled his eyes and whispered, "You're killing me here, Dennis.

"Don't trip on it, he's my brother," Christopher told his cell mate, causing him to shrug and shift his concern to a half-eaten bologna sandwich.

I wavered over posting bail. I thought he deserved a few days in the slam, but leaving him with these losers didn't exactly feel right.

Holding up his soggy sandwich, he pleaded, "Come on, man, I can't eat this shit. I gotta get outta here."

"All right," I said, agreeing to post the required 10 percent for his release. "But from now on, you're on your own. Get yourself a public defender, pay back my five hundred bucks, and lose my phone number."

I was thoroughly fed up with Christopher and his lifestyle. I was aware he was abusing drugs, but didn't realize that he was seriously addicted to crystal methamphetamine. Known as *ice* or *glass* on the streets, it was highly addictive. Meth users, known as *tweakers,* craved the immediate burst of energy followed by a state of acute alertness coupled with euphoria and increased self-esteem. Tweakers would be spun out for days on end, finally crashing for several days only to awaken in a state of paranoia and delusion. The drug had exploded onto the scene in the Valley in the '90s. Still, I hadn't fully appreciated the horrors attendant to its use. Not yet, anyway.

Christopher thanked me for posting his bail. By the way he hung his head, I could tell he was embarrassed to have to ask the favor. I quickly got up and left, pretty much writing off both him and my five hundred dollars.

I didn't know it then, but that was the last time I'd ever speak with my youngest brother.

When Christopher went missing that week in June of 2003, my brother Dan was sure something was wrong. Christopher had been in the habit of calling him at least once a week. It wasn't until Sunday afternoon, the twenty-ninth of June, during softball practice at Hjelte Park in Encino, that I became concerned. Johnny Rio, my Akita–wolf hybrid, was with me as usual. As I was tying his leash to the fence along the third base line, I was overcome with an eerie sense of foreboding.

"Something's not right," I said, turning to one of my teammates. "My kid brother's been missing for about a week. I'm starting to get worried."

"He's probably holed up in an air-conditioned motel somewhere with a couple of broads while you're out here sweating your nuts off," he said.

"Yeah, that would be him all right," I said as I laced up my cleats.

I trotted out to the infield but did not feel all that relieved. I had been taught to trust my instincts, and right now they were telling me something was wrong.

Three days later, Christopher's decomposed, bullet-riddled body was recovered, sealed inside a trash barrel in a storage facility in Van Nuys, less than two miles from where I'd been mindlessly fielding ground balls.

It was Wednesday morning, July 2, when my brother Dan called. I was driving northbound on Interstate 5 in Santa Clarita.

"I've got a bad feeling they just found Chris's body in a storage unit in Van Nuys," he said. "You need to head down there right away, Dennis."

My sister Laura had received a call from Debbie Wilcox, a friend of Christopher's. A woman named Carolyn Vasquez had noticed a foul odor coming from a sealed barrel in her storage unit and suspected the worst. Laura immediately called the LAPD Devonshire detectives who were handling Christopher's missing-person case.

I scribbled down the address, *15500 Erwin St., Van Nuys*. It was the first of hundreds of notes I would eventually compile in haphazard fashion while trying to determine what had happened.

I could hardly speak.

"I'll call you when I get there," I said curtly, and hung up.

I pulled off the highway and stopped on the side of the road for a minute. My insides felt like they were clamped in a vise. I couldn't remember the last time I had cried or prayed. I pleaded with God to please, please not let it be my brother. I wanted it not to be true more than I had ever wanted anything in my life.

My father was serving his sentence at the Federal Medical Center in Rochester, Minnesota. He had undergone a quadruple bypass and suffered from severe coronary disease. His cardiologist had declared his condition terminal. I'd been trying to obtain a compassionate release so he could die at home, but that endeavor did not appear very promising. That situation was stressful enough. Now my kid brother might be dead. A wave of nausea surged throughout my body in a visceral, gut-wrenching sensation.

I took a deep breath and looked in the rearview mirror. In that split second, I realized my life had changed, and changed forever. I knew without knowing that it would be my brother's body in that barrel, and all the prayer in the world was not going to change that fact.

I proceeded south on the 5 to the 405, doing well over the speed limit. It wasn't long before my grief turned to rage. I wondered what son of a bitch could have done this to my brother. I tried maneuvering into the fast lane. A frail, elderly woman in a '60s mint-condition Lincoln Continental leisurely cut me off without bothering to signal. I narrowly missed slamming into her. A mere fifteen minutes ago, I would have dismissed the act as simple carelessness. Now I was overcome with a blind hatred for an unknown killer. I stomped on the accelerator and sped past her car, mouthing a few choice epithets in her direction. Though it was the dead of summer, she was curiously dressed in a black hat and veil, with a fox stole wrapped around her neck. I could hardly believe my eyes when she flipped me the bird. It was like being flipped off by your grandmother. Her reaction seemed so utterly incongruous with her age and her strange attire that I couldn't help but laugh.

It would be a long while before I laughed again.

Within minutes, it was Christopher I was cursing, for having descended into that hellhole of a life.

Although it seemed like an eternity before I arrived at the Sherman Oaks MiniStorage, it had been only about twenty-five minutes. The facility was cordoned off with yellow crime-scene tape. The parking lot and street were teeming with uniformed police officers, detectives, motorcycle cops, black-and-white cruisers, and TV news vans. Local news and police helicopters circled overhead. The scene was strangely surreal. Everything seemed to be moving in slow motion.

I parked down the street and walked over to the yellow ribbon. I motioned to a uniformed motorcycle officer.

"My name is Dennis Walsh. I think that may be my brother's body in there," I barely managed to say with a lump in my throat.

I handed him my business card. He glanced at the card and looked back at me suspiciously but said nothing. The last thing I looked like was an attorney. I had been running errands when Dan called and I was dressed in jeans, boots, a Cleveland Browns T-shirt, and a Cleveland Indians ball cap.

"Don't go anywhere, I'll be right back," he said, just as a dark blue SUV pulled up bearing the LAPD logo with BOMB SQUAD written in bold lettering.

The motor cop returned shortly with a plainclothes detective. White haired, with his shirtsleeves rolled up, he appeared disarmingly avuncular despite his shoulder holster and LAPD detective shield clipped to his belt. "I'm Detective Fleming. I'm sorry I can't tell you anything yet, we're waiting on a search warrant and the coroner," he said. "We might need you to identify the body. Can you stick around for a while, please?"

Hearing him verbalize what I had feared caused me to choke up. Somewhat embarrassed, I struggled to fight back the tears.

Damn it, I thought. *Where the hell are my sunglasses?*

I hoped I wouldn't have to identify the body. I didn't want to remember Christopher that way, but agreed to wait. I lit up a Churchill Maduro. The occasional cigar usually calmed me down. This one didn't stand a chance. While I was pacing back and forth in front of the storage facility, it struck me that just a couple miles away on Sepulveda Boulevard was the 777 Motor Motel where my family had stayed the first night we arrived in the Valley, almost thirty-seven years to the day.

Thoughts of Christopher as a child ricocheted across my mind. I pictured my mother bringing him home from Saint Ann's Hospital in Cleveland, where all the Irish-Catholic women had their babies. I remembered his christening, how proud I was to be chosen as his godfather. I recalled three-year-old Christopher feverishly pedaling his plastic trike down the driveway. It had probably been thirty-five years since I saw him clutching the little stuffed lamb he called Lambie Pie and carried everywhere, but the image flashed by as if it were yesterday. Memories of my brothers and me teaching him to play ball in the street on warm summer evenings until my mother sharply whistled us home for supper filled my head. I hoped none of the reporters, cops, and onlookers who crowded the street noticed the tears streaming down my face.

Christopher was only seven when I left for the navy. I was too busy drinking beer and chasing girls to have spent any time with him that year. He was just my kid brother, and I was a typical self-absorbed teenager. He and my brother Bobby had tagged along with my mother to my navy boot camp graduation ceremony in San Diego. My girlfriend had come down as well, so I didn't pay much attention to my little brothers. I felt guilty as I recalled seven-year-old Christopher holding on to my mother's leg, wearing my crisply rolled sailor hat while staring up incredulously at his big brother in his navy whites.

We grew up in the Porter Ranch section of Northridge. Our neighbors, the Martins, leased a ranch in the foothills of Granada Hills. I could still see four-year-old Christopher sitting on the curb in his cowboy hat and boots, waiting for Chuck Martin—who'd always stop to take him along to feed his horses. It was a small kindness in the midst of our father's frequent absences that I had never fully appreciated until this moment.

Similar thoughts flooded my mind in a kaleidoscope of images. As I walked over to my car to get my Ray-Bans, my thoughts turned to my father. Christopher's murder was the obvious result of the path our father had chosen. It was his fault, I thought. Had he been home setting a good example for his sons, maybe my brothers would have become cops and firemen instead of blindly following in his wayward path.

"If Bobby had stayed on the force, he probably would've become chief of police," a detective who had worked with my father told my uncle Tom.

No matter your opinion of Robert Walsh, no one could deny that he was bright and charismatic—traits his son Christopher had inherited. I could picture my father softly singing "Danny Boy" to my brother Dan and "Too-Ra-Loo-Ra-Loo-Ral" to my sister Laura when they were babies. Yet he was the same man who had sat in the car at L.A. International Airport when Ray Ferritto put a bullet in the back of Julius Petro's head while a jet roared overhead. Now, thirty-four years later, his son had been murdered.

Julius Petro may have been a hard-core hoodlum who had once pulled a knife on Ray Ferritto, tried to get a contract to kill my father, and was muscling bookmaker John "Sparky" Monica, but did he deserve to be killed? His family probably didn't think so. I guess what they say is true: What goes around comes around. My mind was forever filled with conflicting thoughts about my family.

My cell phone rang and jolted me back to the moment. It was hot and sticky. I felt nauseated and could taste my own bile. It was Dan, calling for an update. I filled him in, as I would do time and again for the next five hours or so. Detective Fleming soon appeared with a nondescript woman he introduced as Carolyn Vasquez, the lessee of the storage unit who had noticed the foul odor and called the police. The detective excused himself and left.

"I'm so sorry for the loss of your brother," she said.

I thought that was odd, since my brother's body had yet to be identified. I may have believed that it was my kid brother's body in that storage locker, but I resented her for seeming so assured. I sensed she knew something more, but was still overwhelmed by the entire situation. I let her remark slide without comment. Instead, I heard myself mouthing what was to become my signature phrase.

"There are four brothers left, and we're coming," I said. "Anybody who had anything to do with the planning, the murder, moving the body, or the cover-up is going to answer for it. Make no mistake about it—and you can tell each and every one of those assholes out there—nobody walks on this case. Nobody!"

Carolyn appeared somewhat uncomfortable upon hearing the admonition. Before she could reply, I took a long draw off my stogie, rudely blew a cloud of smoke in her direction, then turned and walked away. I should have peppered her with questions; instead I let my anger get the best of me. It would not be the last time.

I had no idea that I had just embarked on a four-and-a-half-year nightmare of an odyssey that would almost completely consume me.

Dan called back and informed me that an attorney by the name of Barry Cohen was telling the police that he represented the Walsh family. As if that wasn't enough to grab my attention, Dan said the police were leery of this character.

"Get a hold of this prick and have him meet me down the street at Wendy's on the corner of Sepulveda and Erwin. Tell him he can't miss me, I'm wearing a Cleveland Indians ball cap," I told Dan.

I continued pacing in front of the storage facility for another fifteen minutes or so until Dan called to confirm the arrangement. It was around 3 P.M. when I walked into Wendy's, but the place was still fairly crowded.

At the back of the restaurant a large individual, who had to be every bit of three hundred pounds, motioned to me. "Dennis," he called out.

He began to speak rapidly as I strode toward him. I didn't know what he was saying, and I didn't care. Normally I tend to speak in a low voice. Right now, however, nothing seemed normal.

"Shut the fuck up," I roared without thinking.

To my surprise and utter chagrin, everyone in the restaurant shut up. Without breaking stride, I continued on, taking a seat across from him. He attempted to speak again.

"I told you to shut the fuck up," I said, very calmly. "I'm going to ask you a series of questions. The first time I think you're lying, I'm gonna splatter your head all over that fucking wall."

By now beads of sweat dotted his forehead, his shirttail was hanging out, and his rumpled tie was askew. "I'm a friend of Christopher's. You shouldn't be talking to me like that," he stammered.

"Hey, asshole," I said, thrusting my face forward. "My brother's body is stuffed in a barrel like a piece of trash about a hundred yards from here. I'm not in any mood for any horseshit, and by the way, don't ever tell anyone that you represent the Walsh family. If anyone represents the Walsh family, it's me. Understand?"

As it turned out, Barry Cohen meant well. He *had* been a friend of Christopher's. He was facing disbarment and would soon be surrendering himself to federal prison on mail fraud charges. He was such a pathetic character that my anger gave way to pity. He provided some insight into my brother's lifestyle that was an eye-opener for me. It was nothing, however, compared to what I would later learn about Christopher and his downward spiral into a crystal meth–induced hell.

I thanked him for meeting with me, and made my way to the restroom. I splashed cold water on my face and stared into the mirror. I looked like hell.

"Dennis, Dennis," I said, shaking my head with disgust.

That was the second time that day I had let my emotions govern my actions. I made a mental note to tone down my demeanor in the future. It was a good lesson for me at this early stage, and would serve me well, at least most of the time. Still, the white-hot fury that had overtaken me would become my constant companion over the next four and a half years.

On the walk back to the storage facility, I repeated my vow that whoever killed my brother would pay dearly. *Mark my words, Christopher,* I said to myself. *Nobody walks on this one, not if I can help it.*

My friend Jolene's brother, Kenneth Bacon, was murdered over thirty years ago in Granada Hills. The case remains unsolved. Whatever it took on my part, my brother's murder was not going to become a cold case. Not if I could help it.

I wandered around aimlessly for hours before Detective Fleming mercifully informed me that I would not be needed to identify the body.

"We're not going to open the barrel until we get it over to the coroner's office. Hopefully, they can make a formal identification and we'll know, one way or the other," he said.

I didn't need to wait for a formal identification. It was what it was.

It was my family that was usually on the wrong end of the long arm of the law. Now I wanted the cops to make the case, the system to work in our favor. Although I loved my father, I strove not to be like him. I was the one son who had rejected the criminal life. I respected the rule of law. Still, I knew then and there that I was fully capable of avenging my brother's murder in a lethal manner. They say the apple doesn't fall far from the tree. I guess I was my father's son, no matter what—bachelor of arts degree, juris doctorate, and all. That's just the way it was, like it or not.

All day long, my father's voice had resonated in my head: *Do what you think you're big enough to do.*

Well, there was no doubt I *was* going to do whatever I had to do—whatever I thought I was big enough to do—whatever the consequences.

I drove home from the storage facility in a daze. For the first time in eleven years, the long drive up the winding canyon to my little rural town in the mountains of the Angeles National Forest afforded me no relief from the suffocating congestion of urban life.

We decided to keep my mother and Christopher's kids in the dark. They didn't need to know, at least not yet. My mother was seventy-five and already sick with worry since Christopher had gone missing. His son, Shane, was ten years old, with copper-colored hair and a perpetual grin. Blond-haired Ashley was nine and cute as a button. They had inherited their parents' Irish looks. They were way too young to lose their father.

Christopher had never married their mother, Michelle O'Halloran. They had recently separated after a tumultuous relationship. Like him, she had a serious drug problem. I know he loved his kids, and I believe he still loved her. Things were not all that good in my brother's world, as I would later find out.

When I finally arrived home, I was eagerly greeted by my dog, Johnny Rio, and Frank the Cat. I scooped up Frank and hugged him and Johnny Rio, a little longer than usual. I cracked open an ice-cold Heineken, fed Frank and Johnny, and heated up dinner. I didn't eat much and did not bother to check my phone messages. I grabbed another beer and eased into an overstuffed leather chair in the den, with my cat on my lap and my dog at my side.

While growing up, I had always feared something might happen to one of my brothers or sisters. Now, all these years later, something terrible had happened. I felt helpless.

It struck me how different Christopher had been from the rest of us, beyond not getting tagged with a traditional Irish name. He was the youngest and the obvious favorite of my parents. I recalled my mother abruptly leaving the other kids at the dinner table to take six-year-old Christopher to McDonald's because he didn't care for roast beef and potatoes. Tim and I remembered our family being on welfare, eating potato pancakes every night for a month while our father was in prison.

My parents were actively involved with Christopher's Little League and Pop Warner teams. But then again, there were also long periods when my father was either in prison or on the lam. Those long absences without a father figure proved especially harmful to Christopher. I blamed myself and my father for not being more involved in Christopher's life.

My first big case out of law school was defending eighteen-year-old Christopher on a felony assault with a deadly weapon charge. He had gotten into an altercation after taking exception to racial insults directed at two of his African American high school football teammates. He broke the bigot's arm with a eucalyptus branch.

In the hallway of the San Fernando Courthouse, I tried to talk some sense into him. "Look, either clean up your act now and go to school to make something of yourself or wind up like the old man and spend your life in and out of jail," I told him.

I could see he was scared. He said all the right things. "Yes, sir. I want to go to college like you did. I don't want to go to jail," he replied.

I couldn't forget that comment. None of my brothers had ever referred to me as *sir*.

I thought I had made some headway with the kid and continued to prepare for trial. On the day of jury selection the DA announced that the People were unable to proceed, due to the unavailability of the victim. Some time later, I learned that Tim, Dan, and Bobby had convinced the victim that it was not in his best interest to appear and testify. Ultimately, I guess their way made a bigger impression on Christopher than mine.

As I sat in my den that evening, the phone rang several times, but I let it ring. I was physically and emotionally spent. My kid brother was dead and my father was in prison again, along with my brother Bobby. I wondered if the craziness would ever end.

I retrieved another cold Heineken and reflected on the events of my father's arrest on June 12, 2000. Aldo Santore, a neighbor of my parents, called to inform me that the house was being raided by various agents from the DEA, LAPD, and FBI. Later I learned that Bobby was arrested simultaneously in Cleveland, along with twenty-eight others across the country, including Phil Christopher, Ronnie Lucarelli, and Eugene "the Animal" Ciasullo. Phil Christopher is notorious for the 1972 United California Bank robbery in Laguna Niguel, one of the largest bank heists in U.S. history, allegedly netting thirty million dollars in jewels, cash, stocks, and bonds. Ronnie Lucarelli was a member of the Cleveland Mafia. Eugene Ciasullo was a well-known Cleveland mob enforcer.

The feds estimated the ring had transported over twelve million dollars' worth of cocaine over a two-year period. They had enlisted the services of Bobby's friend, an American Airlines employee. Bundles of cocaine were slipped into passengers' luggage in Los Angeles and removed at Cleveland Hopkins Airport before the bags were placed on the conveyor belt.

I was aware of the apartment my father kept at the Carlyle, a high-rise on the shores of Lake Erie on Cleveland's west side. I stayed there while attending the 1995 Braves–Indians World Series. He and Bobby were traveling back and forth from L.A. to Cleveland quite frequently. I just assumed the old man was bookmaking. The news that he was the so-called mastermind of a major drug-smuggling ring left me speechless. He was seventy-one years old, had a bad heart, and suffered from severe diabetes. It was beyond my comprehension that he would risk going back to prison.

I made several trips to Cleveland over the following year to assist in negotiating their pleas. My father was sentenced to twenty years, basically a life sentence for him. Bobby got thirteen years, but would wind up doing only three years and nine months. Since then, I had been doing yeoman's work trying to get my father a compassionate release.

I snapped out of my reverie. By now, Christopher's body was probably on a slab at the coroner's office. My father and brother Bobby were in prison, my poor mother and Christopher's kids were blissfully unaware of the tragedy that had befallen our family, and I was out of Heineken. I poured myself a shot of Jameson Irish Whiskey and trudged upstairs with Frank the Cat and Johnny Rio at my heels.

2

I JACK PEOPLE

I AWOKE EARLY THE NEXT MORNING, even before Johnny Rio could nuzzle me awake. For a brief second it seemed as if it had all been a bad dream, a horrible nightmare. Then reality hit me like a cold slap in the face. It was true, all right. My brother *had* been murdered and his body *had* been stuffed in a trash barrel. I had to fight to drag myself out of bed. I would wake up with these exact same thoughts every morning for months.

A small article in the *Daily News* with the heading LOCKER MAY HAVE MISSING MAN IN IT was not very informative. It was going to be a long day. I had been a runner for years. With all the demands of practicing law and the constant turmoil with my family, running was the only thing that kept me sane. After two cups of coffee strong enough to float a horseshoe, Johnny Rio and I walked up the mountain road to a dirt road that led back into the wilderness. We ran for several miles at a faster-than-usual clip, then jogged home. I felt as if I could have run forever.

I checked my messages and returned a few calls. My brother Tim and sister Kathy were driving from Vegas to Phoenix to be with my mother. Dan and Laura were waiting for them to arrive before breaking the news. I was anxious to direct my attention on one person: David Michael Steinberg.

When I had been pacing in front of the storage facility, Dan reminded me about an incident in January that I vaguely recalled—something about a shooting at the Chatsworth town house where Christopher lived with Michelle and their kids. As far as I knew, nothing had come of it. Or so I thought. Christopher had recruited his friend, David Steinberg, to help him move some furniture, including a cumbersome sectional couch. He had split up with Michelle and was moving out.

The events of that January day would turn out to be an integral part of the murder investigation.

A neighbor, Alex Dixon, an off-duty L.A. County deputy sheriff, had pulled into the alley that separated ground-floor garages in a row of two-story town houses. The deputy, wearing sweat clothes and flip-flops, walked over to see if everything was okay. Steinberg pulled out a pistol and exchanged fire with the deputy, though no one was hit. Steinberg hopped over a wall and fled into the night. A woman neighbor claimed that Christopher had threatened her the day before. He was arrested and served thirty days on the misdemeanor threat charge.

My heart sank when Dan told me that Christopher had moved in with Steinberg a couple of months after the shoot-out.

"What the hell was this idiot kid thinking?" I asked. "How did he even know this prick?"

They had met at Granada Hills High School twenty years ago. Dan told me about meeting Christopher a few months earlier at the Country Deli in Chatsworth. David Steinberg, Jeffrey Weaver, and someone called Cowboy had accompanied him.

"Steinberg and Weaver were both strapped," Dan said.

He meant they were carrying sidearms. For some reason, they had made sure that Dan was aware of it.

This was the first I had heard of David Steinberg, Jeffrey Weaver, or Cowboy. My stomach began to turn. The agita, as my father's friend Ray Ferritto used to say.

"I took Chris aside and hollered at him," Dan said. "I asked him what the fuck he was doing hanging around with these imbeciles."

Christopher had just brushed it off with a smile, telling Dan not to worry about it, he could take care of himself. Dan said Steinberg looked irritated when Christopher brought up the shooting-at-the-deputy incident.

"What's worse than a nigger with a badge?" Steinberg had sneered.

The more I heard, the sicker I felt.

"Dennis, this kid was afraid of Steinberg. He had been calling Chris a rat because he didn't get charged. Chris carried a copy of the police report in his briefcase, took it with him everywhere. It was highlighted where Chris said he refused to cooperate with the cops. He thought he needed to carry it," Dan said.

Neither Dan nor I knew that the arresting officer who had written the report was Detective John Fleming, who was now investigating Christopher's murder. Detective Fleming was about to become a central figure in my life.

Dan also told me that he had received a series of phone calls from Steinberg after he returned to Phoenix.

"Your brother's out of control. . . .

"He's all spun out every night. . . .

"I can't take much more of this shit."

Dan was filled with remorse for not taking Steinberg more seriously.

"This idiot was pissing me off. Finally, I told him to handle it. Dennis, I meant fistfight Chris or evict him. Quit calling me and bitching about it like some sorta pussy. I never thought he'd kill the kid," he said.

I wanted to scream out loud. When Christopher had been missing, I wasn't aware of any of this. I was always the last to know. My family's mantra was, *Don't tell Dennis.* My father and brothers had no problem getting into one jackpot after another without consulting me. Inevitably, though, I would be dragged in for the cleanup.

Five months after the shoot-out, on June 24, 2003, charges were filed against Steinberg and against Christopher as an accessory. Six days later, on June 30, LAPD detectives arrested Steinberg at his apartment. Two days later, on July 2, Christopher's body was discovered. The five-month delay in filing charges proved to be fatal for Christopher. Had Steinberg been arrested earlier, he would not have had the opportunity to kill the only witness to the shoot-out.

Steinberg was charged with two counts of assault with a semiautomatic firearm and one count of being a felon in possession of a firearm. Steinberg, believing he was still on parole, consented to a warrantless search of his apartment. The LAPD, Steinberg, and his parole officer were all unaware that his parole had expired on March 9, posing a potentially serious problem for the prosecution. It was to be the first of many strange twists and turns that this case would take.

During the search, the police recovered a laser sight and a Rolex watch. Items that would have no particular significance until Christopher's body was recovered two days later.

I wasn't sure just yet who had murdered my brother, but it sure as hell looked like Steinberg had the motive, the means, and the opportunity. Steinberg surely had to be climbing the walls in county jail, knowing that his victim's body lay stashed in a storage unit before he could dispose of it. Obtaining a conviction for murder was generally more difficult without a body.

I grabbed a cup of coffee and logged on to the L.A. County Sheriff's Department Web site, clicked on "Inmate Information," and typed in Steinberg's name. The details seemed to leap off the monitor. This David Michael Steinberg character suddenly began to take shape in my mind. Age: 35. Born: December 12, 1967. Height: 5 feet 7 inches. Weight: 175. Eyes: Brown. Hair: Brown . . .

Although bail had been set at ninety-five thousand dollars, the good news was that there was a parole hold. Steinberg wasn't going anywhere—lucky for him. I don't know if I could have controlled myself, let alone my brothers, if he made bail. He was scheduled to be arraigned at the San Fernando Courthouse on July 15. It didn't take much to talk Tim and Dan into driving in for the hearing.

Next, I ran Steinberg's rap sheet. I was surprised to find an arrest for lewd conduct and a couple entries regarding harassing, annoying, or molesting children. A kidnapping charge had been reduced to a misdemeanor in 1989. He had been released from prison on February 7, 2002, after being sentenced to sixteen months for auto theft and possession of a deadly weapon: brass knuckles. On April 17, 2002, he was returned to prison for a parole violation and was released on May 1, 2002. U.S. Marshals arrested him for a parole violation after the shooting-at-the-deputy incident, but since charges were yet to be filed, he served a little over a month in federal custody.

I pulled up an appellate decision, *United States v. David Michael Steinberg,* which detailed Steinberg's 1992 arrest for conspiring to purchase ten kilograms of cocaine with counterfeit currency. Steinberg was to supply the counterfeit cash. His coconspirator, who agreed to procure the coke, Jamie Schulz, was a confidential informant. During a wiretapped phone call, Steinberg boasted to Schulz, "I jack people." Schulz testified that he understood that to mean robbing drug dealers or using counterfeit money to purchase drugs. Either way, it was a dangerous game. Robbery victims were usually pistol-whipped or beaten savagely. Drug dealers who had been jacked did not file a police report.

I jack people was a phrase that grabbed my immediate attention. I was beginning to get a sense of the depth of Steinberg's treachery.

At the time of Steinberg's arrest in '92, two loaded handguns were found on the floor of his van. Schulz was fortunate to have been cooperating with the feds; otherwise, odds were Steinberg would surely have jacked him.

He was convicted of conspiracy to possess cocaine with intent to distribute, using or carrying a firearm during a drug-trafficking crime, conspiracy to possess and transfer counterfeit currency, possession of counterfeit Federal Reserve notes, and transferring counterfeit Federal Reserve notes. He was sentenced to twenty years in federal prison. In 1996, the U.S. District Court reversed his conviction on the grounds that the government failed to turn over Brady material, legalese for exculpatory evidence. The U.S. Attorney's Office opted not to retry the case. Steinberg was released, free to resume his criminal endeavors, and ultimately free to murder my brother.

What a lucky bastard this little prick Steinberg is, I thought, *and how unlucky for Christopher.*

Later that day, my sister Laura called. The coroner's office had officially identified the body as Christopher. While they may have relied on scientific measures to formally make the identification, two tattoos—a green shamrock and a depiction of Christopher's husky wolfdog Jake— were all the confirmation we needed. Laura was softly crying, yet her sobs roared through my head. I cut her short. It was up to her to break the news to our mother. Dan called the prison chaplains to notify my father and brother Bobby. By the time Tim and Kathy arrived in Phoenix, my mother was a basket case. I could not bring myself to talk to my mother just yet. My heart ached for her and for Christopher's kids, but I didn't know what I could possibly say to ease her pain.

I suppose subconsciously I had yet to accept the cold, hard reality of the situation. The horror of having a family member murdered in cold blood cannot be fully appreciated until it is experienced. It's not a good club to be in. You're not asked to join; you're just in.

My mother would never acknowledge Christopher's free fall into a chaotic life of addiction and crime.

"He's got a job now. Why do you always want to bad-rap him?" she would counter whenever I launched into a tirade about his drug use.

A few hours later, I bit the bullet and dialed my mother's number. If I had been avoiding the issue of my brother's demise, a big dose of reality was about to be rammed home.

The conversation went about as I had expected.

"Mom, it's Dennis. Are you okay?" I asked.

"Why would somebody do this to my boy?" she asked. "He was doing better, I thought. I've been praying for Chris. Dennis, you get your brother. I don't want him down there at the coroner's any longer than he has to be."

My mother was crying. She didn't deserve this. She had suffered a ton of grief over the years due to my father's escapades. I was used to fixing situations. This was one I couldn't fix. I wasn't much comfort to her. I was just trying to remain composed.

"Did you eat today? I worry about you, Dennis, you're so thin," she said.

I kept myself lean and fit, but nonetheless, in my mother's eyes I was forever undernourished.

"I'll talk to the coroner, Mom. I have to go," I managed to say. "Don't worry, we're gonna get these bastards, one way or another."

That was my way of dealing with it. I canceled an appointment with a client. The heartache in my mother's voice was difficult to bear.

Tim and Dan must have felt likewise. Not wanting to sit idly by while my mother and sisters cried all day, they headed for L.A. They were both pretty revved up when I called. I made it clear that since we couldn't lay hands on Steinberg, we really had no choice but to let the cops handle the investigation. Besides, I wanted every responsible party arrested and charged. I didn't want any mistakes. Despite my skill as a legal mouthpiece, my two brothers didn't seem all that impressed.

"You'd better be right about no bail, Dennis," Tim replied, "because if this motherfucker hits the streets, you'd better get the fuck out of my way 'cuz I'm gonna kill the cocksucker ten minutes later and feed him to that wolfdog of yours."

The next day, articles in the *Los Angeles Times* and the *Daily News* reported that a man's body had been recovered wrapped in plastic and duct tape in a trash barrel in a Van Nuys storage unit. Detective Mike Oppelt was quoted as saying that the body may be linked to the January 29 shooting at the deputy sheriff. I interpreted it to mean that the police were looking at Steinberg for the murder.

I met Tim and Dan at the Martins' in Northridge, next door to where we had grown up. The Martin family was gathered for a Fourth of July barbecue. My brothers had stopped and met up with Peter Kinsler, a friend of Christopher's who was a small-time Vegas flimflam man and prescription drug peddler with ties to the porn industry. At times, Christopher had acted as his bodyguard. Kinsler had given them his business card with the names of those people he said were responsible for Christopher's murder. The names *Christina Karath, Fat Jeff Lever, Troy Wilcox,* and *Shankster* were scrawled on the back of the card.

"Who the hell are these people? Who the fuck is Shankster? And what about David Steinberg, why isn't he listed?" I asked.

All my brothers knew was that Christina Karath was Christopher's girlfriend at the time of his murder, Jeff Lever was probably Jeff Weaver, Shankster was some kind of Nazi Low Rider, and Troy Wilcox was a dope-dealer friend of Christopher's. It was Wilcox's wife who had called Laura regarding Carolyn Vasquez and the storage facility.

I was familiar with the Nazi Low Riders, a neo-Nazi white supremacist prison and street gang affiliated with the Aryan Brotherhood. The gang had been responsible for numerous violent attacks on minorities, especially African Americans.

Here we go, I thought. Only that morning it seemed like the cops might have made Steinberg for the murder. Now it was shaping up to be more like a whodunit.

Dan had already spoken with Troy Wilcox, and with Cowboy, another of Christopher's friends. It was clear that Tim and Dan liked Steinberg for the murder. There was no doubt in my mind that if Steinberg wasn't behind bars, he'd be dead by now.

"Dennis, this kid Cowboy was Chris's right-hand man," Dan said. "Steinberg made sure he wasn't around when he killed Chris."

I took Wilcox's phone number and walked next door in front of our old house. I sat on the curb where Christopher used to sit and wait for Chuck Martin to take him to the ranch. I dialed the number and reached Wilcox. Cowboy was with him. Each expressed his condolences and professed to have loved Christopher. They had no doubt that Steinberg was the killer. They were willing to help out if they could, but neither wanted to speak with the police. When I pressed for details, neither was all that forthcoming.

Troy Wilcox was downright blunt. "Look, I have a wife and kids. I have my own business doing work for the studios. I have a nice house up in Granada Hills, and yeah, maybe I do sling a few drugs, but I don't need any headaches, if you know what I mean."

I told him that I could appreciate that and would be grateful for any information they could provide. Then I repeated the admonition that I had given to Carolyn Vasquez. "Here's the way it is: You can tell all those assholes out there, there's four brothers left, and we're coming. Anyone who had anything to do with the murder, the planning, or the cover-up is going down. If anybody's thinking about getting one of us, they better get us all. We aren't going away," I said calmly.

He agreed to get back to me. I did not want to pressure anyone—not yet, anyway. Frankly, I didn't care about Wilcox's situation. If he had information, sooner or later he was going to give it up, whether he knew it or not.

It wasn't until after dark when most of the Martin family had left that my brothers and I could sit on the patio and talk with Chuck. The more we drank, the more difficult it became to contain our emotions. Chuck teared up, recounting the times he had taken little Chris, in his cowboy hat and boots, to the ranch. He told us how Christopher had recently come by to repay the one hundred dollars he had borrowed, a debt that was seriously overdue. Chuck wept as he spoke of throwing the money on the ground, telling Christopher he should have come to him months ago if he couldn't repay the loan. It wasn't the money; it was the principle.

Christopher was shattered. He picked up the money and began to cry. "Mr. Martin, you don't know what I'm into. You have no idea how bad it is. Please take this money," Christopher pleaded.

Chuck was so overwhelmed that he hugged Christopher, telling him he would always be welcome there. He would never see Christopher again. He was relieved that Christopher had left on good terms. I envied him.

Tim and Dan, especially Tim, began to discuss in lurid detail the ways they would wreak vengeance upon the murderers.

"We need to kick some ass and knock down some doors so these scumbags know they fucked with the wrong family," Dan said.

Tim was somewhat more graphic. "When we get these motherfuckers, I'm gonna tie 'em to a chair and kill a couple of their relatives right in front of 'em so they know how it feels, then I'm gonna beat 'em to death with my bare hands until their heads are nothing but bloody pulps, and then I'm gonna piss on their fucking corpses."

"Holy shit, Tim," I said. "I'm glad you're not mad at me."

My brothers' rage began to feed off itself. I lost track of how many felonies they were proposing to commit. Luckily, Chuck was there to act as the voice of reason. They didn't want to hear much of my talk about letting the system work. After all, I wasn't really one of them. I was the big brother, the lawyer, the square. I kept talking and Chuck continued to reinforce what I was saying. Our family didn't need any more heartache. My brothers were hurting as much as I was and only needed to vent. They knew that I was estranged from Christopher. They didn't know if I was fully on board.

I attempted to reassure them. "I guarantee nobody's gonna walk on this case. Nobody is gonna kill our brother and not pay for it. If the cops don't put these fuckers away, I'll ride to hell and back with Bobby and you two. We'll do whatever we have to do. End of story," I said.

My assurances seemed to calm them both down. On the other hand, I knew that I had to handle it and handle it properly, or else. I was sitting on a powder keg.

The next evening, my brothers and I met with some of Christopher's old friends at Los Toros Mexican Restaurant in Chatsworth. I was at the bar when our friend Barry White let me know that Peter Kinsler had just shown up and that Tim and Dan had bounced him out on his ear.

I had no objection, but Tim felt he needed to explain. "He don't belong here, Dennis. This is for us and Chris's old friends. He's dead because of pukes like Kinsler," Tim said. "Bartender, my brother'll have another Irish whiskey."

I knew what Tim meant. Christopher had abandoned his lifelong friends in favor of lowlifes who did not deserve his trust. He should have been with people he could trust with his life. People like Barry White, who was like another brother to us, rather than the likes of Peter Kinsler.

A couple days later, newspaper articles announced that the body in the barrel had been identified as Christopher John Walsh, thirty-seven,

of Chatsworth. The brief accounts seemed woefully inadequate to describe the tragedy that had befallen my family.

Over the next few weeks, things began to heat up and heat up fast.
Tim and Dan were interviewed by homicide detectives at Devonshire
Division. Perhaps the first time either had been in a police station without being cuffed. Afterwards, Dan informed me how Detective Fleming
had politely requested our cooperation.

"We know about your father's connections with organized crime. We
know your father and your brother Bobby are in prison. We really don't
need to be finding bodies all over town. You need to let us handle this
case," Detective Fleming had said.

"We told him, yeah, they could handle it, just like you said, Dennis,"
Dan said, not sounding all that sincere.

"Who the fuck do they think we are, anyways, the James gang?" he
asked.

It wouldn't be too long before that characterization almost became a
reality.

A couple of days later, I received a call from Troy Wilcox. "Hey, I
paid Chris's storage bill and went through his stuff. His kids will be glad
to know that his Pop Warner trophies and his Granada Hills High football helmet are in there," he said.

His tone seemed gleeful, which angered me. "What storage unit?"
I asked.

"Public Storage on De Soto in Chatsworth," he said.

I was dumbfounded. I had not been aware of another storage unit.
Despite my resolution to control my temper, I was livid. "Hey, asshole," I
shot back, "what the fuck are you doing in my brother's storage unit during the middle of a murder investigation?"

Wilcox responded, "I know you're a lawyer and you like to hear yourself talk, but if you shut the fuck up a minute, I'll tell you what I was in
there for."

I bit my tongue. "Yeah? I'm listening," I replied.

He explained that he believed Christopher had stolen some ecstasy tablets from him and thought they might be stashed in the unit. Ecstasy was another popular illegal drug that induced euphoria.

His explanation did not sit well with me. "Listen tight, jerkoff," I said. "I don't know if you were in there looking for ecstasy, the murder weapon, or something else, and I really don't give a flying shit. It sounds like tampering with evidence. I'm letting the LAPD know. So go get your own lawyer and see if he shuts the fuck up while you do all the talking, asshole."

I hung up without waiting for his reply. My plan of remaining calm was not proceeding as I had hoped. I made a mental note to jam up this wiseass prick if I ever had the opportunity; then I reported the incident to the homicide detectives. I dropped by Devonshire Division and left Peter Kinsler's business card in an envelope addressed to Detective Fleming.

A few days later, Cowboy called and things began to add up.

"You can't trust Wilcox," he told me in earnest. "Weaver's his dawg, and Weaver's more involved than you know. He was jealous of Chris, he hated him."

Cowboy admitted that he had gone with Wilcox to the De Soto storage unit and that Wilcox was only looking to recover his stolen ecstasy. He did not want to talk on the phone. We agreed to meet at Twain's coffee shop in North Hollywood. I instructed him to look for the only guy in the joint wearing a Cleveland Indians ball cap. I hung up and phoned my brother Dan.

"Dennis, these idiots are bad news. Why don't you wait until me and Tim come in to town," he suggested.

"No," I told him. "It'll be okay, but just in case it's a setup, I'm taking two guys with me."

"Good," Dan replied. "Who?"

"Smith and Wesson," I said.

Dan laughed and insisted that I call him after the meeting. Maybe he thought I was kidding, but I wasn't. I borrowed my buddy Dave Bullard's nickel-plated, ivory-handled .375 Magnum and shoulder holster. I'd borrowed the rig once before, after having a beef with some members of the Crips. I had done some target shooting with it in the Angeles National

Forest, and was confident that I could hit what I aimed at. Cowboy sounded sincere enough, I thought, but Christopher had sold these people short and now he's dead. I wasn't going to make the same mistake.

I made a point to arrive first, like my father had schooled me. I grabbed a booth where my back was to the wall, another survival tactic compliments of the old man. I was about nine when, instead of dropping me off at Sunday Mass, he took me to a bar where he met with Frank Velotta. He ordered me ginger ale and sat me in a booth.

"Always sit with your back to the wall," he instructed me. "Keep your eyes open and always be aware of your surroundings. That way you won't be a mark," he informed me before joining Frank at the bar. A *mark* was someone who got taken advantage of, one way or another.

Soon enough, a stocky guy in his mid-thirties walked up and introduced himself as Cowboy. Tattoos and shaven heads appeared to be all the rage with these hoodlums. I have to admit, it did give them a menacing look.

I had made the decision to dress down and not speak like a lawyer when I met with any of these people. Showing up in a suit and tie and coming off as Christopher's attorney big brother was not going to get me anywhere. The Cleveland Indians ball cap, jeans, and roughout cowboy boots I wore would become my trademark. As they say, I had to walk the walk and talk the talk.

Cowboy was about six feet tall and probably weighed in at about 220. I eyed him up and down, but couldn't tell if he was packing. During lunch, he poured out a tale that made my head spin. He was an ex-marine. His father was an L.A. attorney. He had gotten hooked up with my brother, Jeff Weaver, Troy Wilcox, Shankster Gangster, and David Steinberg doing collections and credit card fraud. The common thread that bound them all was crystal meth.

"Dude, we were constantly spun out," he told me. "We'd be up for days on end and then crash for days. I still got a real bad problem with that shit."

I sat and listened as Cowboy talked.

I hadn't been an attorney for five minutes when my father felt compelled to dispense some advice: "You'll learn more by listening to people than listening to yourself. Too many attorneys don't know when to shut up and listen," he had said.

Over the years, it had proved to be sage advice.

Cowboy spoke very matter-of-factly. Steinberg promoted himself as a criminal mastermind. He was putting together a "crew." He was going to get them "the keys to the Valley." They had regular meetings. Certain members of the crew were designated "captains." The crew would be run like the Mafia. He made it appealing, made it seem glamorous. They had recently engineered the heist of a large amount of tools and construction equipment. Despite the nice score, things weren't going so well between Steinberg and his roommate, Christopher. They argued constantly. Cowboy had to separate the two after Christopher returned home to find his loofah in Steinberg's shower. Chris was so incensed, he had told Steinberg, "I'm gonna kill you."

Cowboy laughed when he told me that Chris had repeated this so often to people that his nickname became I'm Gonna Kill You.

"I told your brother he shouldn't be saying that shit. Especially to Steinberg. He's done hard time. You don't back a guy like that into a corner," he said. "Chris would just laugh and say Steinberg could go fuck himself."

David Steinberg did not tolerate any challenge to his authority. Christopher said and did as he pleased. It was a recipe for disaster.

He described Jeffrey Weaver as a bloated skinhead who was an insatiable hog when it came to crystal meth, women, and food. He was known as Fat Jeff, Fat Boy, or Sharkey. He sported a full-sleeve tattoo of a woman on his arm and bore a scar on his left buttock from a shotgun blast. He was insanely jealous of Christopher. Weaver was a follower, who was clearly enamored of Steinberg. He had ingratiated himself with Steinberg to become his "right-hand man."

According to Cowboy, Shankster Gangster was Shane Wilson, a high-ranking member of the Nazi Low Riders, who had been in and out of prison. Each of his earlobes bore a swastika tattoo. He was a *shot caller,* meaning he had the authority to designate who got viciously beaten or killed for running afoul of the nefarious prison gang. He was a longtime friend of Weaver's and had just started hanging around with the crew.

"If you run across him, be careful. He always packs," Cowboy warned. "He knows more than he's saying, but I don't think he was in on the killing. Watch out for Troy Wilcox. He's telling people not to cooperate with the cops or with the Walsh brothers."

It was the first of hundreds of times that I would hear the term *the Walsh brothers.* It wouldn't be long before that term would spread like wildfire throughout the sordid underworld of the San Fernando Valley, taking on epic proportions. Maybe Dan's crack about the James gang wasn't so far off.

"What's the deal with this Carolyn Vasquez broad?" I asked. "At the storage unit, she said she was sorry before Christopher's body was even identified."

"Her husband's in prison and she got nailed on some kind of federal case. She's been banging Steinberg," he replied.

"Cowboy, let me ask you, are you afraid of Steinberg?"

"He's dangerous, real dangerous," he answered.

No kidding, I thought. *He's graduated from jacking people to killing people.*

Cowboy finished his cheeseburger and wiped some tears from his eyes. "I was always with Chris, always. My girlfriend wouldn't let me go out that day. We went to Magic Mountain. That's the night they got him."

Other than Steinberg, he wasn't ready to elaborate on who *they* were. Still, he sounded sincere.

I took a shot at finding out just how comfortable he felt with me. "Do you mind if I ask what your real name is, Cowboy?"

He bit into a french fry, placed what was left of it on his plate, looked me straight in the eye, and reached into his pants pocket. I calmly slid my right hand up my belly to my chest just in case I had to reach for my piece, which was holstered under my left armpit. A week or so ago, I was playing softball; now I might have to make a life-or-death decision in a blink of an eye. I was relieved when he pulled out his wallet and handed me his driver's license.

His name was Marlon Gene Grueskin. I'd eat my hat if that was an alias. I wanted to trust him; now I did. Even though I could sense he had more to tell. I would have to gain more of his trust.

Before I left, he told me there were other people with information. Some were afraid of the killers, some didn't cooperate with the cops, and others a combination of both. He candidly admitted he had no desire to speak to the police. I understood. He didn't want to be on Front Street. Not many criminals would. He preferred the information to come from others, so I didn't press him to go to the police. Not yet. He promised to see what he could do about getting some of these people to speak with me.

I handed him my business card. "Anyone can call me day or night. If need be, I can be anywhere at any time," I told him.

He smiled. "I don't doubt that, dude," he said. "The whole time you been talking to me, I've been tripping. You sound so much like Chris, it's scary."

Cowboy's assistance would prove to be invaluable.

Cowboy provided the name of a porn actress, Cameron Cain. She had been in contact with Christopher shortly before he went missing. Chatsworth was the pornography center of the country. My brother had worked at odd jobs for porn director Rob Spallone, who arranged for the actress to meet me at El Presidente, a Mexican restaurant in Mission Hills.

Blond and very attractive, Cameron Cain spoke in a distant, distracted manner. I thought she might be high. She said Christopher was with Steinberg on either June 21 or 22. He was supposed to meet her, but never did. He had given her the keys to his DeSoto storage unit. She gave them to Jeff Weaver after Christopher went missing. That explained how Troy Wilcox had gotten the keys. Weaver said he had helped move the body.

What she knew made her a material witness.

"Would you mind speaking to the homicide detectives, Cameron?" I asked.

She had the look of a deer caught in the headlights.

"These fuckers are relying on people like you not coming forward. You said you liked Christopher. Do you want his killers to walk?" I asked.

She reluctantly agreed to speak with the police, then hurried off. I called Detective Fleming and gave him her contact information.

I had intended to contact Jeff "Fat Boy" Weaver. Now I really wanted to speak with him. Before I could track him down, I got word that he had gotten rolled up on a parole violation and was in custody. I could wait. I was pleased he was cooling his heels behind bars, just like his crime partner, Steinberg.

On July 14, twelve days after my brother's body had been recovered, I received a call from Robert "Mouse" Hayes. He admitted to having dropped out of the Nazi Low Riders after entering into a relationship with Desiree Manthe, who had a biracial child. She and Amy "Trouble" Sheeley had picked up Steinberg as he fled down Topanga Canyon Boulevard after the shoot-out with the off-duty deputy. They drove Steinberg to an apartment where Mouse was staying.

"He was out of breath and bug-eyed," Mouse said. "He told me to turn on the news. He had just shot it out with a fat nigger."

"Mouse, will you talk to the cops?" I asked, fully expecting him to decline.

"Fucking right I will. Garbage like Steinberg don't belong on the streets," he said.

Quite an indictment from someone who had spent over half his life behind bars.

"I already talked to Detective Fleming. I'm not afraid of Steinberg. Tell Fleming I'll testify in court. I can take care of myself," he continued.

He was cooperating, so I didn't press him. I didn't need to know the specifics. I knew the less involvement I had with these witnesses, the better. At trial, any defense attorney worth his salt would argue that every witness I had spoken with was tainted. I would have to be extremely careful.

The next morning I met Tim and Dan at the San Fernando Court-house. Tim was a foreman for a commercial masonry company. Dan was a superintendent for a residential builder. They had finally come to real-ize that crime doesn't pay.

We went up to Department C. Tim and Dan took seats in the gallery. I was dressed in a suit and tie. The bailiff and clerk knew me to be a lo-cal attorney, so I had no problem approaching the counsel table. A bai-liff soon brought Steinberg through a side door from lockup. He was handcuffed and in a blue county jail jumpsuit. His hair was razor cut. His features were sharp. His dark, cold eyes scanned the courtroom. Maybe it was just the contempt I had for him, but to me he looked like a sewer rat that had been cornered. The bailiff sat him in a wooden chair against the wall next to the lockup door.

Once the bailiff left to chat with the clerk, I casually walked up to Steinberg, leaned over, and whispered in his ear. "You're in my ballpark now, asshole. Take a good look. I'm your worst fucking nightmare," I informed him.

I had to restrain myself from smashing his face in. I was so close, my nose was assaulted with his pungent scent. County jail inmates don't get to shower every day and usually reek. His head jerked back. He looked up, obviously perplexed. He had never met me. His eyes darted across the courtroom until he caught sight of Tim and Dan, both of whom were glaring at him. Dan had rolled his tongue, holding it clenched between his teeth. Tim was biting his lower lip, while nodding his head deliber-ately with his index finger pointed toward Steinberg. They looked like a couple of psychotic Irish thugs right out of the Westies. Steinberg's eyes widened and the color drained from his face. He had made the connec-tion all right.

I took a seat in the gallery with my brothers. All three of us contin-ued to mad-dog Steinberg as the bailiff led him to the counsel table. His public defender requested the Court to trail the matter to another date. I waited until the prosecutor left and the bailiff was leading Steinberg back to the lockup before I approached the railing.

In a low voice I called out, "Hey, Deputy."

With Steinberg in tow, the bailiff leaned over. "Yes, Counsel?"

"You might want to segregate him from general pop," I said, keeping my voice low so only he and his prisoner could hear me.

"Why's that?" the bailiff inquired, somewhat bewildered.

"Because he likes to pull his prick out in front of little kids," I answered.

The deputy hustled Steinberg out of the courtroom before Steinberg could respond. My heart was pounding. To be that close to the creep who probably shot my brother and stuffed his body in a trash barrel and not be able to lay my hands on him was almost more than I could stand. Taunting him over his lewd-contact beefs was the least I could do.

As I turned to leave, his public defender asked, "What was that all about?"

To my regret, I said, "Maybe you should mind your own business," and walked out.

"You shoulda bit Steinberg's fucking ear off," Dan said through clenched teeth.

We caught up to the prosecutor in the hallway. I introduced myself and my brothers, but didn't mention my confrontation with Steinberg. I didn't think she would have appreciated it.

"I'm Stephanie Sparagna," she said while extending her hand. "I'm so sorry for your loss."

I expressed my concern that my brother's murder might get swept under the carpet because of his lifestyle. The Deputy DA wore glasses and clutched her case file with both hands to her chest. Her looks and demeanor reminded me of a schoolteacher.

"Your brother didn't deserve to die like that. I promise you I will treat this case as if it were the President of the United States who had been murdered," she assured us.

I didn't know at the time how true to every bit of her word that Deputy DA Stephanie Sparagna would be.

As we walked away, she pointedly wagged a finger in our direction. "I don't want any amateur sleuthing on this case. Let us handle it, please."

Despite her broad smile, it was very clear that she was *telling* us and not asking us.

I went down to the second floor to apologize to Steinberg's deputy public defender, Karen Richardson, for rudely telling her to mind her own business. I had no intention of apologizing for what I said to Steinberg.

"I'm sorry," I said, "your client murdered my brother and I guess I lost my head. I apologize for speaking to you like that."

I didn't realize that the prosecution had not yet disclosed that Steinberg was a suspect in my brother's murder. His public defender immediately contacted the DA's Office to find out what was up.

It wasn't long before Stephanie Sparagna let me have a piece of her mind. "Dennis, they didn't need to know we're looking at Steinberg, but you just tipped them off. You need to let me handle this case. I don't need you jeopardizing this investigation. Do you understand me?" she asked.

Her rebuke stung. I felt terrible that I had forced her to show her hand to Steinberg's PD. It wouldn't be the last time, however, that I would be on the wrong end of one of Stephanie Sparagna's stern reprimands.

3

HANDLE IT

JOHNNY RIO AND FRANK THE Cat kept me company while I sat in the leather chair in my den and stared ahead vacantly, something I had done quite a bit lately. All I could think about was my brother's murder. Whenever I tried to watch a ball game or a movie, I was quickly lost in thought, oblivious to whatever was on the screen. Once again my thoughts drifted back to my father. Our relationship was a complicated one. It would have been easy to write him off years ago if he were nothing more than a criminal. As the eldest child, I could remember him in a different light, unlike my brothers and sisters.

In the mid 1950s, we lived in four-unit apartment complex on Lakeview Avenue, in downtown Cleveland. My maternal grandparents lived downstairs. One day I was in the courtyard with my twelve-year-old uncle, Tommy, and some kids from the neighborhood. Tommy was my mother's youngest brother. Five of us kids had trapped a big gray rat in a trash can. The rodent was frantically running in circles.

My uncle Tommy announced, "Let's get your dad."

He raced over to the wooden steps and hollered, "Hey, Bob, come down here. Hurry up."

My father was either on his way to his shift or had just gotten home.

He trotted down the steps wearing a white shirt and tie, his service revolver perched in a leather shoulder holster. My father walked over to the trash can with our little band trailing behind him. "Stand back, kids," he warned.

He reached into his holster, pulled out his pistol, and fired one shot, dispatching the frenzied rat. I had never heard a gunshot before. My ears were ringing. All five boys were speechless. My dad was a policeman, and although I may have been only four years old, I was damn proud. As I grew older and his life took a different turn, I could always picture my father at a time when I looked up to him—dressed in a suit and tie with a navy blue cashmere overcoat, a gray fedora pulled stylishly low on his brow. He carried a badge and a gun. He stood for all that was right and just. My brothers and sisters were too young to remember that version of our father.

Shortly after that incident, in early 1957, my father left the Cleveland PD. There was no explanation. All of a sudden my father was no longer a policeman, and that was that. He soon fell into the company of a group of local hoodlums, mostly Italians from the Collinwood area. As a policeman, he had arrested a few of them, like Frank "Skinny" Velotta, time and again. Sooner or later, they were back on the streets, usually with wads of cash. That must have appealed to him. In 1961, he was arrested by the same Cleveland cops with whom he had once worked. He was convicted of counterfeiting twenty-dollar bills. We were living in Highland Heights on the east side of Cleveland. My parents had five children, and my mother was pregnant with my brother Bobby. Christopher had yet to be born. We were unaware that our father had taken up a life of crime.

He took me and my brother Tim aside. "I'm going to Germany on government business. I need you two loogans to help your mother out when I'm gone," he told us.

Tim and I swallowed the story, and off he went. Not to Germany, of course, but to the federal penitentiary in Milan, Michigan.

A few months after he left, Tim called me into the bathroom and locked the door behind us. "Look what I found under Mom's pillow," he said with tears in his eyes. He handed me an envelope addressed in my mother's impeccable handwriting to

President John F. Kennedy
1600 Pennsylvania Avenue
Washington, D.C.

I opened the envelope and read the letter my mother had written to the young Irish-Catholic president.

Dear President Kennedy, it began,
I am the mother of six children. We are an Irish Catholic family. My husband is in federal prison. If there is anything you could do to help . . .

I stopped reading and carefully folded the letter and put it back in the envelope. My mother's heartfelt plea shook me to the core. I could feel the anguish in her every word.

I was trembling when I handed the envelope back to Tim. "Go put this back under Mom's pillow," I told him, "and don't ever mention this again, not to anyone."

Tim did what I asked. To this day, we have never discussed that letter, nor have I ever mentioned it to my mother. Apparently, that's a trait common to the Irish. We seem to keep a lot buried deep inside us. I went to my room and curled up in bed. I put a pillow over my head and sobbed until I fell asleep. I don't know if my mother ever mailed that letter to President Kennedy.

My mother would take the bus to visit my father, sometimes taking a few of the younger kids along. She never took me or Tim. We were old enough to know what a jail was. We managed to survive on food stamps. Frank Velotta dropped off money from time to time. Our parish pastor, Father O'Brien, would bring over baskets of food on the holidays. My classmates at Saint Paschal Baylon's Catholic grade school were either unaware of the situation or chose to spare me the humiliation. There were a couple of times, however, when some insensitive students in other classes mentioned my father being in prison just loud enough so that I would overhear. It hurt me deeply, but I was too embarrassed to respond.

After about two years, my father was released from federal prison. The first Sunday home, he donned a suit and tie and accompanied the entire clan to Mass at Saint Pashcal Baylon Church. It was unprecedented. The old man never went to church with us. Years later, it occurred to me that he was making a statement to the community: He was back and he was not too ashamed to appear in public, and if you didn't like it, you could go fuck yourself. The next time I would see him in church was at his funeral.

One night after I had been sick and missed a day of school, my buddy Charlie Ibold phoned. "Hey, Walsh, Sister Mary Corleen told the class that we could have a nice day since you were absent and we shouldn't laugh at your jokes when you came back, because you're not funny and she said, 'Mark my words, Mr. Walsh will be in prison by the time he's eighteen years old.'"

A hell of a thing for a nun to tell my classmates. No doubt she was aware of my father being an ex-con.

Screw her, I thought.

I began to steel myself against what people might have to say about my father.

Once we relocated to California in 1966, the old man didn't miss a beat. He hooked up with a ring of ex-Cleveland hoodlums. They engaged in various criminal activities, including commercial burglaries, loan sharking, bookmaking, and contract killings. They were affiliated with Jimmy "the Weasel" Fratianno, an ex-Clevelander described by *Life* magazine as the "West Coast Executioner." Ovid Demaris would mention my father in his biography of Fratianno, *The Last Mafioso,* but misspelled our last name as *Walch.* My mother took some comfort in that, assuming that no one would make the connection. The general public may not have noticed, but it caused my father to become infamous in the organized crime world.

Things seemed to get better for my family, at least for a time. To a young kid from Cleveland, the San Fernando Valley in the '60s was glorious. Orange and lemon groves, resplendent in the bright Southern California sun, dotted the countryside. The Valley was ringed by majestic mountains, offering a spectacular view in all directions. Beautiful weather, palm trees, chaparral, horse ranches, and swimming pools galore came as a welcome respite from the harsh Cleveland winters and brutally humid summers. The money was good. My father drove a Cadillac De Ville and bought us a home in the upscale Porter Ranch area. It wasn't too long ago that we survived on food stamps. Now I watched as construction workers dug up our backyard for a swimming pool.

Some of my father's bookmaking clients were actors James Caan and Chuck Connors, and producer Danny Arnold. He began to socialize with comedian Allan Drake, whose first wife, Janice, had been gunned down by two members of the Genovese crime family while in the company of mobster Anthony "Little Augie" Carfano in 1959. Allan's friend, Gordon Mills, managed singer Tom Jones. Jones's son, Mark, would spend the day with Christopher, Bobby, and Laura playing and swimming at our home. My parents and Ray Ferritto and his wife sat center stage while dining at the Ambassador Hotel's Cocoanut Grove, enjoying the performance of headliner Connie Francis. Afterwards, the women were escorted backstage to meet the famed singer. The move to California seemed to be paying off.

It didn't take long, however, for my father and his crew to catch the attention of the LAPD's elite Organized Crime Division. The FBI had tipped them off that Robert Walsh was a known associate of West Coast Mafia figures. In January 1967, my father, Frank Velotta, Ray Ferritto, Richie Viccarone, and Theodore Ricci were indicted by the L.A. County Grand Jury for conspiracy to commit burglary on an Alpha Beta market on Balboa Boulevard in Granada Hills.

An official LAPD intelligence report claims the crew was additionally responsible for "recent 459's of five Alpha Beta Markets, the Torrance Post Office and the San Fernando Post Office," 459 being the penal code section for burglary.

The report also notes:

Robt. Walsh cases the prospective jobs and generally carries the tools. Frank Velotta is the wire man to bypass the alarms. J. Petro assists in the planning only—The type of businesses which suspects prefer are supermarkets, discount stores, and banks. Money or jewelry has been the object.

The report describes the crew as

a loose knit commercial burglary group composed primarily of Italians from Cleveland area or top hoods from the East. Travel nationwide by air or car . . . using roof drill w/wood bit or pulling lock cylinders from doors w/vise grips. Have ability to bypass any alarm in professional manner. Lately have been attacking E-rated safes w/torch by burning small hole in face & fishing content. Use expensive radio equipment to monitor police frequencies & communicate.

The Alpha Beta burglary made all the newspapers but was not a big topic of conversation at our house. I was in high school at the time. Usually when friends asked what my father did, which wasn't often, I'd say, "I don't know, why don't you ask him," and that would be the end of that.

I had something on my mind about the burglary but didn't know how to broach the subject. One morning my father was driving me to school when a guy in a car that we had just cut off while changing lanes pulled up next to us, honked his horn, and sped away. I didn't exactly know what had happened, but once I saw the smile on my old man's face, what followed was no surprise. That particular smile meant something other than joy.

When we got to the intersection of Victory and Sepulveda, my father threw the car into park, hopped out of the car, and yanked the offending motorist by the tie until his head was out of the side window. I couldn't hear what my father said, but it was clear that he had made his point.

When he got back in the car, I asked, "What did that guy do, Dad?"

"He was making obscene gestures," he explained very matter-of-factly.

"I guess he'll think twice about doing that again," I said, causing my father to smile.

It was a softer smile, not *the* smile. Feeling a sudden sense of camaraderie with the old man, I blurted out, "Hey, Dad, the papers said you did that Alpha Beta burglary on a Friday night, and I remember you being home that night on the couch. We were watching *The Wild Wild West.* What's the deal?"

His head swiveled so fast, I thought I had just made a huge mistake. "You're gonna be late for school today, my boy," he said, obviously pleased.

The next thing I knew, I was in the office of renowned criminal defense attorney Barry Tarlow, telling my story.

I testified at his trial at the Van Nuys Courthouse, where I would later practice as an attorney. I told the jury that my father was at home snoring on the couch the evening of the burglary while we watched TV. Although I testified truthfully, my father was convicted and wound up serving eighteen months in Chino state prison.

While I was still in college in the '70s, my father sent me to Texas after I had prepared a motion to quash a detainer warrant so he could be released from prison without being extradited. I met with a young DA and the judge in the judge's chambers.

The judge, an old-timer with white hair and a thick matching mustache, read over my motion requesting the Court to dismiss the warrant on procedural grounds. "Now, let me get this straight, boy. You haven't started law school yet?"

"Not yet, Your Honor," I replied, hoping he was not going to toss me out because I was not a lawyer.

He turned toward the young prosecutor. "Looks like the boy here has you over a barrel, Billy," he said with a wry grin.

The judge dismissed the warrant. I returned to California, too late to take my final exam in a history class. I had to repeat the class next semester. My father wrote from prison and thanked me, saying he was proud of me.

After he was released from prison, I made the mistake of inquiring about his plans. "Hey, Dad, are you finally done with all this gangster stuff?"

"Mind your own business. What did you do, besides write a goddamned brief?" he replied.

So much for the old man being proud of me.

Julius Petro, a known mob enforcer on parole for bank robbery, who had served time on death row in Ohio before being released on a technicality, would occasionally drive me and his nephew to Notre Dame High School in Sherman Oaks. Julius looked like a Warner Bros. gangster right out of central casting. He wore his jet-black hair slicked back. Dark and swarthy would be an understatement. Ten minutes after he shaved, it looked as if he hadn't shaved for a couple of days. On January 10, 1969, his body was found with a bullet in the head in a car in the parking structure across from the United terminal at LAX. Nine years later, Ray Ferritto told LAPD detectives that he and my father lured Petro to the airport by telling him they had some hot diamonds they needed to move. Petro was in the driver's seat with Ray seated behind him. My father was sitting in the front passenger seat. According to Ray, he shot Petro in the back of the head with a pistol supplied by my father. The shot was muffled by the noise of a jet engine. He claimed he received five thousand dollars and my father was paid fifteen hundred dollars by John "Sparky" Monica. Murder charges were filed against Sparky in June 1978. He was killed in an automobile accident before the case got to trial.

Murder charges were not filed against my father in Los Angeles until 1981. At that time, he was already on the lam. He was accused of masterminding a scheme in which a retrofitted air force transport plane that had been stolen out of Burke Lakefront Airport in Cleveland would be used to smuggle four tons of marijuana and over 200,000 Quaaludes out of Colombia into Hammond, Louisiana. He and my brother Tim were charged with bank fraud and embezzling a total of $610,000 from the Hibernia National Bank in New Orleans to finance the drug smuggling. Charges were subsequently filed in Ohio for the smuggling case. He posted bail but failed to appear at trial in New Orleans in 1981. He remained a fugitive at large for more than three years.

At my law school graduation ceremony in 1982, I spotted two conspicuous FBI agents who must have been expecting my father to show up. My mother and my sisters had made the trip to Santa Clara. Kathy and Laura were snapping photos of us with me in my cap and gown.

I attempted to tease my mother. "Hey, Mom, go ask those feds if they want to be in these pictures."

She was not amused. "Oh, for Christ sake, you think that's funny? What the hell's wrong with you?" she asked, while my sisters tried not to laugh.

I think it was our Irish sense of humor that helped us get by. My mother has a great sense of humor, but not when it comes to my father's line of work.

The old man was finally arrested in Florida in 1984. As a fugitive, he had used twenty-five aliases, six dates of birth, and a phony airline identification card. The headline of an article in the *Daily News* in Los Angeles read LONG-SOUGHT L.A. MURDER SUSPECT TAKEN. Much to my mother's chagrin, this time they spelled the name Walsh correctly.

I made several trips to New Orleans and to Cleveland to meet with my father, his attorneys, Assistant U.S. Attorneys, and FBI agents. As an attorney, I had access to courthouse lockups where he would be shackled in handcuffs and leg irons. It's not very pleasant to see your father in chains. Thankfully, the rest of my family saw him only in visiting rooms without the chains.

In 1985, he was sentenced to fifteen years in federal district court in Louisiana for jumping bond and three counts of embezzling. Tim pleaded guilty to bank fraud and received probation. In Ohio, my father was sentenced to an additional ten years, to run consecutive to the fifteen-year Louisiana sentence, for the smuggling case. The U.S. Attorney's Organized Crime Strike Force filed a sentencing memorandum seeking a maximum sentence due to my father's "wide range of criminal activities, including the threat of physical violence against prospective government witnesses and contract murder."

My father called me from the Federal Correctional Center in Springfield, Missouri, and expressed concern for his safety. Several inmates had approached him in the yard and accused him of being a rat.

"A guy just got shanked in the chow line the other day," he informed me. "Call Russell Bufalino and ask him to straighten this out, and do it right away."

The old man was certainly not a stool pigeon. I had sat in on a meeting with the U.S. Attorney and the FBI in New Orleans, where he refused a deal in exchange for testifying. I knew it had to be a serious threat for my father to make this request. Invoking Bufalino's assistance was not something my father would do on a whim. This was going right to the top of the food chain. Russell Bufalino was the head of the Bufalino crime family out of northeastern Pennsylvania. Called the "Quiet Don," he was known even to FBI agents as a real gentleman. It's said that it was he who had hired Irishman Danny Greene to shoot Crazy Joey Gallo at Umberto's Clam House in New York City's Little Italy. Some say he was involved in the disappearance of Teamster president Jimmy Hoffa. Maybe it was just coincidence that he had driven from Pennsylvania to Detroit the same day Hoffa was last seen at the Red Fox just outside the city.

I knew he was more or less retired at that time. Frank Velotta put me in touch with him.

When I called the old capo, he was mystified. "I can't believe this. Your father's one of the last stand-up guys around. Tell him not to worry. I'll take care of it," he promised.

A few weeks later, my father called and related that the Quiet Don had taken care of the matter. "About seven or eight of these pricks came up to me and apologized, saying they had gotten the word." He laughed. "I told them, 'Eight people testified against me and each one of their names ended in a vowel, so all you Guineas can go fuck yourselves.'"

Despite the stiff sentencing, my father served only eight years in the federal penitentiary.

Prior to being released, he had me contact Ray Ferritto to ask if Ray intended to testify against him in the Julius Petro murder case. Ray had turned state's evidence in a case for the 1977 murder of Cleveland gangster Irish Danny Greene. Greene had drawn the ire of the Cleveland Mafia and instigated a mob war by attempting to take over the union rackets. Ray and Ronnie Carabbia had parked a "Joe Blow" car wired with an

improvised explosive device next to Greene's car while the Irishman was
visiting his dentist. A Joe Blow car was a vehicle that had been stolen or
purchased with phony identification so that it could not be traced and
could be readily ditched when necessary.

Ronnie detonated the bomb as Greene entered his vehicle. The Irishman was blown to smithereens. Ray was arrested and agreed to testify
after learning there was a contract out on his life. His testimony would
ultimately lead to the unraveling of the Cleveland Mafia. He was flown
to L.A. to plead guilty for the murder of Julius Petro. In exchange for his
testimony, he spent less than four years in prison for both murders. He
was paroled and placed in the Witness Protection Program but chose to
drop out.

When I called Ray, sometime in 1992 or 1993, I did not know how he
might react. His voice told me that he was pleased to hear from me. We
chatted for a while before I got to the point of the call. I reminded him
that the first time I ever drove on the freeway was with him on the way to
Dodger Stadium after I had just gotten my driver's license.

"I guess I shoulda had you driving when we offed that Irish prick,"
he said.

Ray was referring to killing Danny Greene. After Ronnie Carabbia
had detonated the bomb, Ray made the mistake of speeding away. A
woman who had heard the explosion had written down a partial plate
number from Ray's car. That was the beginning of the end of the Cleveland Mafia.

When I eventually got around to the Julius Petro murder, Ray told
me that the L.A. District Attorney had tried to have him ordered to appear in California to testify, but a Pennsylvania judge refused to allow it.

"Tell your dad not to worry, I ain't coming out there," he promised.

I thanked him. I had heard that the Mafia had placed a $100,000
price tag on his head. I couldn't help but ask about it. "Ray, are you all
right? Aren't they gonna send somebody for you?"

"Don't worry about me, Denny," he replied. "Whoever they got coming for me, better be as good as me."

Ray never did come to California. My father was never held to answer for the murder of Julius Petro. Charges were dismissed after I requested a speedy trial and the DA was unable to produce Ray to testify. My father was paroled in 1993. As usual, it didn't take long for him to get back in the saddle. He succeeded in avoiding arrest for about seven years until he was apprehended in June of 2000 along with my brother Bobby on the cocaine-smuggling charges.

The Cleveland *Plain Dealer* reported that DEA Agent David Gorman, who had been assigned to tail my father in Louisiana in 1979, was aware of my father's prior police experience with the Intelligence Unit of the Cleveland PD.

He was good—really good. He was an absolute master at picking up surveillance officers. He would make me look like a sissy back then because he knew so much.

Reading this made me smile. I recalled driving to school with my father one morning when I was about twelve or thirteen.

"Don't turn around. Just look out in the sideview mirror," he instructed. "See that green Plymouth a few cars behind us? That's LAPD undercover," he informed me before I could answer.

In a few minutes, after a few quick maneuvers, we were tailing the Plymouth.

"That's how you lose a tail." He grinned while stepping on the gas pedal and honking as we sped past the befuddled cops.

After my brother's murder, I suppose it should have been easy to hate my father, but I didn't. I was bitterly disappointed in him. He was not an easy guy to hate. Assistant U.S. Attorney Ron Bakeman told me he could sit and listen to my father's stories all day, just as several FBI agents had told me over the years. Cleveland attorney Angelo F. Lonardo, who represented him on the last case, told the *Plain Dealer,* "When you meet him you can't help but like him. He is such a nice guy. He has a smile that will light up a room." Over the years, I had introduced only three of my girlfriends to my father. Afterwards, each one of them remarked on his "beautiful" blue eyes and his charming personality.

No matter the situation, my father never lost his sense of humor.

When he was being questioned by two U.S. Marshals after being apprehended in Florida, one of them was a little put out by my father's particular line of patter. "Bobby, you wouldn't shit a country boy, now, would you?"

I can imagine my father's grin as he sarcastically replied, "No siree, not in the country."

He always sent money home when he was gone. He paid for my law school tuition. Still, no amount of money could have atoned for the tremendous amount of grief his family had endured. He was obviously proud of me, even if he never told me directly. When notification that I had passed the California State Bar exam was mailed to my parents' house in November 1982, I received word to come by. I was living with my girlfriend in Woodland Hills. He was on the lam but had been secretly living at home for a couple of years. He kept the car in the attached garage and would lie across the backseat while my brothers transported him to and from another car that he kept across town. My mother had called and mentioned a specific code word that meant the old man wanted to see me. When I arrived, he was sitting at the kitchen table in his bathrobe. He had penciled out the word *Esquire* on a piece of paper and was holding it up for me to see. He was grinning from ear to ear.

It had slipped my mind that the bar results were due that week. I had recently subscribed to *Esquire* magazine and thought that he was upset over getting billed.

He stood up and walked over to me. "You passed the bar, Counselor," he said. He leaned over and kissed me on the cheek.

I was stunned. I couldn't recall my father ever having kissed me.

When I had hernia surgery in San Jose while I was away at law school, I woke up in the hospital recovery room to the sight of my smiling father standing over me with Frank Velotta at his side. He was on the lam at the time, but he still came by.

Around that same time, I was involved in trying to get some funding for a business venture. Frank Velotta had arranged for me to meet with Tony Spilotro in San Diego.

When my father telephoned and learned of the meeting, he exploded. "Get on that phone and cancel that meeting. I didn't send you to law school to be running around with any Outfit guys. I walked away from a score with that fucking lunatic. Stay away from that green-eyed piece of shit, understand?"

The Chicago mob was known as the Outfit. In mobster speak, *green-eyed* meant "greedy." Tony "the Ant" Spilotro had been skimming from Vegas casinos. The Kansas City family was not too pleased. A few years later, Spilotro and his brother were found bludgeoned to death in a corn field in Illinois. When I saw the 1995 movie *Casino,* featuring Joe Pesci playing a character based on Spilotro who puts a guy's head in a vise, I understood that my father was keeping me out of harm's way.

My father may have allowed my brothers into his world, but he was adamantly against me becoming a part of it. Nevertheless, that was the world I came from.

Within a week or two after Christopher was murdered, my father called. I had been expecting his call. Usually we discussed his case or bantered about the Indians or the Browns. This conversation was markedly different. He got straight to the point. There were no tears. He was not going to crack in front of me. He asked me to tell him everything I knew and then followed up with questions. He grilled me like he was still a detective. I told him that the principal shooter, Steinberg, was in jail, and that we needed to let the cops and the DA handle the case. I told him that he needed to put Tim and Dan in line. They were champing at the bit to knock down doors and kick some ass.

"Don't worry, I'll tell them to do whatever you say," he agreed.

He asked how things were going with his request for a compassionate release. It had already been a year since his Mayo Clinic cardiologist reported that he had at best eighteen months to live.

"It doesn't look good," I informed him.

I knew what he was angling for. He wanted out so he could handle things his way. His way would have nothing to do with due process.

Suddenly his voice took on a menacing tone. "I can't be there, understand? *Handle it,*" he ordered.

His tone could be demanding, but this time it offended me. "Oh, I'll handle it, all right," I fired back, "but this is the last of your fucking messes that I'm cleaning up."

There was a pause in the conversation. I think I surprised him. I know I surprised myself. We'd had our disagreements, but I had never spoken to him like that.

"What are you saying, that this is my fault?" he asked.

He didn't have to raise his voice for me to know that he was furious. I may have been a grown man and an attorney to boot, but I was still his son and he did not appreciate the challenge to his authority.

"Yeah, that's what I'm saying," I replied without hesitation. "If you had been home teaching your kids right from wrong instead of running around all over the country with all those Guineas and whores, this kid might not be dead!" I yelled.

I slammed the phone down without waiting for a reply. I didn't regret what I'd said, but regretted having to say it.

A few weeks later, my aunt Mary Ann told me that she had spoken with my father. She said he was in tears, sobbing over my brother's death. He told her what I had said. It had hurt him very deeply. He thought I hated him. She told him I didn't hate him but that I was disappointed in him. I was glad she did. I never spoke with him again. His heart finally gave out two months later. He died alone in the shower at the Federal Medical Center in Rochester, Minnesota, on September 29, 2003.

4

ASHES TO ASHES

THROUGHOUT JULY, I JUGGLED MY law practice with running down leads, as I would continue to do for months to come. Most people I spoke with were in the life, as they say. They were the dopers, thieves, porners, and drug dealers who populated my brother's world. Some offered information; others merely wanted to talk. Information was the key. I began to create a network for gathering information, all the while making it known that my brothers and I would not rest until Christopher's killers were arrested and convicted.

"Nobody walks," I promised, over and over again.

Any information that seemed like it might be pertinent was shoveled to the homicide detectives. I dealt mostly with John Fleming and his partner, Brad Cochran, two veteran detectives. When they were unavailable, David Holmes, a younger detective working the case, usually took my calls. The detectives listened to what I had to say and politely thanked me. They, on the other hand, did not share any information with me. I understood. They could not risk having information leaked onto the streets.

I was constantly on the phone, in the streets, or at the county jail.

"The cops don't care about your brother's murder" became a constant refrain.

"My brothers and I care," I would tell them.

Cowboy was right. It soon became apparent that there were witnesses with pertinent information. Witnesses who feared the killers or who did not want to be considered rats.

My task was clear: I had to convince them to come forward. That would prove to be easier said than done.

Cowboy steered me to Kenny Williams, a dope-dealing gun aficionado who was a friend of Christopher's. It took a series of phone calls before I could convince him to meet with me and my brothers at O'Grady's, an Irish bar in Granada Hills. Barry White, a friend who had grown up with my brothers, was with us. Barry could always be counted on to have your back. Tim had stuffed the jukebox full of quarters. Smokey Robinson's "Tracks of My Tears" was playing when Kenny walked in.

Tim's choice of music was not lost on me. He and I had grown up listening to the Motown sound. Much to the amusement of his friends, Christopher had inherited his big brothers' love of those tunes even though by then the songs were golden oldies.

Kenny was rail thin and wore his hair long like a musician. He was as nervous as a shithouse rat. He wanted to know if Christopher was killed with a .22-caliber gun. I told him I didn't know, the cops weren't sharing any details.

"The reason I ask," he said, "is because just before Chris went missing, he gave me a .22 Colt Challenger pistol to hold on to. The switch on the laser sight was broken. They call me Mr. Gadget, so he probably figured I would clean it up and repair the switch, which I did."

He said he gave the gun to David Steinberg, as Chris had instructed him. He had loaded it with .22 rimfire cartridges.

I didn't pay much attention to that last detail. I was fixated on the pistol. The matter of the cartridges would later turn out to be an important part of the puzzle.

Then Kenny related some even more startling information. "Steinberg asked me about making a silencer, so I told him how," Kenny said.

"Holy shit," I blurted out. "Kenny, you gotta go to the police with this shit, please."

"You know what I do for a living, don't you?" he asked. "That's pretty much career suicide, not to mention me probably catching a bullet in the head."

Tim got up abruptly and ordered a shot of tequila at the bar. I could see the fury in his eyes. He was ready to drag Kenny by the hair down to Devonshire Division.

I could hardly be mad. Kenny Williams was a likable sort. I could understand his reservation. I didn't want anything to happen to him or anyone else who was willing to cooperate.

Dan tried his best to close the deal. "Kenny, anybody so much as drives by your house and blows his horn is gonna catch a world of shit. I promise you," he said while the jukebox played the Temptations' "Ain't Too Proud to Beg."

Kenny finally agreed to speak with the homicide detectives and left O'Grady's like his house was on fire. Later that evening he called me. "I really don't appreciate you setting me up with those undercover cops," he said.

I had to laugh. I was the one who usually got made for a cop. I doubt that anyone had ever mistaken Tim, Dan, or Barry for cops. It took another series of phone calls to calm him down.

I was on my way to Jack in the Box in Granada Hills to meet Kenny when my buddy Jim Cavanaugh called. He was a cop working for a local police department. He just happened to be out and about serving subpoenas.

"What the fuck are you driving?" I inquired.

"I'm in a Crown Vic. What the fuck do you care?" he asked.

"Never mind," I answered. "Get your worthless ass over to Jack in the Box on Chatsworth. I'll meet you there in ten minutes."

We had known each other since we were teenagers. Like Barry White, Jim Cavanaugh could always be counted on.

I spotted his black Ford Crown Victoria in the Jack in the Box parking lot. The vehicle practically screamed *cops*. I got in on the passenger side.

"What's up, Sergeant Friday?" I inquired.

"You tell me, Matlock," he said.

"Just sit here and keep your big Irish trap shut," I replied.

Christopher was prone to boasting about our father's organized crime connections. I thought it wouldn't hurt to let these people know I was working both sides of the fence.

Kenny strolled up a few minutes later. When he saw me exit the unmarked cop car, he stopped dead in his tracks. "What the fuck?" he said.

"Don't ask," I answered. "Kenny, if I wanted you rolled up, your house would have already gotten tossed. If those were cops the other night at O'Gradys, don't you think they'd have been wired up and I wouldn't have to keep begging you to go down to the cop shop?" I asked.

Cop shop was street lingo for "police station." It didn't hurt to talk the talk.

"I don't know what your deal is," he said while nodding toward Cavanaugh, who was seated in the Crown Vic talking on his radio, "but Troy Wilcox called and told me to play dumb, which really pissed me off, so I've decided to talk to the po-po."

Po-po was a street term for "police." I thanked him and told him not to worry, that it would all work out, despite not being really sure of anything.

While hurrying over to my car, I yelled my thanks to Cavanaugh.

"Aren't you even gonna buy me lunch?" he asked.

"I'm in a hurry. Go fuck yourself," I shot back.

I was relieved when Kenny finally called and confirmed that he had given a statement to Detective Fleming.

Cowboy called to inquire if it was all right if he and Troy Wilcox attended Christopher's funeral services.

"You're welcome to come," I responded, "but tell that Porky Pig piece of shit that he can show up at his own peril."

A few days earlier, I had been staking out Troy Wilcox's house on Woodley Avenue. Through binoculars I observed him to be short and stout. He looked to be every bit the bag of wind that he had sounded over the phone. I didn't gain much other information, but did learn not to sit in the driver's seat on a stakeout in a residential neighborhood. Two women from the Neighborhood Watch approached my car to inquire what I was up to. From then on, I would sit in the passenger seat with a newspaper. It worked like a charm. Neighbors assumed that the driver was inside one of the houses. The old man would have been proud.

On July 18, Detective Fleming called. Christopher's belongings needed to be removed from the storage unit where his body had been recovered. I met Detectives Fleming and Cochran at Devonshire Division. I sat in the backseat of a beige unmarked police car while we drove to the Public Storage that Troy Wilcox had rifled through. The units were outside, allowing us to drive right up to the bright orange metal door. The detectives cut the lock with bolt cutters and rolled up the door, exposing mounds of clothing and toys belonging to Christopher's kids. It was heartbreaking to look at those toys. The detectives conducted a brief search of the unit but found nothing evidentiary.

We then made our way over to the Sherman Oaks MiniStorage in Van Nuys, where Christopher's body had been recovered. Until then, I had only seen the multilevel storage facility from the street. The manager punched in the security code to open the gate. Detective Cochran said the security cameras had not been in operation around the time the body was recovered. We drove slowly into the cavernous four-story structure. It would have been eerie under normal circumstances, and now it was even more so. The facility was dimly lit, almost completely dark in some of the narrow hallways that branched off the main ramp that snaked up and around to the various levels. We stopped on the second level and walked down one of the hallways to Unit 2420. It was as dark and dank as I imagined the catacombs to be. A metal roll-up door on the front of the unit with a sliding latch mechanism on the right side was secured with a padlock. One of the detectives opened the lock and rolled up the door. Being in the very spot where that weasel Steinberg had abandoned my brother's body was almost overwhelming. I managed to compose myself. I did not want to crack in front of these two veteran cops.

Detective Fleming spotted a black briefcase that was lying on the floor. He picked it up and opened it. "Have you ever seen this briefcase before?" he asked.

"No," I replied.

"The manager says whatever is left here in the morning is going in the Dumpster," Detective Cochran informed me before they left.

Detective Fleming took the black briefcase with him without further comment. It would turn out to contain a crucial piece of evidence.

The dismal surroundings affected me so profoundly that to this day I don't remember how I got possession of Christopher's white Ford Explorer that day. It had been towed from the carport behind Steinberg's apartment the night he was arrested. Somehow it had been released from SID, the LAPD's Scientific Investigation Division, into my possession. I began loading it up with the contents of the storage unit.

It was plenty hot outside, but it was roasting inside the facility. I hauled whatever I could grab down the hallway to the Explorer. I probably filled that vehicle up five or six times, driving each load across the Valley to the Public Storage unit in Chatsworth, unloading it, then driving back to Van Nuys. I took some comfort in wearing a cheap pair of Christopher's sunglasses I had found in the console.

The Explorer's exterior was completely coated in filmy gray fingerprint dust. It seemed as if everyone on the road was eyeballing me. By the fourth trip to Chatsworth, I was thoroughly exhausted. While stopped at an intersection, I noticed the driver in the lane next to me looking a bit too intently at the dusty Explorer.

"What the fuck are you looking at?" I asked the poor bastard, causing him to quickly avert his gaze.

On the way back for the final load, I stopped at a liquor store and bought a six-pack of Heineken and a bag of ice. After finally finishing my task, I plopped down inside the storage unit and cracked open a beer. I was drenched in sweat and too beat to cry. That beer probably tasted better than any beer I've ever had or ever will have.

I offered up a toast to my departed brother. "I don't know what exactly happened, Christopher, and maybe I was a pretty shitty big brother, but I promise you whoever did this is going to pay. If you can hear me, I just might need your help. Nobody's walking on this one, baby bro."

I wanted to get out of this place that had become my brother's tomb, but then again, I didn't. His body had remained here, cold and alone, after his killers disposed of him. It was only right to stay a bit longer, have another beer. The brew caused me to perspire even more profusely. My thoughts turned to the macabre as I imagined the fluids slowly draining from Christopher's rapidly decomposing body.

"Somebody just bought themselves a first-class ticket to hell!" I yelled.

I fired the empty beer can against the storage wall and left without looking back.

The manager of Steinberg's apartment at 12659 Moorpark Street was anxious to clean the unit and rent it out. Some of Christopher's belongings remained there. After getting the okay from Detective Fleming, I met Cowboy at the apartment. It was a two-story complex of maybe ten or twelve units. I stood in front of the door, marked with a brass number *4*. I pictured my brother walking through that door for the last time, not knowing that he would never walk out. Cowboy was already inside. I walked in with more than a bit of trepidation. This was where Christopher had drawn his last breath. Cowboy pointed out where the couch had been. A section of carpet had been removed by the LAPD. I figured the spot had been saturated with blood. My mouth was so dry, I could have spit dust. I fought off the image of my brother lying on the couch and forced myself to go to a place in my mind devoid of emotion. I had to get through this. I let Cowboy have a broken dresser and a few pairs of Christopher's shoes. I took an accordion file filled with paperwork. It contained mostly bills and receipts dated months before the murder. I assumed the cops had already gone through it and taken what they needed. I didn't spend much time there at all. I couldn't.

The accordion file contained a check for twenty thousand dollars from a production company payable to actress Dana Delany and an application for a money market account in a name I didn't recognize. Later I learned that Steinberg had been in the process of opening the account to deposit the stolen funds in the name of his daughter. I turned the paperwork over to the police and notified Dana Delany's office of the matter.

Steinberg appeared in court again on the thirtieth, two days before Christopher's funeral. I made sure he saw me. I glared at him and didn't care that he ignored me. Just by being there I was sending a message. Steinberg was still wearing a dark blue jailhouse jumpsuit. Blue signified main line, general population.

I approached the bailiff. "Hey, Deputy, this puke shot it out with a deputy sheriff and they're looking at him for my brother's murder. How come he's still in general pop?" I asked.

"Don't worry, I already called Men's Central. He'll be in high power tonight," he said.

High power meant the third floor, maximum security. The 3000 block was reserved for the most notorious offenders, mostly killers and high-level gang members. High-power inmates wore orange and were shackled during transportation and attorney visits. Visits and phone calls were restricted. More use-of-force incidents by jailers occurred on the third floor than on any other unit in the L.A. county jail. It would be a real wake-up call for Steinberg.

Gary Schimmel, Steinberg's friend who had signed the Moorpark Street apartment lease, was in the anteroom between the courtroom and the hallway. I heard Steinberg had been calling him from county jail.

"Next time you talk to Shitberg, ask him how he likes his new digs. Tell him, 'Compliments of Dennis Walsh,'" I said.

Letting Steinberg believe I was behind his transfer to high power couldn't hurt.

On the thirty-first, I barely had time to finish my legal work and make arrangements for Frank and Johnny Rio to be fed while I left town to attend the funeral. I threw my shaving kit, some clothes, and a bottle of Jameson in the car and lit out in a hurry. Somehow I avoided the California Highway Patrol, but my luck ran out around 5:30 P.M., a few miles after I crossed the Arizona border. I had located an oldies station on the radio. The Four Tops' "I Can't Help Myself" was blaring, probably inducing me to goose the gas pedal just a tad.

"Fuck me!" I cursed as soon as I glimpsed the red lights in my rearview mirror.

Fuck me was right. The female Arizona trooper who pulled me over was not in good humor. "Seventy-five miles an hour not fast enough for you, sir?" she asked.

She returned to her cruiser to run my driver's license.

A few minutes later, she delivered the bad news with a stereotypical deadpan delivery. "Mr. Walsh, I clocked you doing a hundred and three miles an hour, and in Arizona anything over one hundred is a criminal offense," she informed me. "I'm going to have to arrest you and take you to jail. You can go to court in the morning. Please step out of your vehicle."

Somewhere my brother Christopher must have been laughing his ass off. His big-shot attorney brother was finally getting hauled off to the hoosegow.

I had to think fast. I grabbed the newspaper clippings and a copy of the obituary with details of the funeral that lay on the passenger seat. I handed her the paperwork and nervously explained the purpose of my trip. I didn't dare tell her I was a lawyer. Most cops have experienced a grilling or two by defense attorneys on cross-examinations.

"I'll never make it to the funeral tomorrow," I pleaded while she intently perused the information.

"What's that?" she asked, pointing to the bottle of Jameson on the front seat.

"It's Irish whiskey for the wake," I replied, holding up the bottle so she could see it was unopened.

"All right, Mr. Walsh," she said. "I'm very sorry for your loss. I'm still going to write you up for a hundred and three. I won't make it a criminal offense, but I suggest you slow down or you might be attending your own funeral."

I thanked her and breathed a sigh of relief. It was around 7 P.M. when I arrived at my mother's house. Many relatives and friends of the family were already gathered there. Christopher's kids, Shane and Ashley, had made a little shrine with flowers and a picture of their father in the backyard. I hadn't seen my mother for a while. She looked haggard, but was busy attending to the guests. I quickly made the rounds, then settled in with my brothers, a few of Christopher's old friends, and my bottle of Jameson. They all got a kick out of my brush with the law. I filled everyone in on what I knew about the ongoing investigation. The night was mostly filled with laughter and stories of Fin, or Finny, or Finnegan, as they lovingly referred to Christopher.

Late in the evening, Tim, Dan, and Barry White pulled me aside. We huddled across the pool in the corner of the yard while the others swam, sang, and carried on.

"Dennis, we're worried about you being alone on the streets in California. Barry's gonna shadow you. He'll have your back wherever you go," Dan said.

"Just call me, Dennis. Whatever you need, I'm there," Barry promised while spitting out a wad of chew and yanking up his shirt to expose the handle of a silver automatic pistol sticking out of his waistband.

"I thought my mother told everyone to check their weapons at the front door," I joked.

Barry was loyal. He would be there, if need be. The old man had taught us to value a trusted friend, but to only place that trust judiciously. One day in the visitors' room at Terminal Island federal penitentiary, I had noticed a Latin phrase penciled on one of his legal files.

Fide sed cui vide it read. Beneath it he had written, *Trust but take care whom you trust.*

"Remember this," my father said. "When the shit hits the fan, there won't be too many people around to help you mop it up."

A small group of us continued drinking until 4 A.M. Most of the conversation centered around Tim's thoughts on killing Steinberg in progressively gruesome scenarios. Even though I had polished off most of the Jameson, I barely felt its effect when my sister Kathy woke me up only three hours later. Normally, I would have been hungover for three days, but not this day.

As I drove over to Saint Anne's Catholic Church for the funeral Mass, it occurred to me that Christopher had been born at Saint Ann's Hospital. I got there just as the Mass was starting. My family was packed into the first few pews. Friends of the family occupied the following rows. I sat alone in the back of the church. The result of having been shoehorned into the middle of the congregation one too many times as a kid.

After Mass, I followed the caravan over to the cemetery. Half of Christopher's ashes were to be interred and the other half would be spread at a spot in the White Mountains where Christopher loved to spend time.

Since the morning after my brother's body was recovered at the storage facility, I had kept myself busy with my law practice and tracking down leads. I hadn't allowed myself time to grieve, and I had no intention of breaking down in front of my family now. My resolve withered, however, at the cemetery. I was about to walk over to console my mother when a kilted Irish piper appeared. Once I heard the first few mournful notes of "Amazing Grace," I froze. It shook me to the core. The shrill wail of the Irish uilleann pipes is intended to mimic the keening voices at traditional Irish wakes. It is said to be a reflection of the Irish soul. The dirgelike sound of the bagpipes coupled with the sight of my mother and sisters crying was almost too much for me. I not only wept like a schoolgirl, but began to shake uncontrollably as well. The reality of my brother's murder had finally hit home. Dan's wife, Julie, latched on to my arm and stood with me.

After the interment of half the ashes, we retired to my mother's house for a typical Irish wake. The drinking and storytelling continued into the night. Both my father and my brother Bobby called from prison. There were plenty of people eager to speak with them, so I did not pick up the phone. After our last conversation, it was no surprise that my father did not ask to speak with me.

The next morning, my uncle Leo, Tim, Dan, my nephew Danny, my cousins Tommy and Scott, and I squeezed into Dan's Cadillac Escalade. We drove to the Mogollon Rim in the Coconino National Forest to spread the remainder of Christopher's ashes. A few of us drank beer from an ice chest in the backseat. The scenery was spectacular once we got up into the White Mountains. As jokes and good-natured insults flew, I clutched the plastic box containing Christopher's ashes tightly.

Dan finally pulled off the road after a few hours. He looked at me standing next to his SUV, polishing off a can of Heineken. "You fuckers were drinking beer while I was driving?" he asked incredulously. "I thought you were supposed to be a lawyer, for Christ's sake."

We walked to a spot laden with pine trees overlooking a canyon. The view was stunning. It was no wonder Christopher loved this place. I handed the container to Dan to do the honors. Just at the moment he scattered the ashes over the side of the canyon, a gust of wind came out of nowhere and blew the ashes backwards. I was covered in powdery gray ash. My relatives thought it was all pretty hysterical, as I'm quite sure Christopher would have.

I managed to laugh and wipe the ashes from my face while my cousin Tommy brushed them from my shirt and jeans. For some reason, I left my Tribe cap on my head, still plastered with ashes. Somehow it seemed to afford me some comfort on the long ride home. Although those ashes would finally wear away, I can say for certain that they remained on that cap for over six months. Just ask an old crystal meth cook by the name of Don Mercatoris.

THE QUEST

5

AND WE NEVER CAME

THE MONTH OF AUGUST PROVED to be not only fiercely hot but also a hotbed of activity with respect to the murder case. Steinberg remained in county jail, but murder charges still had not been filed. I was getting antsy. Cowboy had been calling with bits and pieces of increasingly compelling information.

The word on the streets was that Steinberg had shot Christopher. According to Kimmi Balmes, Shane Wilson said when he and Jeff Weaver arrived at Steinberg's apartment, he told them he had just shot Chris Walsh. Wilson said Christopher was still alive, "gurgling" on the couch. He had been telling people, "You don't wanna know what happened to Chris Walsh." Weaver had told Kimmi, "If the cops get Diane, they might as well execute me." Diane Stewart had said Weaver showed up "white as a ghost" and confessed to taking Christopher's Porsche sunglasses, remarking, "He won't be needing these." They put the body in the refrigerator and then in a trash barrel, which was wiped down with WD-40. They had rented a U-Haul truck to move the body.

The thought of my brother lying helplessly on that couch and "gurgling" sent chills through my body. Weaver's comment made it clear that Diane Stewart, aka Alexandra Quinn, was a key player in this caper.

"I don't think Kimmi will ever talk to the cops," Cowboy told me, "but she liked Chris a lot. I'll see if she'll at least talk to you and your brothers."

I had already spoken with Detective Holmes to let him know what I had been hearing about Shane Wilson. Detective Holmes had an easy-going, affable manner. I got a kick out of how he usually prefaced his response by saying, *Oh, really.*

"Oh, really," he had said. "We know all about Shankster Gangster. He's a real dirtbag. I'd love to put him away for good, but we need something to go on."

It looked like I had my work cut out for me.

I got busy and learned that Kimmi Balmes was a thirty-four-year-old dancer at Eros Station in Van Nuys, a place where men went to watch women dance nude in private rooms. I went down to the county jail to see Lee Martin, a friend of Christopher. Lee had gained some notoriety for escaping from the Van Nuys Courthouse during the middle of a trial. According to him, years ago, Kimmi had witnessed an ex-boyfriend—who had just been released from prison—blow her current boyfriend's brains out at her kitchen table. She hated guns and would probably be sympathetic. She rented a house in Mission Hills with her husband, Indian Gary Balmes. Weaver had been renting a room from them before he was arrested for a parole violation.

Diane Stewart was infamous in the porn industry. She emigrated from Canada with a falsified passport and found work in adult films under the name "Alexandra Quinn." She had been under the age of eighteen when many of her movies were filmed. More than seventy videos had to be pulled off the shelves all over the country when it came to light that she was a minor.

I pulled up a few trailers from her more recent movies. Not all that attractive, she capitalized on her specialty, double penetration. Visiting her Web sites caused my computer to contract a virus and crash. It took an entire day to install new anti-virus programs and remove and reinstall various other software programs. I cursed her all day long.

On August 12, I met with Kenny Williams. He gave me the chip from

Christopher's cell phone and Alexandra Quinn's business card. The chip contained all Christopher's phone contacts. He said Steinberg attempted to have Magic Mark Prines, a magician, rent a U-Haul truck when Christopher was missing. He agreed to see if Magic Mark would speak with me. I passed all the information on to the homicide detectives. I dropped off the phone chip and business card at Devonshire Division.

Tim and Dan were in town on the fifteenth to track down Shankster Gangster and extract some information. August 15 was about to shape up into a barnburner of a day.

"Tim and I can handle this," Dan had said. "You don't need to get your ticket pulled. "We're gonna sit this fucker down and put a blowtorch to his face and see if he tells us we don't want to know what happened to Chris."

"I don't mind grabbing this prick and slapping him around a bit, seeing as how he won't be calling the cops, but there's not going to be any blowtorch. We're just looking for information. If the son of a bitch wants to leave, we let him leave. I'm not gonna catch a kidnapping beef over this. Steinberg would just love that."

I knew if I was there, things would not get out of control.

Dan, Tim, and Barry White met me at the El Presidente Mexican Restaurant in Mission Hills. Cowboy had agreed to meet us. We snagged a couple tables on the outdoor covered patio. That spot was about to become my new "office." Cowboy and his girlfriend, Brandi, arrived a few minutes later. I got up to use the men's room. When I got back, Tim whispered that Brandi had told them how she once worked Weaver up the ass with a dildo.

"That's what happens when I leave things up to you, Tim," I said.

I took over the questioning. It quickly became clear that it was Brandi who had elicited the information from Kimmi.

"Look, Brandi, all this is good shit and I appreciate you talking with us, but Kimmi's really the one I need to talk to," I said.

"I just talked to her. She's home now. Let's go see her," she said.

She didn't have to say it twice. I flung a couple of twenties at the waitress. We piled into our vehicles and followed Cowboy and Brandi the few blocks to Kimmi's house on Sandra Street. Brandi went inside and came out a few minutes later with Kimmi. She was in a housedress and wore no makeup. There was something going on with her teeth. Crystal meth tended to wear away teeth and gums. She certainly didn't look like an exotic dancer. She nervously peered around as Brandi introduced us. She asked if we could go somewhere else. We reconvened at El Presidente.

Kimmi was something of an airhead, but seemed genuinely upset over Christopher's murder. We sat riveted as she sipped a strawberry margarita and confirmed what Cowboy and Brandi had told us.

From time to time, while the others sat mesmerized by Kimmi's tale, I would sneak out to the parking lot to call the homicide detectives. It was late on a Friday afternoon. I spoke alternately with Detectives Sasha and Kaiser, relaying information as Kimmi related it. Coincidentally, Detective Craig Sasha had placed the cuffs on Steinberg at his apartment.

"I've made a lot of arrests," he told me, "but Steinberg had the coldest eyes of anyone I've ever collared. When we took him down, I was kind of hoping he would reach."

It was around four o'clock. At any moment, the detectives would be heading home for the weekend. I made my pitch by tugging at Kimmi's heartstrings.

"My mother and Christopher's kids are heartbroken. Steinberg's counting on people like you not to cooperate. If people don't step up to the plate, these bastards are going to walk. Is that what you want, Kimmi?" I asked.

I almost fell out of my chair when Kimmi agreed to speak with the homicide detectives.

"I'll call them right now," I told her. "If they're already gone, can I pick you up first thing Monday morning?"

"If I don't do it now, I might not ever do it," she said.

I called to inform the detectives that we were en route. On the way to Devonshire Division, I blew through two red lights.

"Hey, Mad Max, take it easy," Kimmi said.

I sat in the lobby while she gave her statement. Afterwards, I took her home. I gave her my business card, thanked her profusely, and left. She promised to keep in touch.

I swang back over to El Presidente, where Barry and my brothers waited. I dialed Shane Wilson's number and left a message to call me. Dan made arrangements for Christopher's girlfriend, Christina Karath, to meet us at the Stovepiper Lounge, a bar in Northridge. She had been avoiding us up until now. I told Dan to call her back and find out what she was driving.

"I don't know if this broad can be trusted," I said in the Stovepiper parking lot. "This would be a great time for an ambush while we're all together. Barry, stay here and call me when she shows. She's driving a white Mustang convertible. Keep your eyes open and call me if any suspicious-looking characters turn up. I don't want anyone walking in this joint that we're not ready for. *Capisce?*"

"Don't worry, Counselor, I got it covered," Barry said.

After about an hour, my cell phone rang.

"The eagle has landed," Barry said.

My brothers were pretty oiled up by this time from drinking all afternoon at El Presidente. They were in a lighthearted mood, chatting amiably with Christina. Her black hair and sharp features evidenced her Greek heritage. She came from a well-to-do family, but supported herself by dealing drugs. I drilled her with questions. She confirmed much of what Kimmi had told us. She said Steinberg shot Christopher with a pistol in the back of the head and that he did not die right away. Cloud Pierson helped clean up the apartment. She had seen Steinberg in a U-Haul truck with a girl she thought might have been Tanya around the time of the murder. Porn actress Diane Stewart had said Weaver admitted to removing Christopher's expensive Porsche sunglasses from his head.

"There's something else about Steinberg," she said. "It was weird. Chris would find little items of his in Steinberg's bedroom. Then one day he went ballistic when he found his loofah in Steinberg's shower. It seemed like David had some kind of sexual fetish for Chris."

"That doesn't surprise me," Dan said. "I heard he got turned out when he was doing federal time. That's how he got by in the joint, being somebody's bitch."

She claimed she was afraid for her life and did not want to cooperate with the police. Troy Wilcox had suggested that she avoid talking to the cops if she wanted to keep slinging drugs. Nonetheless, I kept pounding away.

She reluctantly agreed to speak to the homicide detectives. "I'll do it, but you're going to get me killed," she said.

"They'll have to go through us first," Dan said.

"Christina, are you more comfortable after meeting Christopher's brothers?" I asked.

"I find you very intimidating," she said without a trace of a smile.

She insisted on paying the bar tab and left. My instincts told me not to trust her.

"Let's go find Shankster Gangster," Tim announced. "I wanna see how tough this Nazi Low Rider punk is."

The Le Cannon bar in Woodland Hills, where Shane Wilson's ex-wife, Tiffany, tended bar, was our next stop. Barry, my brothers, and I entered the bar separately in intervals of two to three minutes. The plan was to sit apart from one another, drink some beer, and wait for Wilson to show up. After an hour and a half or so, I decided to cut it short. Dan and Barry were shooting pool. I walked over to the bar.

"What'll you have?" Tiffany asked as she wiped down the bar.

I slapped my business card down on the bar. "My name is Dennis Walsh. Your ex-husband is involved in my brother's murder and I'm looking for him," I told her.

"Shane didn't have anything to do with that," she protested. Her wide eyes suggested otherwise.

"Tell that prick we're coming," I said. "We'll be back."

I walked out the door with my brothers. Barry had already gone to his car. Once outside, I was accosted by two burly muscular bouncers.

"Wait a minute," the one with a shaved head called out. "What's going on?"

Luckily, I spied Tim approaching the bouncer with his tongue rolled up.

"I got this, Tim," I said sharply.

Thankfully, Tim held his ground.

"My younger brother was murdered. Her ex was involved and we're looking for him. This is something you two really don't want to be involved in," I said.

Tim had circled over toward the other bouncer. They couldn't see what I saw. A shiny red dot glistened from the middle of the bald bouncer's forehead. I realized it was coming from Barry's laser-sighted pistol.

"We aren't looking for any trouble," I told the bouncer.

The laser dot suddenly disappeared.

"Let's go," I told Tim and Dan.

We walked over to Barry's car.

"Jesus, Barry. What the fuck?" I asked.

"I wasn't gonna cap that big prick," Barry explained. "I was just checking my sights."

We were all pretty played out after the day's excitement and agreed to postpone rousting up Shane Wilson until the next day. On the drive home, I checked my phone messages.

Shane Wilson had called. "I'm sorry about your little brother," his message began. "I didn't have anything to do with killing him. I'll be glad to talk to you anytime."

The time of the message was 10:16 P.M., just a few minutes after we had left the bar.

I dialed his number. This time he picked up. He continued to deny any involvement whatsoever, which did not endear him to me.

"You made too many mistakes, asshole," I told him. "You told people my brother was on the couch gurgling. You told people they didn't want to know what happened to Chris Walsh. My brothers and I want to sit you down and have you tell us we don't want to know what happened to our brother."

"I know about your family," he said. "Why don't you guys handle it yourselves instead of calling the cops?"

"Hey, asshole, you're lucky we aren't handling it ourselves, because you'd be dead already," I responded, barely able to contain myself.

"Well, I don't cooperate with the cops," he informed me.

"Listen, you white trash hillbilly motherfucker," I hollered. "Mark my words—you're gonna sit on a witness stand and sing like a goddamned canary or you're gonna ride a murder beef straight to hell!"

One of us hung up. I don't recall who.

It took me about fifty minutes to get home. I fed Frank and Johnny Rio and dived into bed without bothering to eat dinner. A couple hours later, I was awakened by the deafening ring of the phone only inches from my ear. It was Tim. He was drunk and he was sobbing. I sobered up in a heartbeat. My brother Tim was as tough as nails and not given to tears.

"Dennis, I can't sleep. I keep thinking of Chris lying on that sofa waiting for his brothers to come through that door and we never came. Dennis, we never came."

My head was pounding and I felt nauseated. "Tim, you can't dwell on this shit or it'll eat you alive. We've got a lot to do. We have to stay strong. Get some rest. I'll call you in the morning," I said, not knowing what else to offer.

I went to the bathroom and puked my guts out. Tim's words—*and we never came*—would continue to haunt me to this day.

6

STRAIGHT THROUGH THE GATES OF HELL

T HE NEXT MORNING, I WAS catching up on some legal work when Kimmi Balmes called. Diane Stewart was in custody at the Van Nuys jail on a petty drug beef and waiting to get bailed out. I had been trying to contact her for weeks, and so had the detectives. Weaver's lament, "If they get Diane Stewart, they might as well execute me," had catapulted her to the top of my list of people to see. It was Saturday, and the detectives were off for the weekend. Detective Fleming had given me his cell phone number. I caught him at home.

"I'm heading down to the Van Nuys station," I told him. "I don't want her bailing out before you get there."

I figured he would probably call the desk sergeant and have them keep her on ice until he got there, but I wasn't taking any chances. If she did bail out, I intended to tail her and find out where she, as the cops would say, "laid her head at night."

I hopped in my car and sped down the canyon out of the mountains. I had put Johnny Rio in the backseat. The harrowing seventeen-mile ride through the winding canyon was enough to cause him and his breakfast to part company. I heard him retching as I dialed Shane Wilson's number.

I didn't have time to stop and clean up the mess. Shankster Gangster picked up the phone as I was southbound on the 405 just past Newhall.

"Hey, asshole," I said, "Diane Stewart just got hooked up. I'm on my way over to Van Nuys jail to see that she sits tight until the homicide cops get there. Remember what your buddy Weaver said about the cops getting her."

My cell phone lost reception as I was going through the pass into the Valley. I redialed Wilson's number several times, but he wasn't picking up.

I found a parking spot near the Van Nuys police station and hurriedly wiped up the vomit in the backseat. Johnny Rio and I sprinted over to the jail. I tied his leash to the staircase railing and ran up the steps. I planted myself in the lobby until Detective Fleming arrived.

On the drive back, Kenny Williams called. Magic Mark Prines had some information. I held my cell phone to my ear with my shoulder while I steered with one hand and jotted down notes with the other. I had begun keeping notes, putting together a half-assed journal of handwritten entries detailing meetings and phone conversations, names, telephone numbers, and addresses. "Half-assed" because I was usually writing on the fly, scribbling away while driving or juggling business calls.

Monday morning, I called Detective Cochran at 7:55 A.M. to relay all I had learned over the last three days. As usual, he listened and thanked me without much comment.

A few days later, I called Magic Mark—from a pay phone per his request to Kenny.

Like my family, he was originally from Cleveland. He said he was a professional magician. Christopher had been acting as a quasi-manager, trying to line up some work for him. He was clearly terrified of Steinberg.

"Listen, you've got nothing to be afraid of. I guarantee you that anybody who had anything to do with the planning, the murder, moving the body, cleaning the apartment, or the cover-up is going down. Nobody but nobody is gonna walk on this case," I assured him.

My tone may have been a little too emphatic. He didn't seem to be all that reassured. He said that while Christopher was missing, he drove Steinberg to a house in La Cañada owned by actor Ving Rhames that was under renovation. Despite it being a sweltering summer day, Steinberg wore a heavy coat zippered to the neck and seemed to be concealing something. Before hanging up, he grudgingly gave me permission to give his phone number to the homicide detectives.

The next day, I received a letter from Michael Gougis, a staff writer for the Los Angeles *Daily News*. He was requesting some background information about Christopher and Steinberg. He also wanted to know "who attended Mr. Steinberg's last court appearance and shouted at him, 'I'm your worst nightmare'?"

I called his office and left a message that I had no comment at that time. On August 25, an article with his byline, titled MISCHIEF LED TEENS TO BIGGER PROBLEMS, appeared in the newspaper. It featured a picture of Steinberg holding a California state prison placard under his chin. I tacked it to the wall next to the prayer card from Christopher's funeral, which carried an Irish blessing. Not that I needed any further motivation, but I wanted to see this bastard's face every day.

The name of Irish Mike O'Hickey turned up on my radar screen. He and Christopher had been involved in some sort of confrontation. I had tracked him down in Glendale. He and his wife, Marta Wilson, were staying at the Days Inn. Thinking he might be hostile, I parked across the street and dialed his number.

His wife answered. "I'm sorry about your brother," she said. "I liked Chris a lot. I don't know anything about his murder. Mike's not here right now, but I'll tell him to call you." Her voice seemed distant, and she appeared eager to get off the phone.

"I really don't have time to jerk around with you people. I'm right across the street and can see your room from here. Tell Mike not to make me come looking for him. I'll be expecting his call," I said.

The line was silent.

"Look," I said, "I need all the help I can get, but I promise you if I find out either of you are lying to me, I'll walk you straight through the gates of hell."

I thought I delivered the message very calmly. It was not my intent to alarm her. I had other matters to attend to, so I hit the road. My gut told me Irish Mike would be calling soon.

I finally caught up with him at the county jail after he phoned to let me know where he was. It was Saturday and the attorney room was closed. I was sandwiched between a slew of women and whining kids in the public visiting room. Mike turned out to be a very interesting character. His shaved head and numerous tattoos belied his gregarious personality. His manic mannerisms suggested he might be bipolar, probably the result of years of drug abuse.

"Your brother came after me one day with a gun," he told me. "I hollered out, 'Chris Walsh, are you here to kill me?' Chris started laughing and we hugged it out."

He was eager to be of assistance, providing details on Steinberg and Weaver. He suggested that I contact Marta, who could assist me until he got released. "I'll call her and tell her to talk to you, but take it easy with her." He laughed. "You sounded like Chris on the phone. You scared the holy shit out of her."

I took Mike's advice and gave Marta a call. I apologized immediately for frightening her. I expected to hear the ramblings of a strung-out doper chick. Instead, she was bright and articulate. Her voice was sweet in a way that made it seem she just had to be attractive. She was truly fond of Christopher. She knew Steinberg as Frankie. He carried a pistol in a hollowed-out book. She wanted to help, but wasn't too keen on cooperating with the authorities. She had already spoken to Detective Fleming regarding witnessing Steinberg pull a gun on Moises Tovar.

I felt I could trust her. Marta Wilson would not only become a major source of information for me, but also a close friend and confidante.

My prior warning to Marta proved to be prophetic, except that I was already at the gates of hell.

September 17 rolled around in a hurry. Christopher would have been thirty-eight years old that day. I called my mother. She and my sister Laura had just come back from the cemetery. Though her voice was heavy, she spoke of how nice it was at the cemetery. She asked about my father's compassionate release.

"Tell that guy I'm not leaving him hanging, Mom. I'm working on that and about nine hundred other things. I'll let you know when I hear something," I said.

"What do you mean 'that guy'?" she said. "Don't be like that, Dennis. He's your father."

Twelve days later, I was driving on the 405 when my aunt Mary Ann called. She was crying. "Dennis, your father died," she said.

"Aunt Mary Ann, let me call you back," I answered.

I was too choked up to talk. The old man had been living on borrowed time. Nonetheless, I shed more than a few tears that day. The thought of him dying in prison had tormented me since his arrest. His words, *Do what you think you're big enough to do,* echoed across my mind.

"Ah, fuck," I said out loud. "Don't worry, Pop, I'll get those mother-fuckers that killed Christopher if it's the last thing I do."

I contacted prison officials in Minnesota to make arrangements for my father's body to be shipped to Phoenix. An ex-girlfriend came over that evening to offer some solace. There wasn't much she could do, however, to ease the pain of the conflict between my father and me that would forever remain unresolved.

I felt I had let my father down by not getting his compassionate release. I also felt I had let Christopher down by not being there for him. My father's death only made me more determined to see that Christopher's killers were brought to justice. They say revenge is best served cold, but I was consumed with a white-hot fury that could rear its ugly head without a moment's notice. It would be a constant struggle to keep my emotions in check.

I was beginning to get frustrated with the police. Jeff Weaver had been calling Troy Wilcox from Wasco State Prison.

I got a hold of Detective Holmes. "Weaver's phoning Wilcox from jail all the time," I told him. "How come you guys aren't running any wiretaps?"

Detective Holmes took a second to answer, as if he was choosing his words carefully. "Dennis, all I can tell you is that I can't say we're not running any wiretaps," he said, clearly making his point despite the double negative.

I hung up and immediately called Tim. "Hey, I just got off the horn with the law. They didn't say anything for sure, but I got the feeling they're on the Erie," I told him.

On the Erie was code used by the old man to alert us that the phone might be tapped.

"Tell Dan to keep his lip buttoned on the phone. He's got a mouth like a torn pocket," I said, quoting one of my mother's favorite expressions.

Then I called Dan and told him the same thing about Tim. I didn't want either of them threatening anybody on the phone, whether they meant it or not.

The days began to get shorter and the weather began to cool down. My world was gradually shrinking. I found myself shunning the company of friends. The dopers, thieves, prostitutes, and other assorted hoodlums who had populated Christopher's world became my constant companions. I felt like a cop who had spent too many years on the Vice Squad.

I received a call from an inmate at the Pitchess Detention Center who insisted on seeing me in person. I pulled up his information. He was a twenty-five-year-old Hispanic in custody on a murder beef. I made the drive to Castaic to see what he had to say. We were in a booth, separated by glass. I picked up the phone to speak with him. He looked around, but not in a nervous way. He calmly pulled a piece of paper out of a legal file and held it up to the glass with the palm of one hand. I leaned closer to the glass to read the note, which was scrawled in pencil.

If you want Steinberg's cell to run red, just help me out on my case. My public defender is a worthless piece of shit. Just nod if you are down with this. If I put the word out, he'll be dead by Friday.

There was no doubt that this guy was dead serious. He placed the note back in his file without taking his deep-set brown eyes off me. Over the last few months, I had envisioned many scenarios in which I personally killed Steinberg. Now I was in a position to have his life extinguished just like that.

"I appreciate the thought," I told him, "but I can't do that. If I can't kill him myself, I'm going to let the system take care of him."

"You know where to find me, Counselor. Come back and see me if you change your mind," he said.

I have been in and out of jails for years, speaking with hundreds of criminals, but no other conversation has ever felt quite so chilling.

I flew to Phoenix to attend my father's funeral. His body was to be cremated and his ashes were to be interred next to Christopher's. Services were once again held at Saint Anne's. The priest referred to my father as "a businessman." I'm pretty sure the statue of the Blessed Virgin rolled her eyes. I almost got up to check the casket to make sure I was at the right church. All in all, it was a pretty sedate affair. My family was still numb from Christopher's death.

I was anxious to get back to L.A. The only thing that mattered was getting justice for my brother.

I got a call from Cassondra Raef, a friend of Christopher. "I heard nobody's walking on this case," she said. "I like that. I don't want any of these scandalous killers walking anywhere, either."

I could not count the number of times I had heard the term *scandalous* over the last few months. It was the adjective universally favored by tweakers to describe individuals of whom they did not approve.

It pleased me that my catchphrase, *Nobody walks,* was making the rounds. It meant people knew I was out there. Cassondra was genuinely incensed over the murder and wanted to do whatever she could to help. She had already contacted the LAPD, so I didn't press her for information. I thanked her and told her to keep in touch.

The next day I received an interesting call. "Mr. Walsh, this is Karma," the caller informed me.

"Good karma or bad karma?" I asked.

Karma ignored my attempt at humor. "You're telling people that Shane Wilson was involved in your brother's murder. He's standing here with me. He was in jail when your brother was killed. He just got out," he said.

I had become aware that there were two Shane Wilsons: Tony Shane Wilson (aka "Shankster Gangster") and another Shane Wilson who was a few years younger.

"Yeah, I know. Your guy was doing time at Chino for breaking his own kid's leg. Tell him he's a piece of shit and ask him for his middle name and date of birth. I don't want him getting mistaken for Shankster Gangster and getting caught in a crossfire," I said.

"I'm a street guy, Mr. Walsh, and you're a lawyer. I'm not comfortable giving you that information. I said what I have to say," Karma said, and hung up.

Later on, I learned that Karma was Danny Williams. He carried a business card that read THE ENFORCER. He fancied himself as someone who settled grievances among underworld characters, who tended to shy away from seeking redress through the police or the courts.

It was November 10. Only two months later, this other Shane Wilson would be found murdered execution style, sending shivers through the doper community and adding to the growing notoriety of the Walsh brothers.

Christopher's friends had arranged for a golf tournament to raise money for his kids. A few of my buddies I had known since the third grade flew out early. We drove south and played golf at La Costa for a few days and returned to play in the tournament at Porter Valley Country Club in Northridge. The outing raised six or seven thousand dollars for my niece and nephew. I spent Thanksgiving morning with Johnny Rio hiking in the wilderness that surrounded my house. I took my .12 gauge and shot enough quail to make a meal, but lost even more in the thick chaparral. The golfing and hunting provided a welcome respite from the sordid underbelly of the San Fernando Valley doper world that I had descended into. Soon enough, I was right back at it.

Kimmi Balmes called and delivered the bad news: Jeff "Fat Boy" Weaver was due to be released from prison on his parole violation on December 3. Detective Fleming confirmed the information. Murder charges had yet to be filed, so there was nothing the police could do. The thought of Weaver walking the streets sickened me.

I hightailed it over to the DA's office at the San Fernando Courthouse and paced around the lobby until DDA Sparagna came out.

"Weaver's going to be in the wind, Stephanie, and you're looking at the guy who's going to bring him back. I don't care if I have to sell my house and hit the road. There's nowhere on God's green earth that he can go without me tracking him down," I said.

"Dennis, we have plenty of law enforcement agencies that will find him. Please don't worry. I can't file the murder charges just yet. We're waiting on forensics to come back. You're just going to have to trust me," she said.

I told her the word on the street was that Steinberg was going to walk on the shooting-at-the-deputy case.

"I'm refiling that case and adding a couple counts. David Steinberg isn't going anywhere," she said with conviction.

She could tell I was upset. Her sympathetic tone was reassuring. It was not unusual for forensic analysis to take a while. I felt somewhat better when I left. Trust, but be careful whom you trust, the old man had advised. I needed to trust someone, and for some unknown reason, I did trust Stephanie Sparagna.

Weaver arrived at Kimmi's on December 3, as expected. The date was circled in red on my wall calendar. From the time Christopher's body was recovered, I never knew what would be in store for me each day. I certainly had no reason to know that December 3 would be the first of seventy-eight of the most intense days of my entire life.

After speaking with DDA Sparagna, I didn't feel compelled to barge over to Kimmi's house. I had been pounding the streets pretty hard. Weaver would get word that I wanted to talk to him. I let him twist in the wind.

It took ten days for him to finally call and leave me a message. "This is, uh, Jeff Weaver and I've, uh, been trying to, uh, get with you. I, uh, want to talk to you. I have, uh, a lot to say," he said haltingly.

I called Tim and Dan. I wanted them to be available for conference calls with Weaver where we played "good cop, bad cop, bad cop." I got Weaver on the phone and explained that my brothers and I just wanted information about who killed our brother. As he spoke, it became clear that he was not too bright. He adamantly denied any involvement in the murder, professing that Christopher was his good friend.

"Hang on. Let me get my brother Dan on the line," I said.

I called Dan and clicked Weaver back on the line. As soon as Weaver reiterated his denial, Dan cut him short.

"Hey, you fat bastard!" Dan screamed. "We know you were there. If you don't go to the cops, Steinberg's gonna make you the fall guy, you stupid fucker, and if you're in any deeper, we're gonna—"

I clicked Dan off the line before he could finish his threat.

"You can see he's pretty hot," I said.

Weaver continued to plead his innocence. I tried to reason with him in a dispassionate manner. After a few minutes, I thought it was time to go to the bullpen again and put Tim on the phone.

"You think those tattoos make you a tough guy?" Tim asked. "When I get ahold of you, I'm gonna peel those fucking tattoos off and feed 'em to you. You pussies think you're gonna kill my brother and walk away? I'm gonna gut you like a fucking hog at the slaughterhouse—"

I clicked Tim off before he could finish his thought.

"You can see my brothers are pretty upset. Let me get back to you and set up a time we can meet. In the meantime, I'll try to keep my brothers off your ass," I told him.

Kimmi called later. Weaver felt he could talk with the attorney brother, but the other brothers were "fucking crazy."

When I called Weaver back a day or so later, his tone had changed. He had no intention of meeting with me.

I remained calm, at first. "Look, Jeff, you're not walking away from this. There's only two teams: my team and Steinberg's team. You've got a chance right now to pick the right team—otherwise, I gotta believe your life is gonna get pretty miserable pretty quick, and you're talking to the guy that's gonna be delivering the misery," I said.

"Hey, fuck you," he replied. "Don't get stupid."

That was more than enough to set me off.

"I had somebody watching you up at Wasco in C block. You never even hit the yard, you fat fuck," I said, as my tone grew increasingly hostile. "You've never done Level Four time, candy ass. Now you're gonna ride a murder beef, and I'm gonna be the last face you see up at San Quentin when they jab that hot shot in your arm!" I hollered.

Weaver hung up the phone.

Kimmi called later to report that Weaver had said, "I can't believe that fucking guy's a lawyer."

It galled me to no end that Weaver was out and about, drinking, slamming dope, and getting laid. With Kimmi's help, I began tailing him. Since he had never met me, I was able to get close to him. Afterwards, I would call him on his cell phone and calmly recite his latest activities to let him know I was watching.

"Hey, asshole, last night you were with Ivan at the Mobil station. When you bought that Snickers bar, I was so close, I could have kissed you," I said. "Ticktock, motherfucker."

I would always hang up without giving him time to respond, just for effect. Sometimes I merely recited information that Kimmi had given me and pretended that I was actually watching him.

My calls had the desired effect.

"Those fucking Walsh brothers know my every move," Weaver complained to Kimmi.

One night, Barry White and I were staking out Kimmi's house. Weaver was inside and it didn't look like he was going anywhere soon.

After about three beers, Barry began to get impatient. "Fuck this shit. I gotta piss. I've got four sticks of dynamite. Let's just level this joint," he said.

"That'll be Plan B, Barry," I said. "Let's just sit tight for a while. Here, piss in this," I said.

I handed him a plastic urine container, the type used in hospitals. I had purchased it at a medical supply store after I had to leave a stakeout a few nights earlier to hit the restroom at a Shell station. Just then Weaver came out onto the porch and peered around nervously. His shaved head was illuminated by a yellow light above him.

As soon as he went inside, I dialed his cell phone. "Hey, asshole, the next time you step out on the porch, I ought to blow your fucking head off," I said, and hung up.

Kimmi said Weaver was getting more and more paranoid.

"I can't even take a shit without those fucking Walsh brothers knowing about it," he told her.

From time to time, my buddy Cavanaugh would drive by Kimmi's at night in an unmarked detective car and spotlight the house. It was just one more way of mind-fucking Weaver.

On December 18, Shankster Gangster's friend, Cloud Pierson, who had helped Steinberg clean up the murder scene, was killed in a choke-hold by members of LAPD's Special Investigations Section while attempting to pass a bad check at Ken Crane's Home Entertainment store in Encino. The SIS surveilled known felons with the intent of catching them during the commission of crimes. The elite squad had a high rate of shooting fatalities. Weaver was already paranoid. Kimmi said Weaver was now convinced that I had the SIS kill Cloud Pierson. The rumor spread throughout the criminal underworld like a hot Santa Ana wind in August.

Kimmi called to say that Troy Wilcox was dealing drugs with Peter Kinsler. Wilcox had been referring to Cowboy as "Dennis Walsh's lap dog." I wanted to create as much dissension among these characters as possible. I made a copy of Kinsler's business card that he had given my brothers with the names of supposed killers, which included Wilcox. I sent it to him along with a copy of my fax to the LAPD. I attached a note that read, *Wilcox, I hear you're doing business with Kinsler. He was the first to give you bastards up. It shouldn't be long before all you bastards are behind bars.* I copied Steinberg's rap sheet with the lewd conduct charges and mailed it to Kimmi with a note reading, *Weaver must be Steinberg's bitch.* I hoped it might make Weaver think twice about protecting Steinberg.

Fueled by crystal meth, Weaver's paranoia began to spiral out of control.

Cowboy called on Christmas Eve. "I ran into Weaver at Kimmi's," Cowboy said. "Ivan was with him. He said Steinberg called and said the cops can't make the case. They're gonna beat the case and David was gonna be out soon. He told me if I don't quit helping out the Walsh brothers, I would be the next victim."

I was furious at the thought of Weaver threatening people who were cooperating. I did not want anyone to get hurt.

Ivan Masabanda was a friend of Weaver's, an ex-con who had done sixteen years at Folsom. He had boxed in prison and was a pretty tough character. He was also Diane Stewart's boyfriend. I had been trying to contact Ivan so I could arrange a meeting with Diane Stewart. Apparently, he did not appreciate a message I had left him. He in turn left me a message in which he threatened to kill me if I didn't leave him alone. I could easily have turned the tape over to the LAPD and had Ivan arrested for making a terrorist threat, but chose to handle it another way.

Ivan's older brothers were not happy with his meth use and running around with Diane Stewart. Dan had some connections with the Mexican Mafia. I got Dan on the line and called Ivan back. Ivan delivered an expletive-laden litany of threats. I was impressed by Dan's calm response as he interrupted Ivan's tirade.

"Ivan, this is Dan Walsh. Listen very carefully to me. Weaver thinks he can threaten people because you're his muscle. You can either stop hanging out with him and stay out of our way or your brothers are gonna hear all about the meth and the porn whore. Then the next call you get is gonna come straight from Guadalajara, and believe me, those people will blow your fucking doors off," he said.

Ivan softened up after that. "I'm not looking for any problems," he said. "I don't need to be around Weaver anyways."

I called Weaver immediately. "Hey, asshole, you know what time it is?" I asked. "Ticktock. You're time is running out, and by the way, you're not allowed to play with Ivan anymore."

"What do you mean?" he asked.

"Like I said, ticktock, motherfucker," I replied, and hung up.

Kimmi reported that Weaver was by now completely freaked out.

"This fucking Dennis Walsh, he's got juice with the cops, with the Mexicans, and the Mafia. What kind of fucking lawyer is this guy?" Weaver had asked her.

On New Year's Eve, I stopped at the liquor store and paid close to two hundred dollars for a bottle of Cristal champagne. I met Kimmi at Eros Station and gave her the gift as a token of my appreciation. She had earned it.

Tim rolled into town on January 3. Dan was on his way in from Phoenix. Both were irate over Weaver's threats to Cowboy. Tim and I were sitting in my car around the corner from Kimmi's house. Shane Wilson's black Hyundai was parked out front.

"We don't need these pussies scaring people, Dennis. We need to nip this in the bud. Let's go kick that door down and beat the shit out of these cocksuckers," Tim suggested.

Tim was wearing a black leather coat. I don't know if it was his intent, but he looked the part of a mob enforcer.

"Let's call that Plan 9 from Outer Space, Tim. I don't think the cops or that DA would appreciate us doing that. We'll tail them when they come out, see who they're hanging out with. It's all about information," I said.

Tim slumped back in the passenger seat. His frustration was evident. "I know the old man said to listen to you, but fuck, if we don't do anything, we look like pussies," he said. "Let's crack a few skulls. I know you want to, Dennis. I don't care how many schools you went to, I know you. How big is this fat fuck Weaver anyway?"

"He's about six foot, two-fifty," I said.

Over the last six months, I had been running and working out strenuously. I worked a bag and shadow-boxed to build up my stamina. Most street fights didn't last more than a few minutes and usually ended due to sheer fatigue. It was important to be able to go toe-to-toe with any of these creeps if there was a confrontation. We didn't want to give them the satisfaction that one of the Walsh brothers got his ass kicked. By now I was in tip-top shape, and probably more than a little eager to lay hands on one of these dirtbags.

Weaver, Wilson, and a female finally appeared. As they walked toward Wilson's car, I switched on my ignition. Wilson and the woman got in his car, but Weaver stayed on the lawn. It was obvious they were parting company.

The fervor in Tim's plea for action must have struck a chord in my psyche.

"Fuck it, let's take 'em!" I yelled as I stomped on the accelerator.

We roared around the corner, laying rubber. Smoke was still belching from my exhaust pipe as I slammed on the brakes in front of Kimmi's house. Weaver's eyes were as big as saucers. I saw the look of surprise on Shane Wilson's face as his car lurched forward. By the time I threw my car into park and stepped into the street, Tim was on top of Weaver, pounding the hell out of him on Kimmi's front lawn. Wilson had turned his car around and was driving right at me. He stopped just short and started to get out of the car. I remembered what Cowboy had said about him always packing. It was one of the few times I was not armed. Tim's plan was turning out to be half-baked.

I reached behind my back with my right hand and held it there. "Don't get out of the car, asshole," I told Wilson.

By now, some neighbors had come outside to see what all the commotion was about. The last thing we needed was to get arrested.

"Get in the car, Tim!" I yelled. "Tim, get in the goddamned car."

Tim punched Weaver one more time and got in my car. Weaver lumbered up to Kimmi's front door. His lip was bleeding and his T-shirt was in tatters. A huge lump decorated his forehead.

"That's round one, Fat Boy," I said.

Wilson was motioning me from inside his car. His face bore a look of utter consternation.

I approached the passenger side, where the wide-eyed female was sitting with the window rolled up. "Roll down the fucking window," I said.

"I told you I wasn't involved," the Nazi Low Rider pleaded through the open window.

I could tell from the look in his eyes that he was between a rock and a hard place. It was apparent that he was not in on the killing, but did not want to rat anyone out. If he had been one of the killers or if he was completely free of any involvement, he would have been more aggressive. He never would have sat in the car and watched his buddy get his face rearranged. I knew enough about him to know that he wasn't a pussy.

I also knew that there was only one person Shane Wilson cared about, and that was Shane Wilson. He didn't stick his neck out for anyone.

"I told you that you made too many mistakes, motherfucker. You told people my brother was on the couch gurgling and that they don't want to know what happened to Chris Walsh. Well, we do want to know, asshole, and we'll be back to find out," I told him.

I pulled my hand from behind my back and made like I was firing a pistol.

"Bang, bang," I said.

As we drove away, Tim was grinning from ear to ear. "Two-fifty my ass. That fat bastard was every bit of two-eighty. Boy, did that feel good. You and I haven't done that shit together since high school. We gotta do this more often," he said.

I was not quite so joyful. "That DA's a real ballbuster, Tim. This is gonna to come back and bite us in the ass," I said.

We drove a few blocks to the Bear Pit for lunch, where we were joined by Dan, Barry White, and Jim Cavanaugh. We filled them in on all the excitement.

"I lumped that fat fucker up pretty good, didn't I, Dennis?" Tim asked.

"I guess so, Tim, but my guy was afraid to get out of the car," I joked.

We wanted to get the word out that Shane Wilson and Jeff Weaver weren't so tough after all. More important, we wanted to let it be known that threats toward people who helped the Walsh brothers would not be tolerated.

I called Cowboy. "Put the word out to all those people that are afraid of these pussies that the Walsh brothers just kicked the shit out of Weaver while Shankster Gangster sat in his car and pissed himself," I said.

The pissing reference may have been metaphorical, but I wanted these so-called tough guys humiliated.

Accounts of the incident spread through the tweaker world like a prairie grass fire. Shane Wilson's ego was massive. He tried to protect his reputation by telling people that he would have got out and fought except that Dennis Walsh had a gun. It didn't matter. Fat Boy and Shankster Gangster had gotten their pants pulled down in public.

7

NOT A BAD DAY'S WORK

EVERY MINUTE WEAVER WAS FREE gnawed at my gut. I wanted him behind bars, yet I felt like I was the one in a cage. I reveled in the knowledge that the pressure was really getting to Weaver. My plan was coming to fruition. Scared people make mistakes, and I wanted Weaver to make a mistake. Word got back to me that he intended to leave town. He was trying to obtain a falsified passport and a gun. The more desperate Weaver got, the more dangerous the game became. The stakes got a lot more serious on January 10, when a tweaker known as "Bounce" found the bodies of the younger Shane Wilson, his girlfriend, Nicole, and her girlfriend at his apartment on Hayvenhurst. Their hands were tied behind their backs. Hoods had been placed over their heads. Each was shot execution style in the back of the head. Weaver was staying at a motel that weekend. I had been in contact with Christopher's friend, Brian Swartz, who was keeping tabs on Weaver for me.

He called later that day. "Dude, I was with Weaver when he got the call about Shane Wilson. He thought it was Shankster Gangster that got snuffed. When he got off the phone, he was all nutted up. He said the Walsh brothers just shot Shane Wilson and that he was gonna be next," Brian said.

The headline in the *Daily News* read TRIO'S SLAYINGS LINKED TO DRUG DEAL. The article attributed the killings to white supremacist gang members due to a drug deal gone bad. Nonetheless, the tweaker grapevine lit up with the rumor that it was the Walsh brothers who killed the wrong Shane Wilson. Marta Wilson related how she had listened with some amusement as a group of spun-out tweakers confirmed the story as gospel. In a brief moment of clarity, one of the dopers had asked the group, "Hey, wait a minute. If the oldest Walsh brother is a lawyer, don't you think they would have killed the right guy?" The question, possibly too esoteric for the tweaker crowd, fell on deaf ears.

I figured the cops had made the connection as well. I called up Detective Katz, one of the detectives assigned to the triple homicide. "Hey, Detective, I heard you guys might be looking at me and my brothers on that triple on Hayvenhurst," I told him.

"Yeah, for about five minutes," he said.

I told him I'd let him know if I heard anything on the streets. The case remains unsolved to this day.

Brian Swartz's assessment that Weaver was "nutted up" was a serious understatement. Kimmi called on Monday morning, January 12. She was pissed that Weaver had taken her truck without her permission early Sunday morning and broken into an adult-entertainment business in Reseda. LAPD officers showed up during the robbery and shot his partner, Keith Wade Clark, in the arm. Clark surrendered, but Weaver escaped. A .45-caliber pistol was recovered at the scene. It looked like Weaver had gotten a gun, all right, and hadn't wasted any time putting it to use. I called the police and told them about Weaver. Detective Holmes put me in touch with Detective Tony Avila of the SIS. Once he confirmed that there was an arrest warrant out for Weaver, I canceled everything and went on the hunt 24/7.

My buddy Dave Bullard lent me a six-foot length of chain. I had my own plans for Fat Boy, and they didn't involve the police. I was going to make a citizen's arrest by disabling him with the chain, tying him to the hood of my car, and driving him up the steps to Devonshire Division. I was perfectly willing to suffer the consequences.

Weaver had seen my black Acura CRX two-door coupe, so I rented a car. Kimmi had already given me a list of motels frequented by Diane Stewart. She said her roommate, Don Mercatoris, was mad at Weaver for leaving his "crimey," Keith Clark, after he had gotten shot. Still, he was in contact with Weaver. Mercatoris was a lifelong criminal, a veteran meth cook. There was no way he would help me find Weaver, unless maybe he caught a major beef. I was casing motels and working the phone day and night. I hit some of the tweaker pads where I'd recently tailed Weaver. A couple of times I missed him by a few minutes. Troy Wilcox admitted that Weaver had called him. According to him, Weaver was still in town and had vowed to "take it all the way."

"What does he mean by that?" I asked, although I knew perfectly well what it meant.

"You figure it out, you're the lawyer," Wilcox replied.

I called Steinberg's friend Gary Schimmel. "David says the DA fucked up the case. She had to refile twice, and it's going to get kicked," he said, referring to the shooting-at-the-deputy case.

"Oh, really," I said. "Tell him the Walsh brothers send their regards. We'll be throwing him a real wingding when he gets out."

All this talk about Steinberg hitting the streets unnerved me. If that happened, I wasn't sure that I would be able to resist taking the law into my own hands. If it wasn't me, it would be my brothers. Every time I thought about Steinberg possibly beating a murder rap, it caused me to take a long, hard look into my own soul. Sometimes I didn't like what I saw.

On January 20, I was at the San Fernando Courthouse for Steinberg's preliminary hearing. I thought Steinberg looked resplendent in his new orange high-power jumpsuit. The hearing was continued once again. He averted his eyes when he caught sight of me. I was still boiling over his comments to Weaver about beating the case and getting out of jail. I had just called my mother to wish her a happy birthday. She was turning seventy-six that day.

"If I could have a wish granted, it would be to have my Chris back," she said.

The prosecutor had already left. Judge Meredith Taylor was still on the bench perusing some paperwork. Steinberg had a new public defender, who was seated at the counsel table, notating his file. The bailiff was in the process of escorting Steinberg to the lockup. I walked over to the railing for a repeat performance of our confrontation last summer.

"Hey, Deputy," I whispered. "You might want to make him a keep away. He likes to pull his prick out in front of little kids."

This time Steinberg chose not to remain silent. "Fuck you!" he rejoined, loud enough for Judge Taylor to take notice.

"Fuck me?" I replied, still whispering as the deputy hustled him toward the lockup door. "You're done, motherfucker." I turned to walk out.

"Who are you?" the PD inquired.

"I'm just an interested observer," I answered over my shoulder, and continued toward the door.

"Are you going to state your name for the record or are you just going to run away?" he asked.

I was just about to exit the courtroom. I turned and flew up to the rail. Judge Taylor looked a bit bewildered.

"My name is Dennis Walsh," I said loud and clear.

I managed to make it out into the hallway before two deputies grabbed me by each arm. Now it was my turn to be escorted, into the attorney conference room.

"We know this guy's a real piece of shit and they're looking at him for your brother's murder, but you can't pull that shit in the courtroom. The judge is pissed off," one of the deputies said. "She's liable to put you in jail."

Just then, the door opened and Cavanaugh poked his head into the room. "Hey, Gino," he said to one of the deputies, "what's going on? This is my good buddy Dennis Walsh."

Cavanaugh was known as "the Mayor" because he knew everybody. He was there to meet me for lunch. Instead, he wound up springing me out of a jam. I promised the deputies that I would not be disrupting the court in the future. That might have satisfied them, but no one had to tell me that this episode would not sit well with DDA Sparagna. I made a beeline out of the courthouse before word got back to her.

I changed clothes and bought Cavanaugh lunch. I kept a duffel bag in my car so I could change into street clothes and my trademark Tribe cap in a hurry. Dusty Urban, a friend of Christopher, called during lunch. Talking Tina wanted to see me.

"She wants to help, bro," he said. "She's driving everybody crazy talking so much about the murder. She wants to see you first, then she'll talk to the cops."

Later that day, I met with Tina Arnone at Beeps, a fast-food joint in Van Nuys. She was petite, with a round face and an engaging smile.

"They call me Talking Tina," she said, "because everyone says I never shut up. Now everyone says I'm talking too much about Chris getting killed and should keep my mouth shut."

I could not help but like her. She was the epitome of a bubbling personality.

She admitted to having a problem with alcohol and drugs while sipping from a straw in a plastic cup. "Vodka and Orange Crush. I call it a Harvey Wall Slammer." She laughed. "I loved your brother. We were just friends, though. He was very protective of me. Sometimes when some of those other creeps would be mean to me, he would get mad at them. He said I was like a little sister."

Soon she began to cry.

"You sound so much like Chris, it's scary," she said. "I hate David and Jeff for what they did to him."

She recounted what Diane Stewart had said about Weaver being white as a ghost. She said Weaver had threatened Diane if she talked. Diane was staying at Jim Anderson's house a few blocks away. Tina gave me his phone number. I asked if she would speak with the detectives.

"Sure. I don't know what's important, but if no one else wants to listen to me, maybe the police will," she said.

I wrapped up what was left of my beef dip sandwich and drove Tina to Devonshire Division. While I waited in the lobby as she was interviewed by Detective Fleming, I finished my sandwich and called Jim Anderson. He said Diane Stewart came and went, but he would call me when she showed up. While I was driving Tina home, she gave me the number of a guy she called Teddy the Tortoise. He claimed to be a friend of Tim's and wanted Tim to call him. When I dropped her off at Beeps, she hugged me and left with tears in her eyes.

A day or so later, Jim Anderson called me to say Diane Stewart was on her way there. I called Detective Cochran and let him know. I sped over and parked down the street, where I had a good view of Anderson's house. I read over a couple of case files until Diane Stewart pulled up in a brown van. I jotted down her plate number as she entered the house. I called Jim Anderson. He said Diane had gone straight to bed. I waited until Detectives Fleming and Cochran arrived. Patience was not one of my few virtues, but if it was connected with Christopher's murder, I could sit and wait for hours on end. I watched them enter the house and emerge with Diane Stewart in tow, though she was not handcuffed. After she got into the backseat of their unmarked detective car, I headed home to get some rest. I hoped she would finally come clean about Weaver.

I called Tim to tell him about Teddy the Tortoise.

"Fuck no, that's Teddy Tourtas," Tim said. "He used to be Sylvester Stallone's bodyguard. He's a martial artist and he's fucking deadly. I watched him lay out eight guys in a bar in Hollywood one night in about six seconds. I heard he's been strung out on heroin for years. He's good people, though, Dennis. His father was a famous wrestler. He'll do anything for us. I'll give him a call."

I went to see Lee Martin again at county jail. I wasn't getting anywhere with a character known as Dennis the Dentist. Dennis Sage was a behemoth, probably six foot four, weighing over three hundred pounds. He got his nickname by carrying around a jar of teeth that he claimed belonged to victims of his beatings. Later I found out he had gotten the teeth from a dentist. Lee suggested that I contact Dennis's ex-wife, Jeannie. She owned a bail bond company and was facing federal charges for narcotics trafficking in Hawaii. He claimed she knew everybody.

Tim had arranged to meet Teddy Tourtas at the Safari Room in Mission Hills. Jeannie agreed to meet us there as well.

Teddy did not look at all like a martial artist. He was thin, almost emaciated. He was clearly glad to see Tim. He was familiar with Shane Wilson, Kimmi Balmes, and many of the characters I had been dealing with.

"When my father heard that it was Timmy's little brother that got murdered, he said it ain't over yet," Teddy said. "I've been telling people I know the Walshes, just stay tuned."

Jeannie showed up a little while later. While I had expected her to be a fat, tattooed biker chick, she was petite and cute. Still, she had that tell-tale wizened, drawn look of a meth addict. She had clearly seen better days. Her arrest had scared her straight. Now she was a born-again Bible thumper. She was eager to be of assistance, especially when I suggested that her cooperation might be of some use in negotiating a plea bargain on her pending case. We exchanged business cards and she left.

"She's a little worn out, but she's got a nice rack on her," Tim commented.

"Hey, Tim, do me a favor and try to stay focused, will you please?" I replied.

Lee Martin was right: Jeannie did know everybody. My world had shrunk considerably. When I attempted to relate my activities to friends, their faces would inevitably go blank as I referred to the cast of characters. Shankster Gangster, Mouse, Mr. Gadget, Irish Mike, Talking Tina, Fat Boy Weaver, et cetera. I was constantly explaining who was who. Finally, I quit discussing the case with them. I could call Jeannie and she would understand what I was talking about. The same was true with Marta Wilson. Talking with them provided an opportunity for me to vent; otherwise, I might have really gone off the deep end.

Jeannie soon called to inform me that Weaver had been calling Little Ricky—Ricardo Veloz. Little Ricky lived in Glendale with his girlfriend, Candy, a part-time prostitute. According to Jeannie, Little Ricky was so strung out on meth that he positioned mirrors all over the house so he could see every room from his chair in the living room.

"Jesus Christ," I said, "sounds like some sort of whacked-out fun house."

She gave me his phone number on the condition that I not tell him where I got it. When I called him, he denied having any contact with Weaver. I told him he was full of shit, that I knew Weaver had been contacting him.

"Hey, man, where the fuck did you get my number?" he asked.

"Wait a minute. I'm looking for some prick involved in my brother's murder, and you ask me where I got your number?" I replied heatedly. "I oughta slap your teeth out just for being an adult named Little Ricky. How'd you like me to drag you out of your house and beat the shit out of you in front of your neighbors?"

"Uh, no," he replied.

Months later, his girlfriend, Candy, told me that after he hung up the phone he turned to her and said, "We're moving to Vegas."

On January 22, Marta Wilson called to let me know that Shankster Gangster had been arrested on felony possession of narcotics for sale. I wanted to make sure he stayed locked up. I drafted a declaration stating that I had witnessed him in the company of parolee Jeff Weaver on January 3 and faxed it to his parole officer, Brian Docherty. I called to see if he had received the fax.

"Shane Wilson's been in and out of prison since he was a kid. Him and his brother are prison bred," Agent Docherty said. "Unfortunately, I can't establish any gang allegations against Weaver to violate Wilson, so he'll probably bail out pretty quick."

"Prison bred," I repeated to myself. Norman Mailer could not have phrased it any more eloquently.

I went downtown to Men's Central Jail and pulled Lee Martin out in the attorney visit room.

He offered a solution to keeping Shankster Gangster in custody. "You're a lawyer. Just swear out an affidavit saying that he threatened your life, they'll violate him for sure," he offered.

"As much as it kills me to see this prick cut loose, I can't do that. I haven't asked anybody to lie for me and I'm not going to start lying myself. I'm probably going to wind up sitting on a witness stand someday, if they ever file the fucking murder charges, and I can't afford to have my credibility jeopardized," I told him.

My attention was temporarily diverted from Shane Wilson when Kimmi called on Saturday morning to inform me that Weaver had been with Don Mercatoris the night before, dealing drugs at the Best Western motel on Sepulveda. She didn't know if Weaver was still there or what room they were in, but said Mercatoris was driving his girlfriend's blue Camaro. I jumped in my rental car and flew down the canyon at breakneck speed.

This time I had the foresight to leave Johnny Rio at home. I pulled into the motel parking lot and circled around back. On the south side of the building, I spotted a blue Camaro. The doors to the rooms on both floors were facing the parking lot, so I was able to park about a hundred feet away and watch. I turned my hat around. My Tribe cap was getting pretty well known by now. Several cars pulled up at various times, and the occupants walked up to a room on the second floor. A short while later, a stocky individual with a shaved head stepped out onto the second-floor balcony and walked down to a car parked next to the Camaro. He was pretty close to Weaver's height and build, but I couldn't be sure it was him. I started my car and inched forward, hoping not to get made. He scurried back up the stairs and into the room before I could creep any closer.

I was armed with Dave Bullard's .357 Magnum and a length of chain. I debated whether to take Weaver down with the chain, hold him at gunpoint, or call the cops. I figured he had probably replaced the .45 he lost in the robbery by now. Weaver was on the run and desperate. He had told Troy Wilcox he was prepared to "take it all the way." There was no telling how he would react. The last thing I wanted was a shoot-out in a motel parking lot. The voice of reason prevailed. I looked around for my journal to get Detective Tony Avila's number. Unfortunately, in my haste, I had left it at home.

"Goddamn it," I said out loud.

I feverishly dialed Detective Fleming's and Detective Holmes's cell phone numbers, which I knew by heart, but neither one picked up. I called information and got the number to the Robbery Homicide Division at Parker Center.

"Detective Kilcoyne," the voice on the other end informed me.

"Kilcoyne? Did you go to Chatsworth High?" I asked.

"Yes, why?" he asked suspiciously.

"I went to high school with you. Anyways, my name is Dennis Walsh and I need to reach Detective Avila, Tony Avila, He's with SIS. He's looking for a robbery suspect that I think is holed up in a motel in Mission Hills."

I was annoyed to have explain it again, but he finally took my cell phone number and said he'd see what he could do.

A few minutes later, my phone rang. It was Detective Avila. "I'm serving warrants on a murder case right now. Are you sure it's Weaver?" he asked.

"No, I'm not," I said, "but it sure looks a hell of a lot like him."

"All right, maintain your position. I'll get some backup and head over," he said.

"Maintain your position," I repeated to myself. "Now we're talking."

I watched a few more dope transactions go down before Detective Avila called back. "I'm out front. Where are you and what are you driving?" he asked.

I told him I was on the south end of the motel in a white Chevy Impala. I gave him the plate number and the plate number of the Camaro and the car that Weaver had gone to.

"I'm in a gray sedan," he said. "Maintain your position until I get back there."

I slid my holster and .357 Magnum under the seat. Just as I spotted the gray sedan slowly approaching, my phone rang.

"Is that you?" he asked.

"Yeah, those are their two cars and they're upstairs in room number 277," I said.

"Okay, thanks. Go across the street and sit tight. I'll call you back a little later," he instructed.

I parked my car across the street and leaned against the stuccoed wall of a dental office. I fired up an Arturo Fuente madero robusto. Pretty soon, all hell broke loose. The Camaro and the other vehicle hurtled out onto Sepulveda Boulevard. One just missed slamming into one of two black-and-white patrol cars that had just arrived with sirens blaring. The police cruisers gave chase.

Wow, I thought while blowing a cloud of smoke. *Now, this is some good shit. I sure hope it was Weaver in there.*

Three or four more unmarked detective cars with red and blue lights swirling sped into the motel parking lot.

It wasn't long before one of the black-and-whites returned and parked on the island in front of the motel in the middle of Sepulveda Boulevard. Someone was in the backseat. I walked up to get a better look. I could see that his hands were cuffed behind his back and it clearly was not Weaver. I assumed it was Mercatoris. I wanted him to get a good look at me in case Weaver escaped or it wasn't Weaver after all. He just might be willing to give Weaver up in exchange for some help, now that he was jammed up on this beef. I pitched my cigar into the street and drove over to the median. I slowly eased next to the black-and-white.

The uniformed patrol officer standing alongside the squad car looked curiously at me. "Are you on the job?" he asked.

I took off my sunglasses. "No, but I'm with Detective Avila. I just want this prick to see who I am," I answered while staring at Mercatoris and pointing to my Tribe cap.

Kimmi had told me he was watching out the window when Tim and I rolled up on Weaver and Shankster Gangster.

"They looked like a couple of Mafia types," he had told Kimmi.

Mercatoris had a perplexed look at first, but I could tell the instant he finally recognized me. "Fuck you!" he hollered.

"Just move it along, sir, will you please?" the uniformed officer politely asked me.

I called Detective Avila. He told me to come around back and meet him outside the motel room. "We're gonna be here for a while, waiting for a search warrant. We caught that other guy, but we're not sure if it's Weaver yet. You can leave and I'll call you later or you can wait around if you want," he said.

"I think I'll just maintain my position," I replied.

It started to get dark. Finally, a detective returned with a search warrant. After a while the SIS detectives came out of the motel room. They were jubilant. The good news was that they found a .45 semiautomatic pistol, a police badge, a police uniform, cocaine, marijuana, and three and a half pounds of crystal meth. The bad news was that the other guy turned out not to be Weaver. He was known as "Bullet" and was wanted on an arrest warrant. Some of the SIS detectives were slapping me on the back and telling me what a great bust it was.

"A fugitive, a parolee with a gun, dope, and police badges. Not a bad day's work," said Detective Avila, grinning.

I felt almost like I was "on the job."

"Yeah, that's all great, but we didn't get my guy," I said. My disappointment was quite evident.

"I promise you, my friend, we will get Weaver," Detective Avila said, emphasizing the word *will*.

I shook hands with the detectives and headed home. All this cops-and-robbers shit was pretty exhausting.

8

TICKTOCK—SEVENTY-EIGHT DAYS

I WAS HOPING TO REST UP on Sunday after all the excitement of the previous day. I had a colonoscopy scheduled on Monday morning. My life had become so hectic, I was looking forward to it. The procedure required drinking a noxious liquid at 3 P.M. and 7 P.M. the day before.

"Whatever you do," my doctor had warned, "don't stray too far from a bathroom."

He wasn't kidding. I took the three o'clock dose and had more or less set up shop in the bathroom. I had just forced myself to swallow the last of the concoction at seven o'clock and was preparing for the evening's festivities when Dusty Urban called. He wanted to meet and talk right away.

"Can this wait?" I asked. "It's sort of a bad time right now."

"This is kinda important, bro," he said.

Throwing caution to the wind, I agreed to meet Dusty at the Mobil station just next door the town house where Steinberg had shot it out with the deputy sheriff. The second dose of my medication had kicked in. It seemed like I stopped at every gas station restroom on the way there. Dusty appeared to be high. He told me that he had seen Weaver driving a white Mercedes on Topanga that he believed belonged to Diane Stewart.

"You gotta be shitting me, Dusty," I said. "I drive all the way down here for that? You could have told me this over the phone," I said.

"Hey, bro, I'm thinking maybe I can find her. They don't know I'm helping you guys out. She might lead us to Weaver. I wanted to see you face-to-face. I don't want them knowing it's me who set him up," he said.

"I like it, Dustman. See what you can find out and let me know," I said.

I promised to come up with a plan that didn't put him on Front Street, then left hurriedly. On the way home I stopped at a gas station, but the restroom was out of order. I rushed into a nearby Chuck E. Cheese's pizza parlor. As I made my way to the restroom, I began to cramp up. The Chuck E. Cheese mascot, a huge gray rat, was dancing in a circle with some small children. To my horror, he grabbed me by the wrists and started to dance. I had no choice but to slam him against the wall and sprint to the restroom. The kids were aghast, but not quite as much as they would have been had I not broken loose from the rat's grasp. Suffice it to say that I am no longer welcome at Chuck E. Cheese.

A few days later, I was on the phone with Jeannie when Gangster Shankster called her on another line from county jail.

"You tell that piece of shit motherfucker that—"

She cut me short before I could finish. "Shh, let me talk to him," she said.

I listened as she took the call without telling him I was in on the conversation.

"Shane, you need to tell what you know about this Chris Walsh thing. I've talked to Dennis Walsh, and believe me, that guy is really on one. Him and his brothers aren't going away. You need to get straight with Jesus Christ and do the right thing," she said.

I strained to hear his reply.

"The Walsh brothers want me to talk to the cops. The cops are gonna try to make me testify or charge me with . . . " he replied.

I couldn't tell if he said charge him with second-degree murder or accessory to murder. Jeannie later told me he said accessory to murder. In any event, he gave no indication that he would cooperate.

I was more than a little upset when Shane Wilson was released from custody the next day, but I didn't have time to mope. Robert "Mouse" Hayes called. He had been in county jail with Cloud Pierson.

"Cloud was gonna be Weaver's alibi. When the cops killed Cloud, it put Weaver up shit creek," he said.

He also told me that Shane Wilson was "in the hat." Somehow he had run afoul of both the Aryan Brotherhood and the Nazi Low Riders. *In the hat* meant he was green-lighted to be killed. If that were true, Shane Wilson would have to be placed in protective custody if he went back to prison. "PC'd up," as they say. His policy on not cooperating with the cops just might change, although I doubted it.

Cowboy called to relate that Weaver had money and was traveling around in a Lincoln Town Car owned by Valley Town Car Service. I called the LAPD and relayed the information.

Later that evening, I received a call from a law enforcement official who identified himself as Agent Scott Barker. "I'm with a special task force with the California Department of Justice. I'm at Kenny Williams's house. He's being arrested for possession for sale. He wanted me to call you. What's going on?" he asked.

"He's a material witness in a murder case," I replied. "He needs to be a K-10, otherwise he's liable to get killed. Get a hold of Detective Fleming or Cochran over at Devonshire Division, they can verify it."

Agent Barker already knew all about the case. Later I would learn that he had intercepted several wiretapped phone calls between Weaver and Troy Wilcox while Weaver was in jail, as well as calls between me and Wilcox. He assured me that Kenny would be placed in protective custody. I hung up and cursed my luck.

"Goddamn it," I swore out loud. Shane Wilson gets released and Kenny Williams gets hooked up. "What the fuck!"

I tossed and turned all night.

Shortly after the motel bust, I got a call from Dan Evanilla, Special Agent with the California Department of Corrections. He was in the business of tracking down parolees at large. By this time, I had gleaned enough information on the streets to have more than a few people locked up.

"I just left Devonshire Division. The detectives said I should give you a call. I hear you're the Charles Bronson of the Valley." He laughed. "I'm looking for help finding Ivan Masabanda."

"I don't know about being any Charles Bronson, but it must be your lucky day," I said. "I'm looking for his girlfriend, Diane Stewart. I hear Weaver's been driving her car around. I'm expecting to hear from Kimmi Balmes to find out where they're shacking up tonight."

"That Alexandra Quinn, she's a real piece of work," Dan Evanilla said. "We're looking for Weaver, too. Call me back when you hear from Kimmi."

After hearing that Weaver was driving Diane's car, I had no illusions that she would be cooperating anytime soon. I had left her several very polite messages appealing to her sense of right and wrong, which went unreturned.

When I learned she was actively aiding and abetting Weaver, my anger got the better of me. "Listen you two-bit whore," I yelled at her voice mail, "unless you want me to drop a dime on you with the Immigration Department, you better get down to Devonshire Division and tell what you know about my brother's murder. Otherwise, you'll be filming porn movies back in Canada."

My bedside manner was steadily diminishing. Needless to say, I still had not heard from her.

Kimmi called while I was eating dinner at the Bear Pit. Diane and Ivan were at a motel on San Fernando Road in Sylmar. I boxed up my dinner and got over there just in time to spot Ivan pulling up in his pickup truck. I watched him carry a pizza box up the stairs to a room on the second floor. I called Dan Evanilla and finished my meal of pork ribs, coleslaw, and baked beans. Dan arrived about forty-five minutes later. A few minutes after that, an LAPD patrol car entered the parking lot. After they led Ivan out in handcuffs, they placed him and Diane in the patrol car. I packed it up and headed home. I was hoping for Weaver to show up, but it was plenty enough excitement for one day.

Back in August, when Shane Wilson had left a message, I hadn't checked my caller ID. When I finally did check, I was shocked to see that the number was registered to Christina Karath.

I called her right away. "What the fuck is Shane Wilson doing with your phone and why didn't you mention that to me?" I asked.

"I, uh, bought a bunch of phones for those guys. I, uh, just forgot all about it," she stammered.

I didn't believe her for a minute. "Get those fucking phone records to me as soon as possible," I told her.

She agreed, but over the next few weeks, kept stalling and finally stopped returning my calls. It became apparent that she did not intend to produce the records. I staked out her house after I received word that Weaver intended to rob her. He was desperate for money to flee to Spain. He believed Christina had a Picasso painting that he could fence. As I said, Weaver was not very bright. I headed home after one of the Crips relieved me and sat on her house.

"If Weaver shows, I'll call your ass, Law Dog, but I ain't calling no cops. I'd just as soon kill the motherfucker. I'm only doing this as a favor to you," he said.

When I first met him, he had wanted to kill me. Eventually he became fond of me and took to calling me "Law Dog." After my brother's murder, he became concerned for my safety. I politely turned down his offer to have "two of my boys ride with you twenty-four-seven."

"No offense, but driving around my little country town with two black guys would draw more attention than I need," I said.

On the way home from Christina's, I stopped at Ralphs market to pick up a few groceries. I noticed my reflection in a mirror in the produce section. My face was covered in stubble. Shaving had become a luxury that I didn't have time for. My .357 Magnum was tucked inside my shirt in my shoulder holster. A woman with a small child in a shopping cart sorted through the bell peppers while her husband wiped the toddler's nose.

Wow, normal people, I thought to myself.

My life had become a cornucopia of dopers, convicts, thieves, and porners. My old life seemed to be a distant memory. I felt like I was tethered to the earth. I drove home, fed my animals, poured a couple shots of Jameson, and went to bed. A little while later, Dan called.

I let him know what I had been up to. I asked how our mother was doing.

"Not too good, Dennis. I just left there. She was looking at photo albums and crying over Chris," he said.

The stress was starting to get to me anyway, but the thought of my poor mother poring over pictures of Christopher sent me into a rage.

I got off the phone and dialed Christina Karath's number. "You better have those goddamn phone records down to Devonshire Division Monday morning or I'll make sure you never sell another bag of dope in this town, you fucking cunt!" I hollered at her voice mail.

Just my luck, her house got raided by the LAPD a few nights later. Christina got arrested. The cops confiscated her voice mail and turned the messages over to Deputy DA Stephanie Sparagna.

The C-word is never a big crowd pleaser to begin with, so it would come as no surprise that Stephanie was not exactly pleased.

Detective Fleming called on the evening of February 3. The DA's office had filed first-degree murder charges against Steinberg and Weaver on February 2, seven months to the day since Christopher's body had been recovered. Shane Wilson and George Jassick were named as accessories to murder. Wilson was arrested earlier that afternoon at his residence on Blix Street. Jassick was arrested at a studio where he was employed about an hour later. They were due to be arraigned the following morning in San Fernando court. My head was reeling. I thanked him and made a series of calls to family and friends. The murder charge against Steinberg included special-circumstance allegations that warranted the death penalty. I was beyond ecstatic.

I was even more elated in court to see Shankster Gangster and Steinberg handcuffed in their orange jumpsuits. Steinberg's bail was set at over two million dollars. I did not know much about George Jassick, except that Troy Wilcox had told me Steinberg had given him a blood-stained sofa when Christopher was missing.

An LAPD news release detailed the arrests and sought the public's help in locating Weaver, describing him as "a career criminal who should be considered armed and dangerous." Weaver's picture was blasted across the television news.

Two days later, Jeannie called to say that Cloud Pierson's mother had said that Shankster Gangster was calling from county jail to have her make three-way calls to Weaver. He was encouraging Weaver to leave town. I alerted the LAPD.

On February 7, Scott Ryan called. Kimmi told him that the manager at her storage unit had called and said a bald-headed guy had been there, trying to get into her unit after he was refused entry to his unit for not paying the storage fee. He asked if it was the guy on TV the cops were looking for. She told him no. I had no doubt that Troy Wilcox and Don Mercatoris had persuaded her to cover for Weaver. I gave Detective Holmes the information.

Later that day, I met with Jimmy Bray at El Presidente. Jimmy was an old friend of my brother Tim and Teddy Tourtas. I was drinking a Heineken when he pulled up on a Harley. His hair was long and unkempt. He sported numerous tattoos and wore a leather vest and motorcycle boots. He was Irish and spoke with more than a trace of a Brooklyn accent. We ordered dinner and talked for a while.

"I was over at Kimmi's when Timmy called," Jimmy said. "That fucker Mercatoris freaked out when he found out I was on the phone with one of the Walsh brothers. I told him the lawyer brother wants to see him. He wants to kill you for jamming him up."

"Get him on the phone and set up a meeting. Tell him I think he can get him some love on his case," I said.

Jimmy dialed Mercatoris's number. "No, they're not coming, just the lawyer," I heard Jimmy say before he hung up. "He'll meet us at the Sundown in an hour," Jimmy said.

That's just jim-fucking dandy, I thought.

The Sundown was a biker bar on Foothill Boulevard in Tujunga. It was notorious for shootings and stabbings. Not even the cops would go in there unless they absolutely had to. Some likened it to Dodge City on a Saturday night—and just my luck, it was Saturday.

Jimmy agreed to meet me at the bar. On the drive over, I called Tim and asked if Jimmy could be trusted.

"I haven't seen him for twenty years, but yeah, I'd say so," Tim said. It was hardly a ringing endorsement.

Minutes later, my phone rang. It was Dan. "Tim just called. What the fuck is going on?" he asked.

I explained what I was up to.

"Is Barry with you?" he asked.

"No, this came up spur of the moment. I don't have time to wait for Barry, besides, you how I love a nice saloon," I said.

"I don't like this, Dennis. Call me later," Dan said, and hung up.

I circled around the Sundown until I saw Jimmy pull up on his Harley. The bar was on an island facing Foothill Boulevard with two streets angling on each side of it. A perfect spot for a drive-by. I parked in back and walked to the front door, where Jimmy was waiting.

He was smiling as he put his hand on my shoulder and whispered in my ear. "I know you're packing, partner, but whatever you do, don't pull that fucking piece out unless you have to. Every motherfucker in this joint is strapped. If you start waving that hog leg around, it'll be like a fucking shooting gallery in there," he warned.

I was carrying Chuck Martin's 9 mm pistol tucked in my waistband. Jimmy must have spotted it. I tugged my shirt down a bit. We walked inside. Mercatoris was not there yet, but Barry was seated at a table, calmly drinking a longneck Budweiser. Dan must have called him. I didn't acknowledge his presence.

I sat on a stool at a round table and ordered a longneck Bud. This definitely was not a Heineken kind of joint. Jimmy went over to the bar, where it seemed like everyone knew him. Soon enough, a guy in his forties with salt-and-pepper hair walked in and approached Jimmy. Jimmy brought him over to my table and introduced him, then walked back to the bar. Mercatoris ignored my outstretched hand and sat across from me. I asked if he wanted a drink.

"You threw me and my girl under a bus, motherfucker," he said while glaring intently at me. "I'm looking at a gang of time because of you."

His girlfriend, Jill Barco, had also been arrested in connection with the motel bust.

His voice was hoarse and raspy. A vein in his neck was pulsating rapidly. He was clearly agitated. I took a swig of my beer. It bothered me that his hands were in his lap, under the table. I kept my eyes on his arms just in case he might pull a gun. I held both hands out with my palms facedown. They were perfectly still. My pulse rate was normally around 56 due to my strict physical regimen. Right now I was sure it had not risen a beat. I was confident that, if I had to, I could blow him clean out of his chair. My only concern was the barrel of the pistol pointing right at my groin.

Just clear the fucking table, Dennis, I thought.

"I was only looking for Weaver," I replied. "I don't have a beef with you. You just got caught in the middle. You knew he was white hot. You oughta be more careful who you're slinging dope with."

Ending my sentence with a preposition did not seem to faze him.

"All you gotta do is help me find Fat Boy. Your attorney can get the DA to cut you and your girlfriend a sweet deal," I said.

"I'm in and out of jail, so I don't make no deals with the cops. I ain't wearing no rat jacket," he said.

"Your buddy Weaver is toast," I told him. "That dumb bastard is gonna get hooked up any day now, so your time is running out. They just upped the ante to murder one. Help me find him, and the DA will show you and your girl some love. Nobody's gotta know but you and me."

"Just so you know. Jeff ain't no killer. He said he put the final bullet in your brother's head to put him out of his misery," he said. "That's one thing I ain't talking about, so don't even bother asking."

That revelation did not come as a complete shock. The word on the street was that Weaver was a shooter. This was the first time I had heard someone actually confirm the rumor.

My calmness vanished. "You see that shit on my hat?" I asked, point-ing to the ashes that still clung to my Tribe cap. "That ain't dust. Those are my brother's ashes, and if you or any other of these motherfuckers think my brothers and I aren't serious, take a good look into my eyes and tell me I'm not dead serious. I've been telling everybody that nobody walks on this case, and I'm telling you right now, nobody, but fucking nobody is walking on this fucking case."

Christopher's ashes had begun to fade from my cap, but were still clearly visible. I had sprayed the cap with Scotchgard a few weeks earlier, hoping it would preserve the ashes just for a situation like this.

Mercatoris was visibly startled. I saw the same look of fear and indeci-sion that I had seen in Shane Wilson's eyes. "I see in your eyes you're seri-ous. I've been arrested plenty, but I've never been cut loose so fucking fast in my life," he said. "I don't know who the fuck you are, but I know you got some juice with the cops. Wherever you go, houses get tossed and people get busted. Now I'm sitting here instead of in a cell."

It seemed like a good time to play on his fear. I pulled out my cell phone and dialed Detective Holmes's number. "Hey, Detective, I'm sit-ting here with Don Mercatoris. If he helps you guys find Weaver, do you think he can catch a break on his case?" I asked.

Mercatoris's head almost snapped off when he heard me say *Detec-tive.*

"Detective Holmes says you can probably get some love from the DA," I said.

"What the fuck?" Mercatoris whispered while looking over his shoul-der. "You call a fucking cop on a Saturday night, just like that. Like what, at his fucking house?"

"What's the difference? I give you my word, no one's gonna know if you help me find Weaver," I said.

"All right, but I'm only doing it for my girlfriend. I don't want her doing any time," he said.

I gave him my business card. He gave me his cell phone number. This time he shook my hand. Mercatoris would either help or I would see to it that he did get "a gang of time."

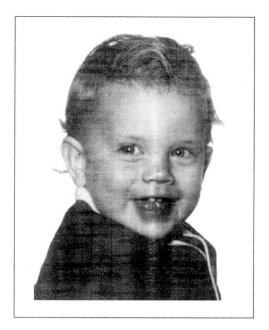

Christopher John Walsh, age 16 months. *(Courtesy Kathleen C. Walsh)*

Christopher John Walsh, age 3 years, 7 months (April, 1969). *(Courtesy Kathleen C. Walsh)*

Christopher John Walsh. *(Courtesy Kathleen C. Walsh)*

Christopher John Walsh, Granada Hills High School. *(Courtesy Kathleen C. Walsh)*

Christopher John Walsh, 2003—shortly before his murder. *(Courtesy Kathleen C. Walsh)*

The author's parents, Robert and Kathleen Walsh (circa 1954 when his father was a Cleveland detective). *(Courtesy Kathleen C. Walsh)*

The author's parents with Mafia hitman Ray Ferritto and his wife at Ambassador Hotel's Coconut Grove in Los Angeles (September, 1967). *(Courtesy Kathleen C. Walsh)*

Troy Wilcox, "Ralphie," Christopher Walsh, Jeffrey Weaver, and Marlon "Cowboy" Grueskin (Mr. Chen's, Encino, California). *(Courtesy Kathleen C. Walsh)*

Jeffrey Lawrence Weaver (Fired the final shot). *(Courtesy* Los Angeles Daily News*)*

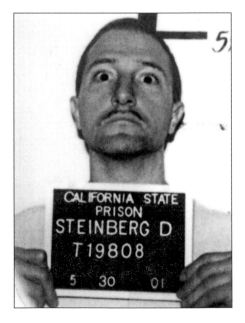

David Michael Steinberg (The principal shooter). *(Courtesy* Los Angeles Daily News*)*

777 Motor Inn (San Fernando Valley motel where the Walsh family stayed in July, 1967). *(Courtesy Craig Endler)*

Steinberg's apartment—the scene of the murder (12654 Moorpark Street, Studio City, California). *(Courtesy Craig Endler)*

Sherman Oaks Mini Storage (site where the Christopher Walsh's body was recovered). *(Courtesy Craig Endler)*

Ramp leading up to the second floor of the storage facility. *(Courtesy Craig Endler)*

The author pointing out Unit #2420. *(Courtesy Craig Endler)*

The author at home in "street attire." *(Courtesy Craig Endler)*

The author. *(Courtesy Craig Endler)*

The author today with Rowdy and his Border Collie, Dusty. *(Courtesy Craig Endler)*

No sooner had I left the Sundown than Dusty Urban called. "I've been trying to reach you, bro. Weaver came to my house. Can you meet me now?" he asked.

He didn't have to ask twice. It was after 10 P.M. by the time I got to the Mobil station on Lassen and Topanga.

"I was in my garage a couple days ago, bro. Weaver and this dude named Ean walked up. Him and Weaver want a video camera to make a porno. He gave me a card with his cell phone number on it. He lives around the corner from me on Golden Canyon with a couple of porn actors, Kid Vegas and Johnny Toxic," Dusty said.

Dusty worked for a company that distributed adult videos. He handed me the business card for DAN THE LIMO MAN with Ean's number scrawled on the back.

"Weaver wants me to get Diane Stewart's server. She needs it for her porn site. I know the guy that has it. I can get it, if you want me to, bro," Dusty said, speaking rapidly while nervously looking around.

"Every cop in the state is looking for Weaver, and he's out trying to make porn movies. I don't believe this fucking guy. Whatever you do, don't give him that server without getting ahold of me first," I told him. "Maybe we can set up a sting and have the cops grab him when he comes to get it."

Dusty was game, but had lost his cell phone and didn't have money to get a new one. I drove him to the ATM and drew out two hundred dollars to buy a new cell phone. He promised to call Ean and give him the new number.

"Keep that fucking phone with you twenty-four-seven" I instructed him.

Before I left, I asked him about a guy named Phillip Miller. I heard that he might know something about the weapon that was used to kill Christopher.

"Is that Big Phil or Little Phil? Or are you talking about Small Paul, or maybe Tall Paul?" he asked.

Time and again I had been frustrated by tweakers who knew one another only by their nicknames. Getting a last name was like pulling teeth.

"What the fuck, Dusty?" I asked. "Am I the only motherfucker in this caper without a nickname?"

Dusty smiled. His given name was Leon.

"Well, it ain't like you been keeping it on the down low. Everybody knows you're coming. You want a nickname, bro? How about 'Josey Wales'?" he asked.

That moniker would have been fine with me. On my way home, I stopped at Devonshire Division and left Ean's business card at the front desk with a note for the detectives. It was almost midnight. I was beat after another hard day on the streets. I managed to sleep in Sunday morning. I was able to catch up on some work. I celebrated Johnny Rio's third birthday by grilling a couple of porterhouse steaks.

"You're eating better than Shitberg," I told my dog.

On Monday, I called Detective Holmes and suggested setting up a sting. I didn't tell him what Mercatoris had said about Weaver being a triggerman. What would be the point? He was never going to cop to it. That decision would be a major point of contention at trial.

Word got back to me that Weaver was in search of a bulletproof vest. He was telling people he would not be taken alive. It confirmed Troy Wilcox's statement that Weaver was prepared to "take it all the way." I let the homicide detectives know. I had been calling the detectives quite a bit.

At one point, Lieutenant Oppelt became a bit annoyed. "Dennis, if you quit calling us, maybe we can get some work done," he had said.

I didn't take offense. I had heard that Detective Holmes caught some grief from Deputy DA Stephanie Sparagna for talking to me and figured the lieutenant was just sticking up for one of his guys.

Detective Holmes gave me the number of U.S. Marshal Tony Burke, the head of a fugitive task force that was assisting the LAPD in apprehending Weaver.

It was already February 9, now sixty-nine days since Weaver had been released from jail and twenty-eight days of being on the run after the robbery. Every minute he was on the street was a minute I was in prison, especially now that I believed he was a triggerman.

I went down to county jail to see Lee Martin and Ivan Masabanda. Lee had received a kite note from Keith Clark, Weaver's crimey in the botched robbery. Kite notes were a means of communication between inmates. Messages were wadded up and passed from inmate to inmate, sometimes tied with dental floss and dangled from tier to tier. Clark believed that Weaver may have set him up. It was information that might ease Mercatoris's conscience for being a rat. I promised Ivan that I would call his parole officer if he would put out some feelers and try to locate Weaver.

I drove over to Kimmi's. Tim had asked me to give Teddy Tourtas two hundred dollars for his rent. Teddy asked me to leave it with Kimmi. Don Mercatoris was out front with Indian Gary when I pulled up. I didn't want to seem too familiar with Mercatoris in front of Indian Gary.

"I'm Dennis Walsh. I've got some money for Teddy. Where's Kimmi?" I asked.

Although Indian Gary shook my hand, his hand was limp. He said nothing, but the contempt in his eyes was evident. He may have wanted to cause me some harm, but no one was going to fuck with a friend of Teddy Tourtas. Kimmi wasn't home. I gave the money to Mercatoris and left.

I had driven only a few blocks when a pickup truck pulled up next to me and honked. It was Don Mercatoris, in Ivan Masabanda's truck, with a female passenger. I pulled over to the curb and waited for him to walk up to my window.

"I'm gonna have my parole officer call you. You can tell him I'm helping out. That's Tammy Romanelli," he said, pointing back to the truck and waving her over. "She thinks you want to help me and Jill out because you didn't mean to get us busted. My phone is dead. You can reach me through her, but she needs money to pay her phone bill."

"How much do you need?" I asked her after Mercatoris waived her over.

"Just twenty to keep it on this month, but fifty would be better," she said.

I knew her to be a small-time speed dealer. I had her write down her number and handed her a twenty-dollar bill.

Tammy called a few days later to say she was with Diane Stewart. Diane would not speak with me but wanted me to know that Weaver did not tell her any details about the murder. I told Tammy I didn't believe her.

"She got beat up pretty bad, but won't say who did it," Tammy whispered. "She's wearing sunglasses to cover her black eye."

Whoever knocked Diane around had probably forced her to call me, but she didn't have the nerve to speak to me directly.

"She's full of shit. Tell her I said, 'Nobody walks.' She'll know what I mean," I said, and hung up.

That alone was worth the double sawbuck I had given Tammy.

A few days later, I contacted U.S. Marshal Tony Burke. I told him about Weaver trying to obtain Diane Stewart's server. He said they had information that Weaver was in Hollywood traveling with a female named Andrea. They had been triangulating cell phone calls and confirmed that he was in the Hollywood area. I gave him some cell phone numbers and the names of some clubs in Hollywood that Ivan Masabanda said Weaver had recently visited. I left a message with Ivan's parole officer and spoke with Dan Evanilla about getting him some help on his case.

I learned from Kimmi that Teddy Tourtas was on a dope binge. She hadn't given him my two hundred dollars yet. I flew over to Kimmi's house and pounded on the door. She was at work, but said the money was in her room. Don Mercatoris answered the door.

"I'm here to pick up that dough I left for Teddy," I informed him. "I'd rather put my money in a pile and light it on fire than see it spent on dope."

I followed Mercatoris into a bedroom. Indian Gary stood in the living room and stared at me. Mercatoris's girlfriend, Jill, was lying on the bed. She did not say a word. Mercatoris picked up a wad of money off the dresser and handed it to me.

"Thanks," I said, and walked out.

Walking into a tweaker flophouse and recovering two hundred dollars was no mean feat. I was sending a message. I could walk into their house and take my money back after having them arrested. I wanted these people to know my brothers and I were not going away, and there was nothing they could do about it.

I called Teddy to tell him why I had taken the two hundred dollars back.

"Yeah, I understand. Hey, I've got Diane Stewart's passport. What do you want me to do with it?" he asked.

"I don't even want to know how you got it, Teddy, but just hold on to it," I said.

Jimmy Bray called. Mercatoris was on his way to meet with Weaver, but didn't know where. Jimmy had been combing the streets, looking for Weaver himself.

"If I find Weaver, I'm gonna leave him in a pile. You can come and scrape him up," he had told me.

I was in the neighborhood and managed to catch sight of Mercatoris pulling away from Kimmi's house in Ivan's truck. I tried to tail him but lost him on Sepulveda Boulevard. It's not easy tailing someone with one vehicle. I had no choice but to pull up right behind his truck at an intersection. I yanked the visor down and covered my face with my hand. I had to fall back before I got made. Getting caught at a red light caused me to lose him for good. Jimmy called the next day to tell me that Mercatoris had met with Weaver at a 7-Eleven in Van Nuys and spent forty-five minutes with him. I was irate. I called Mercatoris and left several not-so-tactful messages.

The last one must have got under his skin. "I hear you're backdooring me and helping Weaver, you broken-down meth freak," I said. "I'm gonna make sure you're locked up for a shitload of time."

"Don says you're leaning on him too hard and he may have to put a hole in you," Jimmy told me. "I told him look how you turned this town upside down since Chris got killed, and that there's three more brothers behind you. I told him he better kill every one of the Walsh brothers if he touches you. Then I told him if he thinks the lawyer is a pussy, he'll put one right between your eyes."

I had to be talked out of going after Mercatoris. Jeannie was the voice of reason. "Dennis, you're a lawyer. You have some credibility going for you. You'd be pressing your luck. You guys already beat up Weaver. Think about it," Jeannie advised.

She was right. I didn't need another altercation.

I called Dusty to see if he was available to try to lure Weaver under the ruse of having obtained Diane Stewart's server. He had a large shipping container, the type normally seen on the docks, at a vacant lot in an industrial area of Chatsworth. It would be a good site for a stakeout. A few days earlier, U.S. Marshal Tony Burke had been receptive to the plan. I dialed his number.

"Funny you should call. We're in Hollywood. We just lost Weaver, we almost had him," he said.

I knew the feeling. I reminded him of the plan involving Dusty. He agreed to meet us at the vacant lot after he and his crew grabbed a quick bite to eat. Dusty and Barry White agreed to head over there as well.

After forty minutes of pacing back and forth across the vacant lot, smoking a Padron, I began to feel vulnerable. My .357 Magnum was in the car. I really didn't know Dusty that well—maybe I was being set up. I felt much better when I spied Barry's green Honda turn onto the block and cruise slowly by. I had taken to referring to Barry as my "shooter." Barry began to circle the block. I was sitting in my car when Dusty's van, with the Stars and Stripes boldly painted on both sides, came blasting up with a black-and-white on his tail. The red and blue lights of the police cruiser were flashing. I watched as one uniformed officer stood at the back of Dusty's van while the other approached his window. I wasn't too concerned, assuming it was a routine speeding violation. Moments later, Dusty was handcuffed and placed in the backseat of the patrol car.

"What the fuck now?" I said out loud.

I jumped out and approached one of the officers.

"What's going on? I'm waiting for the U.S Marshals. We need this guy for a stakeout on a murder case," I said.

"Are you on the job?" the patrolman asked.

All I could say was no, before I was ordered back to my car.

I dialed Marshal Burke and told him what was going on.

"You're kidding me," he said. "Put the officer on the phone, I'll talk to him."

I walked back over to Dusty's van. The cop I had spoken to was none too pleased.

"Officer, U.S. Marshal Tony Burke is on the line and would like to speak with you," I said while holding out my phone.

"Are you on the job or not?" he asked. It was clear that I was beginning to irritate him.

"No, but unless you want to catch some hell with Devonshire Division homicide detectives, I think you should talk to the marshal," I said.

"Get back in your car now or you're going with him," he said while gesturing over his shoulder with his thumb.

I was on the phone with Marshal Burke when the patrol officer walked up to my window.

"Do you mind telling me what's going on?" he asked.

"I've been trying to. I've got a United States Marshal on the phone, he's with a fugitive task force. We're setting up a stakeout. Just talk to him for a second," I said while thrusting my cell phone toward him.

He reluctantly took my phone. I heard the officer repeat, "Detective Fleming, Cochran, Oppelt. Yeah, okay, sure." He handed me back my phone and proceeded to pull Dusty out of the patrol car and uncuff him. "I don't know what the hell you're up to, but good luck," he told Dusty.

As the police drove away, Dusty was incredulous. "How the fuck did you do that, bro?" he asked.

"Never mind, you fucking moron. Can't you even show up without drawing a heat score?" I asked.

"I was late getting here. They pulled me over for speeding, but turns out I got a warrant on a zoning violation for my patio cover I forgot about. I've been arrested a lot, but I've never been set free like that. They didn't even write me a speeding ticket. Thanks, bro," he said.

I had to wonder, *A fucking patio cover? Doesn't anything come easy on this case?*

While we waited for the marshals, I carefully rehearsed with Dusty what he would say to Weaver. The more I talked, the more nervous he became. It was evident that he hadn't even thought about what he might say to Weaver until now. That was typical tweaker behavior. They lived in the moment, except to scheme where their next bag of dope was coming from.

Finally, Marshal Burke and his crew of three showed up in two pickup trucks. We walked over to the shipping container. The plan was to have Dusty call Ean claiming to have Diane Stewart's server, Ean would call Weaver, and we would wait for Weaver to call. Dusty would tell him to come and get the server, that he didn't want it around because he was afraid of the Walsh brothers.

As Marshal Burke flipped through a three-ring binder, I noticed blown-up color driver's license photos of many of the people I had been dealing with. The faces of Kimmi Balmes, Don Mercatoris, Indian Gary, Cowboy, Kristina Karath, Irish Mike, and a slew of others caught me by surprise. I felt like I was on the old *This Is Your Life* show with Ralph Edwards. Dusty identified a photo of Weaver as the person who had just been at his house. It started to get dark. I had turned in my rental car. I raced over to my Acura to move it down the block so Weaver would not spot it. When I returned, the federal marshals were suiting up. They looked pretty formidable in flak jackets with pistols strapped to their thighs. Two had rifles with night scopes and lights.

"Hey, Marshal," I said. "If you guys kill Weaver, Steinberg will lay the murder on him. Can you try to take him down without killing him?" I asked.

It was ironic that I had been in the unusual position of trying to protect Weaver and Shankster Gangster while Steinberg sat in county jail.

"Don't worry, the detectives told me all about it. My guys are crack shots. We won't kill him unless we have to," he promised.

Marshal Burke pulled opened a toolbox in the bed of his pickup truck. It was loaded with various types of weapons and ammunition.

"Hey, Marshal, why don't you deputize me and let me just blow his kneecap off?" I asked.

"I wish I could." He laughed.

"Go find a spot across the street where you can take cover. Come back and we'll have Dusty call Weaver," he said. "Then you can lay low and watch this go down."

I picked out a spot under a truck that afforded a good view of the vacant lot and trotted over to the shipping container. Dusty was beyond nervous. I thought he was about to soil himself. I took him aside to calm him down.

"Holy fuck, do you see all that firepower these guys have?" he asked. "I said I'd help you out, bro, but this is heavy-duty shit. Is this what you call not putting me on Front Street? You got me right in the middle of a shoot-out, bro."

"Come on, Dusty, get your shit together. Don't do it for me, do it for my brother," I said.

"You know, you're as crazy a motherfucker as Chris was," he said while shaking his head. "All right, bro, let's do this."

The six of us huddled in the shipping container. Dusty got Ean on the line. It was Friday night. He didn't know where Weaver was and had no way to reach him. Weaver usually called him. He said he'd call Dusty when Weaver contacted him. Dusty was more than a little relieved. I was more than a little disappointed. I walked over to my car and got a beer.

"Call me right away if Weaver calls over the weekend. We can be ready to roll pretty quick," Marshal Burke told Dusty.

I went home and went to bed. There was no word from Dusty all day Saturday. I decided not to bother him. By Sunday afternoon, I was out of patience. "Dustman, have you heard from Fat Boy?" I asked.

"Bro, you know, uh, my son was going dirt biking in the desert yesterday and he doesn't have a phone, so I gave him mine," he said.

I could hardly believe my ears. I felt like I was ready to stroke out right then and there. These tweakers were going to be the death of me.

"You mean the same fucking phone I gave you two hundred dollars to buy?" I hollered.

"Well, yeah, bro, that's the only phone I have," he said.

"Listen, you stupid crackhead!" I screamed. "Either you get that motherfucking phone back immediately and keep it with you twenty-four-seven or I'll drive down there and duct-tape it to your motherfucking forehead. Understand?"

"Okay, bro, okay," he answered. "Geez, when you get mad, you really sound like your brother."

I called Barry. A few nights before, we had sneaked between the boulders in the Santa Susana Knolls that separated the San Fernando Valley from Simi Valley to stake out Ean's town house. Barry had streaked his face with greasepaint and wore a light strapped to his forehead. He brought night-vision goggles and a six-pack. I had a pair of binoculars. We had a good view into the house, but Weaver never showed. Tonight I wanted to sit on Dusty's house on the off chance that Weaver might show up unannounced.

"Barry, can you meet me at Chatsworth Park in an hour?" I asked.

"Should I stop at the hardware store?" he replied.

That was his way of asking if I needed a weapon. I told him I was good. I rented a car to avoid being made by Weaver and met Barry at the park. We drove the few blocks to Dusty's town house in the rental car and parked on the street. After about an hour, a white Oldsmobile Cutlass slowly pulled into the communal driveway that led back to Dusty's unit. The driver's fat head was closely shaved.

"Holy shit," I said. "I think that's Weaver."

The car eased back onto the street and parked. Barry pulled out his .45. I slowly took my .357 from my shoulder holster and held it in my lap.

"Let's take it real easy, Barry," I said.

The driver exited the Olds and stared straight at us. He began walking toward our car.

"Oh, fuck, he made us," I said.

I cracked my door and got ready to hop out. Barry did the same.

"Keep an eye on his hands, Barry," I said.

As he got closer, I could tell it wasn't Weaver.

"Easy, Barry, it's not Weaver," I said.

The skinhead approached my side of the car. "What's going on?" he inquired.

I opened my wallet and quickly flashed an LAPD business card with a shiny gold shield. "Just keep walking, pal," I replied.

He turned around and began to walk away. Just as it looked like the ruse had worked, he spun around. "No, really, what the fuck's going on?" he asked.

Before I could respond, Barry pointed his .45 straight up and chambered a round. The loud metal clack of the semiautomatic pistol was unmistakable. "He said just keep walking, dick lips," Barry said.

The skinhead threw up his hands. "I'm out of here, man," he said.

He turned and walked away quickly. I watched him enter Dusty's town house, then drove down the street to contemplate our next move. A few minutes later, my cell phone rang.

It was Detective Holmes. "Dennis, I just got a call. We've got LAPD, sheriffs, U.S. Marshals, CDC, FBI, and other local PDs all out in the field looking for Weaver. You know what they're hearing over the radio. 'Who are those guys? What team are they with? Holy shit, I think it's the Walsh brothers.' If it was my brother, I'd probably be doing the same thing, Dennis, but we don't want you getting caught in a crossfire. Wrap it up and go home. We're closing in on him. We'll get him any day now," he said.

While I was driving Barry back to his car, Dusty called. "What's going on, bro? Chris Calopi was just here. He said two guys were out front who looked like cops, but one of them looked and sounded like Chris Walsh," he said. "I told him it was just some security cops I hired since all these fuckers keep stealing from me, but I don't think he bought it."

"I see you got your phone back, you fucking nitwit," I said, but in a lighthearted way.

"Of course, I didn't think I would look so hot with it duct-taped to my forehead." He laughed.

The morning of February 18, I was running late. Steinberg, Wilson, and Jassick were due in Department D of the San Fernando Courthouse for a preliminary hearing. The phone rang at 7:45 A.M. I kept a business line that rang through to my house.

It was Don Mercatoris. "Kimmi's house just got tossed and Indian Gary got busted thanks to you, fucker," he said.

I was surprised to hear from him. He had been avoiding my calls. Jimmy Bray had told me that Mercatoris was with Weaver at a tweaker named Chicky's house on the evening of Valentine's Day.

"Hey, fucknuts, one thing about me—if I set up that raid, you would have seen me standing there when they hauled everybody outside, just like you saw me when they had you hooked up in front of that motel," I said.

Without mentioning Jimmy as my source or anything about Mercatoris wanting to "put a hole" in me. I accused him of helping out Weaver. He denied it and promised to get back to me with information. I played along and told him I would wait to hear from him.

I got to the courthouse and grabbed a seat in the back of the courtroom. The three defendants were led out from lockup and seated at the counsel table in their orange jumpsuits. Weaver's absence grated on me. Shane Wilson turned and caught my eye. I glared at him with obvious contempt. Strangely enough, he responded with a sort of plaintive look, which took me by surprise. It would be another month before I was able to make sense of his demeanor. I didn't, however, have much time to ponder his odd conduct. The preliminary hearing was continued, but the proceedings were hardly over. After the defendants were escorted to the lockup and their attorneys left the courtroom, Deputy District Attorney Stephanie Sparagna stood up and asked Judge Cynthia Ulfig for a court order banning me from all further court proceedings and from contacting any witnesses in the case. Her request took me by complete surprise.

"Your Honor," she said, "some of the witnesses are more afraid of Dennis Walsh than they are of the killers."

When asked by the judge, Detective Cochran stated that some witnesses had expressed some concern. I felt like I had just been suckerpunched.

I stood and asked permission to address the court. "Your Honor, I'm the only family member in California. I need to be able to keep my family informed of the proceedings," I managed to offer.

"Your Honor, it's at the point where Mr. Walsh may well need to retain counsel," said Deputy DA Mike Kraut, who was assisting Stephanie Sparagna on the case.

"Ms. Sparagna advised me that she would be seeking this order, Mr. Walsh," Judge Ulfig said. "I've been watching you all morning, and you seem like a complete gentleman, but I am going to issue the order. You are ordered not to be in the courthouse during any proceeding and you are further ordered not to have any contact with any witnesses in this case. You may arrange for someone else to attend court hearings and take notes for you."

I tried to speak with DDAs Sparagna and Kraut in the hallway.

"We can't talk to you now, Dennis. We're just trying to get justice for your brother," Mike Kraut said, and walked away.

I walked out to the parking lot and sat in my car. Feelings of embarrassment, anger, frustration, and disbelief fought for center stage in my brain. I felt that nobody knew the case like I did. Nobody understood the characters involved and their motivations like I did. Nobody cared about my brother's murder like I did. But most of all, I was worried that witnesses who would otherwise be willing to speak with me might not be willing speak to the police.

I called Detective Holmes. "Oh, fuck," he said. "That's bullshit. Dennis, don't feel bad. All the information you've given us is golden. She's wound pretty tight, but she's a real good prosecutor. Just keep away from any witnesses. Everything is going to turn out okay."

I checked my messages. Cameron Cain, Kimmi Balmes, and Christina Karath had called and wanted to speak with me. I called Scott Ryan, a local tweaker. I asked him to return the calls and inform them that I was under court order not to contact witnesses and to have them contact the police directly.

"Yeah, like that'll happen." He laughed.

Next I had to sheepishly inform my family and friends of what had transpired.

Later I spoke with Detectives Fleming and Cochran. They assured me that Stephanie Sparagna was on top of the case: "She calls us at all hours," Detective Cochran said. "She's got files in her garage and works this case nights and weekends. I think she hates Steinberg almost as much as you do, Dennis."

I felt a little better, but spent most of the day in a blue funk. Being probably the only attorney in the state banned from the courthouse was a dubious distinction. I didn't even bother to hit the Jameson. That would have been like throwing gasoline on a fire.

My two courtroom confrontations with Steinberg certainly had not helped matters. Ironically, it was a few years later that I would discover that it was another character by the name of David Steinberg who was convicted of the misdemeanor lewd conduct charges, and not David Michael Steinberg. I suppose it really did not matter. In my state of mind, I would have confronted him with some equally inflammatory comment.

Marta Wilson called. I told her what had happened. I was not aware that she would be a witness. I knew she had spoken with Detective Fleming, but believed that she merely furnished some background information and was not a material witness. She said Mouse had run into Weaver the day before. I called Detective Holmes to let him know. He did not say anything about Marta being a witness.

Jimmy Bray called. I didn't consider him to be a witness: he was merely trying to help me find Weaver. He said that Don Mercatoris wanted to borrow his motorcycle to meet with Weaver. He offered to let the police put a tracking device on his bike. I put him in touch with Marshal Burke, who said they would consider it.

I changed the voice mail on my business line to say, *"You've reached the law office of Dennis Walsh. If you're calling with information regarding People versus Steinberg and Weaver, please call Detective John Fleming, Devonshire Division Homicide Squad at 818 . . ."* That was not going to be exactly good for business, but I didn't care.

Kenny Williams's girlfriend, Danielle, called and I informed her that I could not speak with her or with Kenny and directed her to call Detective Fleming.

Jesus Christ, I thought, *I just get banned from talking to witnesses, and all of a sudden they have me on speed dial.*

Later that night, my phone rang around 10 P.M.

"Dennis, Detective Holmes. You didn't hear it from me, but Weaver just got arrested about a half hour ago in Hollywood. I thought you'd like to know. I'll have Marshal Burke call you a little later," he said.

I thought I was dreaming. I thanked him and poured myself a shot of Jameson. The agony of defeat and the thrill of victory, all in one day. I called my brothers, sisters, and mother to share the good news.

U.S. Marshal Tony Burke called a little while later. "We thought we had him in a room at the Saharan Motor Hotel in Hollywood around quarter after nine. When we crashed it, only the girl was in there. Weaver came running out of another room with a jacket over his head and fled down Sunset Boulevard. After he climbed onto a balcony on North Fuller Avenue, the resident held him at gunpoint. When I got there, he was crying. He kept saying, 'They're gonna kill me, they're gonna kill me.' I asked him who and he said, 'The Walsh brothers and the SIS.'"

This from the guy who wasn't going to be taken alive. A search of Weaver's motel room netted four cell phones, a California driver's license in the name of Thomas Alvarez, and a birth certificate in the name of Brandon Cook.

I had spent what seemed like an eternity waiting for Weaver to get arrested. Every breath he drew on the streets sucked more of the life out of me. I had become obsessed with the chase. I went upstairs and pulled out my appointment book to count the days he was free to roam the streets. It came to seventy-eight days. It seemed like seventy-eight months to me. In reality, it was only two and a half months. A total of eleven weeks, one day, nineteen hours, and fifteen minutes of hell. I fell asleep and slept the soundest I had in months. I don't recall what I dreamed that night, but I never dreamed it would be three and a half years before the case would get to trial.

THE VIGIL

9

THE MAKING OF A SEA CUCUMBER

W EAVER'S BAIL WAS SET AT one million dollars. He and Steinberg were charged with first-degree murder. Shane Wilson and George Jassick were testifying for the prosecution. My elation was tempered with disappointment from being blindsided by DDA Sparagna. I began to second-guess myself. If anything I had said or done ultimately damaged the prosecution's case, I would never forgive myself. If the killers were acquitted and set free, I had no doubt that I was the guy who would kill them. The peace of mind I had expected to find once murder charges were filed and Weaver was arrested never materialized. Instead, my stress level went off the charts.

Even conducting my practice became a bit of an ordeal. In the San Fernando Courthouse one day, I found myself and my client surrounded by five sheriff's deputies. My client was charged with felony possession of narcotics for sale. He was looking at jail time, and already on edge. The contingent of deputies did little to ease his mind.

"What's going on?" I asked the deputies.

"What are you doing here?" one of the bailiffs inquired.

"I kind of work here," I replied.

My client must have been relieved that the deputies were focused on me rather than on him. I asked him to wait in the courtroom while the deputies ushered me out to the hallway. One deputy pulled out his radio and summoned a sergeant.

"There's nothing going on today in the Steinberg–Weaver case that I know about," I told the sergeant.

"I know, Counsel, but whenever we hear that either you or your brothers are in the courthouse, we're on high alert. From now on, whenever you come to this courthouse, I want you to come downstairs and check in with me first so we don't have any problems," he said.

So there it was. I was already embarrassed for being barred from the courthouse; now I was basically required to report to the principal's office.

The next morning, I was cursing Christopher for allowing himself to get drawn into the hellhole that had destroyed him and continued to affect my life on many different levels. I laced up my jogging shoes as Johnny Rio spun in circles in anticipation of our run.

"Goddamn it, Christopher," I said to myself. "You need to give me some kind of sign that this is all going to turn out all right, before I go out of my friggin' mind."

Ten minutes later, my wolfdog and I were jogging up the road less than a hundred yards from my house. As we approached a large oak tree, I noticed what I thought was a dollar bill at the base of the tree. When I bent over to pick it up, I was stunned to see Abe Lincoln's face. It was a five-dollar bill, a fin.

"Holy shit," I said out loud.

Fin was Christopher's nickname. This was a rural area, and the chances of a five-dollar bill turning up at all, let alone after I had just requested a sign, had to be astronomical. I am not a religious person and I'm pretty sure it was pure happenstance, but nonetheless, I took it to be a good omen. After we finished our run, I tacked the fin next to Steinberg's picture and Christopher's prayer card.

Things did seem to be looking up. My brother Bobby was due to be released from federal prison any day after serving three years and nine months. He had missed both Christopher's and our father's funerals.

On March 4, Steinberg was charged with two additional counts of at-tempted murder in the shooting-at-the-deputy case. That case was con-solidated with the murder case. The prosecution's theory being that Steinberg had killed my brother because he was a witness to the shoot-out with Deputy Dixon.

On March 26, Jeannie attended the preliminary hearing for me. At a preliminary hearing, the State puts on a skeletal case, presenting just enough evidence to convince a judge that sufficient cause exists to hold the defendant over for trial.

Jeannie called to tell me that Shane Wilson was testifying for the prosecution. The news was breathtaking. I cut her short as she inveigled me to attribute my good fortune to divine intervention. Shane Wilson was typical of many inmates who found Jesus while in jail. *Born again until they're out again,* was a favorite phrase among defense attorneys.

"Well, maybe God did have something to do with it," I replied, "but I don't think Shane Wilson needed the Lord to tell him that riding a third strike for life was a bad call."

Perhaps due to my Catholic upbringing, I did express my gratitude to God while gloating over my prediction to Shane Wilson that he would "sit on a witness stand and sing like a goddamned canary." The prosecu-tion now had a star witness. I pulled the tack out of the fin I had found and idly creased it over and over between my fingers while savoring the good news. The notorious Shankster Gangster had at least one prior strike and could have been looking at twenty-five years to life if con-victed. Still, my brothers and I felt the hapless Weaver would be the one to flip. Finding the fin may have been a good omen, but Shankster Gang-ster flipping was more than I could have hoped for.

Detective Holmes told me that he once told Shane Wilson that one day he would sit on a witness stand and testify to save his own skin. "He just sat there and smirked, saying that'll never happen," the detective had related.

Shane Wilson was a career criminal who relished his reputation. He had served time for leading the police on a high-speed car chase ending with a five-hour stand-off with a SWAT team in Canyon Country, and for invading a home in Oxnard and robbing the occupants at gunpoint, among numerous other crimes. As a youth, he was incarcerated under the auspices of the California Youth Authority, where he was recruited to join the notorious Nazi Low Riders. Each letter of a member's NLR tattoo had to be earned by an act of extreme violence. He freely admitted to assaulting witnesses who had dared to testify against NLR members. Wilson *taxed* local meth dealers on behalf of the NLR prison hierarchy. Failure to pay or pay on time was met with unbridled brutality. NLR members prided themselves on their sworn vow not to surrender to the police. The organization had a zero-tolerance policy for breaking the oath. Any Nazi Low Rider who failed to take the opportunity to shoot it out with law enforcement before being arrested faced death in prison. Parole Agent Docherty's phrase *prison bred* was burned into my brain. I had believed that Wilson's massive ego would never allow him to cooperate with the police despite the amount of time he was facing, but now it was really happening. Shankster Gangster was, in the words of Don Mercatoris, going to wear a rat jacket. Maybe Mouse had been right. Maybe Wilson *was* in the hat.

It occurred to me that the plaintive look on his face in court in February had telegraphed a message that was just being delivered now. I appreciated his decision to cooperate but had no illusion that it was anything but self-serving. Shane Wilson didn't stick his neck out for anyone. He did the smart thing and agreed to a sentence of three years in exchange for his testimony.

Most criminals were quick to disparage a rat, quick to tout their own loyalty to their "dawgs," and quick to condemn anyone who even spoke to the police. But when push came to shove, most of them collapsed like a three-dollar card table. It was mostly the Mexicans who held their mud these days, if only because *La Eme,* the Mexican Mafia, would not hesitate to take revenge against their families.

I dialed my brother Dan's number. "Shane Wilson testified against Steinberg at the prelim today. Who'd have thought Shankster Gangster would be the one to play the sea cucumber?" I asked.

I didn't have to explain what I meant. My father had his own special term for rats. *Sea cucumbers*, he called them. He had defined it for me in a letter from prison in reference to the guy who had ratted him out in Florida:

> *Sea Cucumber—the only other animal which, at the first sight of trouble, spews forth their internal organs before collapsing like burst balloons—alive but empty.*

I took particular delight in knowing that Shankster Gangster would now be nothing more than a pariah. He would never again be a shot caller, never again be afforded the respect he craved so much from the denizens of the criminal underworld. Now he was just a rat, a lonely sea cucumber, alive but empty. It was almost like neutering a dog.

Shane Wilson was overly concerned with his reputation. He sought redemption in a three-way call to Don Mercatoris from Beverly Hills jail. Three-way calls from inmates are prohibited. Inmates learn to blow into the phone while the second person dials a third person's number, so the click connecting the third person is not recorded.

Wilson tried to soft-pedal cutting a deal. He told Mercatoris, "I told on myself," rather than saying he ratted out Steinberg. He said he took a deal so he could be with his son. Later Wilson would tell people that he testified only because Steinberg tricked him into touching the trash barrel so that his fingerprints would implicate him.

To this day, the ex–Shankster Gangster, "alive but empty," remains eager to explain his rationale for ratting out Steinberg to anyone who will listen. I didn't care much about his motive. I was just glad he'd decided to tell the truth.

With both Wilson and Jassick testifying against Steinberg, it was beginning to look like Steinberg and Weaver were going down. I finally felt as if I could afford to relax.

My relief was dampened the day after Wilson testified at the preliminary hearing. His attorney had arranged for him to be placed in protective custody at Men's Central Jail. Deputy DA Mike Kraut had called the jail to follow up and make sure Wilson was designated K-10, a keep away.

Testifying was a surefire way to get stabbed in custody, and L.A. county jail was one of the most dangerous facilities in the country. Over the previous five months, five inmates had been killed there. Somewhere along the line, the sheriff's department dropped the ball guarding Shane Wilson.

I was drafting a motion when Detective Holmes called. "You didn't hear it from me, but Shane Wilson just got stabbed at county jail. It's pretty bad, but he's going to pull through. Don't say anything to anyone just yet," he said.

"How the hell did that happen? Wasn't he PC'd up?" I asked.

"He was supposed to be. It looks like the sheriffs fucked up, big-time," he replied.

Wilson had been left alone in a cell in a protective custody module pursuant to court order. Security measures broke down when an inmate named Porfirio Avila was allowed to serve Wilson his dinner. Avila was a hard-core gang member with nothing to lose. He had just been convicted of two murders and sentenced to life without parole, commonly known as an "L-WOP." He was dangerous enough to be designated K-10, a keep away who was not supposed to come into contact with other inmates for their safety. One of his victims had also testified for the prosecution. It was nothing short of sheer lunacy for the sheriff's department to assign an L-WOP any duty that gave him access to the protective custody module. It was a clear violation of sheriff's departmental policy, which required K-10 inmates to be escorted by a deputy at all times.

It was around 4 P.M. when Avila pretended to lose control of the plate of hot dogs and beans he was handing Wilson through the slot in the cell bars. Wilson instinctively leaned forward to grab his chow before it spilled. Avila had concealed a crudely fashioned shiv made of razor blades fused to a toothbrush handle in his right hand. Right on cue, he slashed upward, cutting Wilson from throat to ear, missing his jugular vein by a quarter inch. Shankster Gangster hit the floor and grabbed a towel to stem the blood freely flowing from the five-inch gash. He frantically screamed, "Man down!" again and again. The other inmates began to hoot and holler in a unified attempt to muffle his cries. The word was out: Shane Wilson was a rat, and they had no problem watching him bleed out. Fifteen minutes ticked slowly by before a deputy finally took notice of the rising cacophony of jeers and responded to Wilson's pleas for help. It took more than one hundred stitches to sew up the wound. Had Avila managed to slice Wilson's jugular vein, the prosecution's star witness would surely have bled to death on the cold, damp concrete floor of the protective custody module.

In a May 14 *Los Angeles Times* interview, Wilson discussed the incident and admitted fearing for his life: "I'm a big guy, I'm a bad guy. . . . I was scared for my life. . . . In my world, if you testify, you put your life in jeopardy, bottom line."

Regarding having to testify again at trial, Wilson said, "If I don't, then he could go free, and I could end up dead."

Had Avila successfully carried out his assigned task, Wilson's preliminary hearing testimony would have been admissible at trial. Live testimony, however, is always more powerful. I was glad he survived for that reason and because he had a young son. I knew what it felt like to have your father die behind bars.

There's no doubt in my mind that Steinberg had arranged the stabbing. The authorities shared my belief but were unable to prove it. Shane Wilson filed a civil suit alleging negligence on behalf of the sheriff's department. Three years later, the L.A. County Board of Supervisors approved a settlement in the amount of eighty thousand dollars. To this day, Wilson wears the five-inch scar on the left side of his neck as a permanent souvenir.

A few weeks after the preliminary hearing, I unintentionally ran into Robert "Mouse" Hayes at a client's house in Simi Valley. I was walking up the driveway while he was walking toward his car.

"You know I can't talk to you, Mouse," I said.

"Yeah, don't trip, it's okay," he answered.

"Be careful out there, testifying against Steinberg didn't win you any popularity contests," I cautioned.

Robert Hayes was not only a Nazi Low Rider dropout, but had also testified for the prosecution. Being in the hat put him at constant risk.

"You don't have to worry about me," he replied. He opened his jacket to expose a pearl-handled pistol in a shoulder holster.

I asked my client, Holly Wilkins, what Mouse was doing flashing his gun like that.

"That's my grandpa's Colt .45. He knew you were coming. He said everybody knows Dennis Walsh is strapped. He just wanted to put on a show," Holly said.

I wondered how "everybody" knew I carried a gun. Jimmy Bray would not have put that out there. It must have been Chris Calopi after seeing Barry and me outside Dusty's town house.

The next day, Holly called to say Mouse got arrested and charged with being a felon in possession of a firearm.

"Are you shitting me?" I asked. "Holly, do me a favor. Make sure he knows I didn't drop a dime on him. I'm not allowed to go down there and see him."

The mind-set of these criminals was such that they never believed they got caught due to their own ineptitude. It always had to be that someone ratted them out. I didn't much care for felons carrying guns, but Mouse was definitely in danger. It was a risk he chose to take.

I called Detective Fleming to see that Mouse was made a K-10, knowing that he would probably be too proud to seek protection himself. Steinberg's ability to reach out and touch witnesses was not anything to take lightly.

The two stabbings reaffirmed my decision to carry a weapon. So did a call I received from Detective Fleming. Sheriff's deputies at county jail had confiscated a kite note with Dan's name and the names of several detectives and a DA. They believed it to be a hit list. The note was signed "Silent Thunder," a nickname Steinberg had given himself.

The LAPD had Phoenix police dispatch patrol cars to my mother's and Dan's homes to advise them of the potential threat.

I called my mother. "Mom, you need to just sit tight for a few hours, will you please?" I said.

"I have an appointment to get my hair done," she replied.

Family lore has it that my mother once stopped at the beauty parlor on the way to give birth to one of my brothers or sisters.

"Mom, I don't think they're going to give you a police escort to the hairdresser's, just stay home for a couple of hours until I call back," I said.

The LAPD and sheriff's department tore the high-power cells apart, looking for additional evidence to corroborate the threat, but to no avail. Because the handwriting could not be linked to Steinberg, the authorities were unable to charge him. There was no doubt, however, that Silent Thunder was the nom de plume of David Michael Steinberg.

"Hey, Detective, see what happens when you hang around me? You get yourself on a hit list," I told Detective Fleming.

"Thanks a lot." He laughed.

Shane Wilson recovered from his injuries and was transferred around to local jails in Beverly Hills and Burbank until he was housed in protective custody in Orange County jail.

I didn't look at Mouse the same way I viewed Wilson. Mouse wasn't seeking a deal. He wasn't ratting out a crimey to save himself. He just hated Steinberg. One of the more comical moments of the entire case occurred when, during his preliminary hearing testimony, DDA Sparagna asked him if he committed crimes with Steinberg.

"Let me get this straight," he answered, with obvious indignation, "I commit my own crimes."

The case had been transferred downtown to the ninth floor of the Criminal Courts Building—or CCB, as it is known. Everyone entering the courthouse went through a metal detector on the first floor. Those getting off the elevator on the ninth floor went through yet another metal detector before gaining access to the hallway leading to the various courtrooms. The ninth floor was reserved for high-profile criminal cases, like the O. J. Simpson and Phil Spector trials.

I asked Detective Cochran why this case had been transferred downtown. Brad Cochran was a hard-nosed, veteran detective, and even more reserved than Detective Fleming. His responses to my questions were usually limited to "Yes," "No," "I don't know," or "I can't say." It was like speaking to the *Dragnet* character Sergeant Joe Friday, but I had come to like him.

This time his reply was a bit more informative. "Well, according to the sheriff's department, it's because they can't guarantee the safety of the defendants because of the Walsh family and their known connections to organized crime," he said.

"Really? They ought to be more concerned about protecting inmates in their so-called protective custody than worrying about my family," I answered.

I thought Detective Cochran might have been pulling my leg until one day when Tim, Dan, and Bobby were in line to go through the metal detector on the CCB ninth floor.

"Oh, are you guys the gangsters?" one of the deputies inquired.

"Yeah," Dan answered, "we're with the Crips."

From then on, at every hearing my brothers attended, there was always additional security. I guess they weren't taking any chances with the Walsh brothers.

10

HER BIGGEST CURSE, YET HER
GREATEST BLESSING

IN FEBRUARY 2004, I HAD received notice from the Major Narcotics Division, Bureau of Specialized Prosecutions Division of the DA's office that telephone conversations between Troy Wilcox and me had been intercepted from August 12 through October 10, 2003. He was arrested for felony conspiracy to commit a crime and for the transportation and sale of assault weapons. It pleased me that Troy Wilcox had caught a little heat of his own. *Schadenfreude,* the Germans called it—taking pleasure in another's misery. I could only imagine what expletive-laden pearls of wisdom I had imparted during those wiretapped phone calls. It was one more reason I was not looking forward to the inevitable meeting with Deputy DA Stephanie Sparagna.

Friends and relatives were urging me to contest the court order, but I decided not to. It was never my intent to interfere with the prosecution's case. Judge Ulfig had expressly permitted people to attend hearings on my behalf, allowing me to keep abreast of the judicial proceedings. I was more concerned about witnesses who might be inclined to speak with me but not with the police.

The Devonshire Division homicide detectives seemed to be in my corner. I went down to the station one day to personally meet Detective

Holmes. Previously I had only spoken with him on the phone. He came outside and met me on the steps. The same steps I had envisioned driving up with Weaver tied to the hood of my car. His boyish smile and close-cropped reddish hair caused him to appear even younger than he was.

"Hey, Detective," I said. "I just wanted to meet you so you could see that I'm not some sort of a crackpot. You guys know there's people who won't talk to you. I'm just trying to help out. Detective Oppelt thinks I'm a pain in the ass, but I try to call only when I have decent information."

"I told you everything you've given us is good intel. Don't worry about Oppelt. We were in a meeting the other day, and he said it was bullshit that the older Walsh brother got banned from the courtroom. We don't have a problem with you, Dennis. Just stay away from witnesses. The defense is going to try to make it all about you," he said.

I'd liked Detective Holmes before; now I really liked him. It was good to know that the cops were in my corner.

A few months after the motel bust that netted a fugitive, a gun, drugs, a police badge, and a uniform, I was at Devonshire Division being interviewed by Detective Fleming. I asked for a drink of water. He walked me to a locker room at the back of the station. Detective Holmes was suiting up with a group of cops putting on black vests and what looked to be SWAT equipment.

"David, haven't you picked that fugitive up yet?" Detective Fleming asked Detective Holmes.

"Not yet." Detective Holmes grinned. "We were waiting for Dennis."

The LAPD may have had my back, but I had mixed emotions concerning the deputy DA who had me banned from the courthouse. I resented her for apparently not appreciating that I had convinced numerous witnesses to come forward, but was grateful that she appeared to be true to her promise to treat my brother's murder as if the president were the victim. Somehow, though, I felt like Lee Harvey Oswald. She let me stew for five or six months before having Detective Fleming call me.

"The DA wants to see you. Can you come down to the station tomorrow at two o'clock?" he asked.

I felt a sudden pang of nausea. DDA Mike Kraut's comment that I may need my own attorney had been bothering me for months.

"Hey, Detective, if I'm going to be arrested, just let me know now, will you please?" I replied.

Detective Fleming seemed to get quite a kick out of my response. "Well, not that I know of." He laughed.

I agreed to be there, although his response was not all that reassuring. I called my friend Gary Valeriano to post my bail if I did get hooked up.

"Den, you don't have to call. I'm always ready to post your bail," he said.

"Very funny," I answered.

I wasn't in the mood to have my balls busted.

The next day, September 7, 2004, I was interviewed by DDA Sparagna and Detective Fleming at Devonshire Division. I knew the interview was being recorded. I didn't know if the prosecutor was aware of the little dustup my brother Tim and I had with Shane Wilson and Weaver early in January. It was essential to come clean and not have it sprung on her at trial.

"You know, Stephanie, I think you should know that my brother Tim and I had a sort of confrontation with Weaver and Shane Wilson a few months ago," I said.

Stephanie leaned her head back and stared up at the ceiling while taking a deep breath. She then very deliberately placed her pen on the table and covered her eyes with both hands, her fingers pointing upward as if she was in prayer. After a few seconds, she slid her fingers to the bridge of her nose, barely exposing her eyes.

"Confrontation? What does that mean, Dennis? Like the two of you beat the shit out of them?" she asked without it really sounding like a question.

"Well, basically yes," I answered.

Her hands went back to completely covering her eyes as I related the events that took place in front of Kimmi Balmes's house.

When I finished, she peeked out through her cupped hands. "Is there anything else I should know, Dennis?" she asked with a sigh.

There was not a trace of anger in her voice. She had resigned herself to take her witnesses as they came, warts and all. Her reaction showed me a softer side of her personality, a sort of vulnerability that would forever endear her to me. She cared deeply about convicting these murderers and the thought of anything harming the case truly pained her. I could hear that in her voice. I would never again doubt her dedication to the case.

I recounted my experience with Dusty Urban and the U.S. Marshals. She simply shook her head upon hearing of my threat to duct-tape Dusty's cell phone to his forehead.

In an effort to explain the crude message I had left Christina Karath, I told her what Dan had told me about my mother crying over photos of Christopher and Christina's reluctance to produce phone records.

"Did you have to use the C-word, Dennis?" she asked.

During the interview, she asked me a question that I was unable to answer. I had brought my "journal" with me and began to thumb through it. My "journal" was just a typical green legal file folder. I had been in the habit of carrying it with me just about everywhere.

"What date was that you asked about?" I asked.

"Wait a minute. What is that?" she asked me.

"Oh, it's just kind of a journal with notes that I've made about the case," I answered.

"John, did you know about this?" she asked Detective Fleming.

"No, this is the first time I've seen it," he answered.

Stephanie asked to see the journal. After poring through it for a few minutes, she paused to gather her thoughts. "Dennis, can I have this file or do I have to subpoena it?" she asked.

Her question took me by surprise, although it was perfectly clear she was getting that file, one way or another. Even though I was a lawyer, I had never given much thought to my journal being evidentiary. It was pretty much a handwritten mess intended only for my use. The entire cover was haphazardly strewn with a jumble of names and phone numbers. Had I thought the journal would ever be subject to any scrutiny, I would have taken more care to keep better and neater notes. Stephanie did not have to tell me that copies would have to be turned over to the defense attorneys.

"If you think it will help your case, you can have it," I said, "but it's kind of like my bible. I need to get a copy back."

Detective Fleming agreed to make a copy for me.

Stephanie and I talked after the interview. I wanted her to know that I was only trying to get witnesses to come forward, that I did not mean to hamper her case in any way.

"Dennis, I get it. I've got four brothers. We're Italian—if anything happened to me, they'd be out doing the same crazy shit you're doing. It's really great that you've been able to get me all these witnesses, but I have to convict Steinberg and Weaver in a court of law. You're a lawyer. You know the defense attorneys are going to hammer you on the witness stand. Like it or not, you and your family are going to be put on trial. You tainted every witness by talking to them. I've put a lot of time into this case already and I'm going to do everything in my power to convict these creeps, but if they wind up walking, I'm telling you right now that it'll be through no fault of mine," she said.

The implication was not lost on me. If the killers walked, it would be my fault.

She must have sensed how much her comment weighed on me. "I will say this, though, Dennis. You're my biggest curse, but also my greatest blessing," she said with a warm smile.

The more I spoke with Stephanie, the more comfortable I became. Detective Cochran was right: She had done her homework. She was familiar with all the players. If I mentioned some tweaker or petty hoodlum peripherally involved in the case, she would spit out the information that I had provided to the homicide detectives. She understood the depth of Steinberg's depravity. She realized that Steinberg had killed Christopher not only because they weren't getting along but also because Christopher was an eyewitness to the shoot-out with Deputy Dixon. She got it, all right. Like I said, I'm not a religious person, but Deputy DA Stephanie Sparagna was a godsend. On one hand, I felt as if the world had been lifted off my shoulders. On the other hand, that burden was replaced with the formidable weight of living every moment with the knowledge that it would be my fault if the killers walked. DDA Sparagna did not miss an opportunity to remind me of that burden.

A sound sleep would be nothing more than a memory for me over the next three years.

I tried my best not to speak to witnesses, except that more often than not, I didn't exactly know who was a witness. I wanted to avoid violating the court order and did not want to cause DDA Sparagna any further aggravation. Still, I found it difficult to put myself on ice completely. The order did not forbid me from talking about the case. I talked to anyone and everyone who did not appear to be a witness. I was walking a tight-rope.

Gina Crotts, a friend of Lee Martin, called and began relating how Troy Wilcox had offered Jeff Weaver ten thousand dollars to leave town shortly after the murder. I asked her to contact the homicide detectives and then relayed the information to the police.

I returned a call from a woman named Patti Vandall, who I thought was seeking legal advice. She blurted out that Gary Schimmel kept changing his story before telling me that she was George Jassick's girlfriend. I immediately referred her to Detective Fleming. Despite my voice mail message directing people to contact the homicide detectives, I was contacted on a regular basis.

Lee Martin requested my help in his case in which he was "pro per," acting as his own attorney. He had provided many useful contacts. I was happy to repay the favor by assisting the crime-scene reconstruction expert that had been appointed by the court.

I didn't consider Jimmy Bray to be a witness, either. When his girlfriend called after he had been arrested for possession of narcotics, I had no problem hustling down to the lockup at San Fernando Courthouse to see him.

"Thanks for coming, Counselor. I ran into that prick Weaver yesterday at County. We were chained up, and I couldn't get at him. I told that fat cocksucker that the Walsh brothers sent their regards and that he was dead meat," Jimmy informed me. "He looked like he was ready to shit himself."

Jimmy knew that I had asked other inmates to deliver the message that the Walsh brothers sent their regards whenever they ran across Steinberg or Weaver in county jail. I wanted to make sure neither of them forgot about us.

I was grateful that Jimmy had offered to let the U.S. Marshals put a tracking device on his motorcycle to tail Don Mercatoris. I had no problem agreeing to represent him on the San Fernando case and on an outstanding warrant in Orange County. When my brother Tim came into town, I took him and Jimmy to dinner at Los Toros in Chatsworth.

"Me and a couple of the Walsh brothers, just like the Irish Mafia," Jimmy cracked.

He was more than grateful for my help.

"Timmy, I love this fucking brother of yours. He's a pretty good mouthpiece, but he's gonna get himself killed the way he talks to some of these people. You gotta make him put a lid on it. Before I met him, I thought he was six foot nine. On the phone, he sounds like a fucking gorilla, then I meet him and he's a buck and a half drippin' wet. Ever since Chris got murdered, I haven't been able to sell a fucking bag of dope. This crazy bastard tore this whole fucking town apart," Jimmy said.

"Well, Jimmy, that's my big brother," Tim replied. "We can't take him anywhere."

"Timmy, I ain't shittin' you, he's like a one-man SWAT team. A whole bunch of joints been raided and a ton of people been arrested because of him. He's stepping on a lot of toes," Jimmy continued, as if I were not present.

Jimmy had been moving dope for a major trafficker in the Valley.

"Two of my boss's guys got hooked up and he ain't real happy about it. He wanted to kill your skinny ass, Counselor, but I told him about Chris. He's cool with it 'cuz you're just a civilian, but he told me to tell you to stay the fuck away from his operation," Jimmy said.

I took a long draw off my bottle of Heineken. "Hey, Jimmy, tell your boss to go fuck himself. Tell him until Steinberg and Weaver get convicted, if he or any of his guys get in my way, they're going down," I replied.

Jimmy grabbed me and put me in a headlock. "Timmy, that's why I love this wild man. You crazy Irish fucks are as crazy as me." He laughed while releasing me from his grasp. "And I ain't telling my boss nothin', Counselor. You got enough people that want to put a hole in you."

After Kimmi Balmes's house got raided, she became less enthused about cooperating. One day in the courthouse hallway, Jeannie overheard Kimmi speaking with DDA Sparagna.

"Dennis Walsh had my house raided," Kimmi complained.

"Kimmi, Dennis Walsh does not have the power to have anybody's house raided," Stephanie had responded, obviously annoyed.

Apparently nobody was too happy with my tactics, not Kimmi, Jimmy Bray, his boss, or any number of tweakers and hoodlums on the streets, nor, for that matter, DDA Sparagna. It didn't take Clarence Darrow to understand that at trial, the defense attorneys would attack me like a pack of hyenas on a fresh carcass. I was banking on the fact that every witness would have to admit in front of a jury that all I had asked them to do was to be truthful and to speak with the police, no matter how many times I had cursed them out.

Brian Swartz had helped by keeping an eye on Weaver for me before an arrest warrant was issued. I went to court for him on a petty drug case. I didn't have any qualms about helping out anyone who had helped me as long as they were not witnesses. The court order didn't say anything about potential witnesses.

Then there was the matter of the murder weapon, which the police had not recovered. I assumed it to be the .22 Colt Challenger that Kenny Williams had repaired and given to Steinberg. Finding it might assist the prosecution, but I was also interested in who might have helped Steinberg dispose of it. If I did find out, I would jam them up however I could. I meant it when I told people nobody walks.

I continued to speak with Marta Wilson and even represented her in a civil case. Neither she nor I knew that she would be called as a witness against Steinberg. Steinberg had pulled a pistol from a hollowed-out Bible and pointed it at Moises Tovar in front of her. DDA Sparagna had charged Steinberg for that offense. She and the homicide detectives were playing it pretty close to the vest and not telling me much.

The first time I met Marta Wilson in person, it was at my makeshift "office" at El Presidente. Her friend Chris "Beanie" Ashad was willing to talk to me, but not to the police, about the murder weapon. Beanie had gulped down two shots of Patrón tequila before I arrived. Marta sipped a margarita as I walked in.

I was right, Marta was easy on the eyes. Blond, with a trim figure and sincere laugh, she was an accountant by trade. You would not have guessed that she had been down the crystal meth rabbit hole. Her marriage to Irish Mike was an on-again, off-again affair. Beanie seemed uncomfortable and ordered another Patrón. I chatted with them for a few minutes to put him at ease.

"I didn't know what to expect," he said. "From what I've been hearing all over town, I kinda expected you to hop out of the bushes and kick my ass."

"Well, the night is still young," I said with a smile.

Beanie made it absolutely clear that he would under no circumstances speak with the police. He told me that an old-timer named Dutch West, who was dying of AIDS and had been a sort of mentor to Shane Wilson, had had his car impounded recently and that a pistol was secreted in the dashboard. The rumor was that it might be the weapon that was used to kill my brother. I relayed the information to the LAPD, but nothing ever came of it. It was one of many rumors about the murder weapon.

For seven months, I had been able to avoid focusing on the details of my brother's murder by pounding the streets. The court order severely limited the scope of my activities. The thought of Christopher lying on that couch and "gurgling" with several bullets lodged in his head was more than I could stand. I suppose searching for that pistol was a subconscious attempt to divert my attention from the grisly details of the murder. No matter what I did, where I went, or who I was with, the murder was never far removed from my thoughts.

Once I received word that Aaron Archer was in custody, I called Detective Holmes. Kenny Williams had said Archer originally sold the Colt Challenger .22 to Christopher and felt bad about it. If Detective Holmes ever interviewed him, he didn't tell me.

Some time later, I would discover that the LAPD had swept Ving Rhames's house with metal detectors without any luck. There were rumors that a couple of heroin addicts named John and Priscilla had taken the pistol apart and disposed of the parts in various locations. That turned out to be a dead end. A couple of people told me that Shane Wilson had buried some guns at a house in Canoga Park. I routinely passed the information to the LAPD. Days, weeks, and months rolled by without the weapon being recovered.

An inmate named Robert Dragusica contacted me. He claimed to be an ex–Nazi Low Rider and lifelong friend of Shane Wilson. I went down to county jail to see him. "Bigfoot" was his handle, and it fit. He stood six foot three and weighed around two-fifty. His soft-spoken demeanor provided an odd contrast to his shaved head and numerous tattoos. A few pencil and ink sketchings protruding from a file he carried evidenced his talent as an amateur artist. His orange jumpsuit alerted me to his high-power status. He expected to be out soon and offered to let me know if he heard anything about the murder weapon.

"That was bullshit what happened to your brother. I admire you for what you're doing. I don't care what anybody in here says," he said.

He said Shane Wilson had a habit of burying guns he could retrieve when necessary.

He confirmed what I had heard about the extent of Wilson's ego. "Shane's in love with himself," he said.

We were sitting in the attorney interview room. At that time, there were no glass partitions between the attorneys and the inmates. Bigfoot was handcuffed with the cuffs chained to the narrow tabletop. As we were speaking, a deputy approached with another inmate in handcuffs. I didn't pay any attention.

Suddenly Bigfoot turned his head and yanked on the chain securing his handcuffs. "If I weren't chained up, I'd smash your fucking face in!" he shouted at the startled inmate.

The inmate looked down at me. When our eyes met, my heart stopped for a second. It was Jeff Weaver. He may have recognized my face, but it was probably the Chief Wahoo logo on my Tribe cap that caused his jaw to literally drop.

He turned to the deputy. "That's the brother of the guy I—" Weaver stopped just short of making an admission.

"This fat prick murdered my brother," I told the flustered deputy.

"All right, everybody just calm down here," the deputy ordered, then hustled Weaver to the other end of the interview room.

"Damn it," I told Bigfoot, "that dumb bastard almost admitted killing my brother."

This little episode had to have rocked Weaver's world. I relished any moment of grief visited upon either Weaver or Steinberg, especially if I had caused it.

I drove to the Van Nuys Courthouse when Bigfoot was due in court. The judge released him right there. I picked him up in front of the courthouse. He was wearing county jail whites. I took him over to the Sherman Room and bought him a steak dinner. With his huge size and jail garb, he stuck out like a circus elephant at a church picnic.

"I hope all these people think you're a house painter," I told him as he devoured his steak and baked potato.

I drove him downtown and gave him forty dollars. He had plans to stay with a friend and to get into rehab. The next day, he was back in jail. He had used the money to buy crystal meth. I wrote him a letter and told him that he owed me forty dollars. *I'd rather put my money in a pile and light it on fire than see it spent on dope,* I wrote.

Bigfoot wrote a letter to the DA, claiming to have disposed of several pistols for Shane Wilson. LAPD divers searched the ocean floor off the Malibu Pier several months before the trial without any success.

The murder weapon never was recovered. It may lie forever buried in a concrete footing at Ving Rhames's house. It may be scattered in pieces. It may be in the hands of a criminal. I don't know for sure, but I won't rest until I do.

11

BEWARE THE PATIENCE OF AN ANGRY MAN

THE WAIT WAS ON. SEYMOUR Amster was appointed to represent Jeff Weaver. Frank DiSabatino was appointed to represent Steinberg. Both were experienced criminal defense attorneys. The case was assigned to Superior Court Judge Michael Pastor in Department 107.

In the movies and on television, criminal cases proceed to trial with warp speed. In the real world, a murder case works its way through the criminal justice system to trial at a glacial pace. Generally, prolonging the trial date favors the defendants. Witnesses may die or disappear, memories fade, and stories change. My experience led me to believe that this case would not be tried anytime soon, especially with a savvy defendant like David Michael Steinberg working the system. I had learned to be patient sitting on stakeouts and waiting on tweakers and hoodlums who lived lives devoid of time constraints. Now I would have to patiently bide my time waiting for trial.

In the meantime, I was trying to establish some sense of normalcy in my life. My caseload kept me pretty busy, but sooner or later, this case always pulled me back in. One morning, I was at the lockup in the basement of the San Fernando Courthouse to see a client. Having dutifully checked in at the sergeant's office as required, I pressed the lockup buzzer and was let inside. To my surprise, sitting behind glass waiting for their attorneys were Don Mercatoris and Bullet. After the motel bust, the DA had elected to delay filing charges. Mercatoris had been released. I suspect the police were watching him to find Weaver. After Weaver was arrested, Mercatoris and Bullet were charged for the gun, drugs, and police badge.

Before I could say anything, Mercatoris leapt toward the glass to address me. "Hey, what the fuck are you doing here? I thought you were gonna talk to the DA because you didn't mean to get us busted?" he asked in a loud rapid-fire delivery.

His gravelly voice was irritating enough, but after he had been backdooring me with Weaver, I found his tone especially insulting.

I turned to Bullet. "Listen, I don't even know you. I thought you were Weaver. I'm sorry you got jammed up," I told him.

Bullet just shrugged his shoulders.

I turned toward Mercatoris. "But you, you cocksucker, can kiss my Irish ass. You had your chance, smart guy. Nobody walks means nobody fucking walks. Sit in your cell and think about me every fucking day for years and know I'm the guy that put your ass there!" I hollered.

It must have made quite a sight. I was in a suit and tie and carrying a briefcase. Another attorney who was interviewing his client paused to watch the show. Several other inmates looked on with fascination. The back of the prisoner lockup was glassed in, affording a view from the deputies' station. The commotion caused two deputies to walk over to the lockup door. The last thing I needed was another headache.

I pressed the buzzer to exit but could not resist a parting shot to Mercatoris. "Adios, asshole," I said.

My blood pressure skyrocketed from the jolt of adrenaline coursing through my veins. As I got off the elevator on the third floor less than a minute later, I was met by Deputy DA Mike Kraut.

Son of a bitch! How the hell did he hear about this already? I wondered.

"Dennis, I'm glad you're here. Do you mind testifying at Don Mercatoris's preliminary hearing?" he asked.

His request caused my elevated blood pressure to plummet like a free-falling elevator. I had not been aware that the hearing was calendared that day. "That would be my pleasure," I replied.

Detective Tony Avila and a couple of other SIS detectives were in the hallway in front of Department D. I had to tell them who I was. "Hey, Detective Avila, it's me, Dennis Walsh," I said.

"You look a lot different in a suit and tie," the detective said.

I wished him luck. I had heard that he and a couple of his partners were being investigated for shooting and killing two suspects after they robbed the Northridge Beauty Club in 2003. The SIS had engaged in over fifty gun battles, killing thirty-seven suspects and wounding dozens during its forty-year history. The unit was under constant scrutiny. No wonder Weaver had been terrified.

"Thanks," he said. "We think it's a good shoot. We'll see."

DDA Kraut asked us to take a seat in the courtroom. I purposely planted myself in the midst of the SIS detectives. Soon enough, bailiffs brought the handcuffed Mercatoris and Bullet into the courtroom. My broad smile was met by a dark scowl. The public defenders conferred with their clients and then repaired to the judge's chambers with DDA Kraut. When they returned to the courtroom, it was announced that a plea bargain had been reached. The defendants would waive their rights to trial and plead guilty in exchange for a sentence of ten years in state prison. With good time credits, they would probably serve half the time.

I left the courtroom walking on air. If Mercatoris was going to make good on his threat to "put a hole" in me, he'd have to wait five years. Even then, he'd probably have to wait in line.

On a Saturday in April 2004, I received a call from my sister Laura. Her voice trembled as she informed me of a letter Michelle O'Halloran had received from Kimmi Balmes. Michelle was in prison at a minimum-security camp for writing bad checks.

"Dennis, that Kimmi Balmes girl wrote to Michelle and said Jeffrey

Weaver fired the last shot to kill Chris," she said. "They were torturing him, Dennis."

The words *torturing him* crackled through my mind like a flash of raw electricity arcing across the sky. The white-hot rage that had taken refuge in a corner of my brain immediately enveloped me. Laura cried as she read the letter, making it difficult to comprehend. After she had to repeat several passages, I stopped her.

"Laura, calm down. Can you fax me the letter right away and mail me the original?" I asked.

I listened patiently while Laura recited a myriad of tasks that she had to do before she could drive over to Staples to fax me the letter. Trying to finish the brief I had been drafting proved a futile endeavor. I paced around my house before resorting to doing sets of push-ups until I was exhausted. Finally, the fax arrived.

The letter, in Kimmi's cursive handwriting, dated February 7, 2004, read—grammatical errors and all—as follows:

Michelle,

Hi how are you doing? Well I am sending you these two articles I got off the Internet and in the papers. It just came out they charged Dave with 1st degree murder also Jeff but he is on the run. They have his picture all over the place. They will get him. They also got Tony and a guy named George. Tony & George with access after the fact.

I no its not what you really want to hear but you should no and I would want to no if I was you. So how has camp been treating you? You should be getting out soon. I am sure before all these people go to trial you will be out. Dave's case more than likely will be capitol offence because Chris was a witness in that case and to kill a witness in your case is a capitol offence. I guess the prints came back on all the tests they did. I still don't have a # for you to call. I wish I did. I don't like writing to much cause the case is still open. Dennis his brother is really pushing the issue which you can't blame him its his brother. Any how they are looking for Jeff also for a robbery he just did. So when they catch up with him he's through besides the fact I am way

pisted at him cause he used my truck during the robbery of an adult
entertainment place and I work in the adult entertainment clubs. I
was so pisted it was like what the hell are you thinking and then gets
his crimey busted shot at and left him and ends up with nothing from
the robbery except getting a friend of mine a life sentence. You no it
was him who did the final thing to Chris, Michelle. Dave was making
him suffer alive and Jeff ended it over a period of 2 days.

I really hope that when you get out you file a civil suit against the
assholes. Really Michelle for your children for the loss they have to
suffer not to mention you. Let the kids get something from these ass-
holes. Well Michelle I will keep you up to date on whatever else is
going on. I will mail you a stationery package so you have some
stamps and paper & envelopes.   Kimmi

Tony Shane Wilson went by "Shane." I had never heard anyone on
the street refer to him as Tony. There was no way I could get back to
work. Tim's haunting nightmare of Christopher waiting for his brothers
who never came seemed magnified a thousand times by Kimmi's words,
"Dave was making him suffer alive."

Faxing the letter to Detective Fleming could wait until Monday
morning. I poured myself a couple shots of Jameson, and shouldn't have.
The thought of Steinberg abusing and taunting my brother while he lay
dying almost drove me out of my mind. I fantasized over killing Steinberg in a very savage, primal manner. The more I drank, the darker the
scenario turned. I envisioned beating him senseless, then tearing his jugular vein out with my teeth, spitting it in his face, and watching him die
like he had watched my brother die.

David Michael Steinberg had no idea how lucky he was that the
LAPD arrested him before my brothers and I got ahold of him. On second thought, maybe it was we who were the lucky ones.

The case dragged on throughout 2004 with a series of pretrial hearings.
My friends Jim Cavanaugh and Pat Murphy attended on my behalf and

reported back to me. Cavanaugh's Irish mug was always causing him to be mistaken for one of Christopher's brothers.

After Weaver complained one day in court, Stephanie Sparagna stood up and addressed the judge. "No, Your Honor, he's not one of the Walsh brothers, he's a friend of the family," she explained.

Kimmi Balmes, Cassondra Raef, and porn actress Diane Stewart were subpoenaed by the prosecution and routinely ordered to return to the next scheduled proceeding. More often than not, one of them would fail to appear, causing Judge Pastor to issue a body attachment directing law enforcement to bring them before the court. Detective Fleming would usually chase them down and make sure they appeared at the next hearing, and the order would be recalled.

The fact that Diane Stewart was being hauled in and out of court caught my attention. It wasn't clear if she was cooperating. Neither DDA Sparagna nor the homicide detectives would confirm her status. I didn't have to be clairvoyant, however, to read Detective Fleming's body language to know that Diane Purdie Stewart was not being helpful. According to Ivan Masabanda, she had entered into a sham marriage with a homosexual in order to avoid deportation to Canada. The gay bridegroom was last seen sprinting down San Fernando Road after Ivan had confronted him. I wondered if her immigration woes had anything to do with my having dropped a dime on her with the U.S. Immigration and Customs Enforcement or perhaps Teddy Tourtas holding on to her passport. I hoped so.

Petty thieves, tweakers, and a host of other hoodlums continued to shovel information my way, knowing I would inform law enforcement.

In July, an inmate called with some serious information. "This is an E-fucking-mergency," he confided. "A couple guys in here for murder stole a, a you know, a trans, you know a paper where the court reporter writes down what you say. They stole it from one of their lawyers, the dumb fuck."

"You mean a transcript?" I interjected.

"Yeah, that's it. I seen it. It's got the name of the CI who's a key witness against them and they're reaching out to have him hit. You need to call the cops or he's a dead fucking duck," he said. "The cop is the same cop who's working on your brother's case, David Holmes."

I called Detective Holmes right away to tell him that one of his confidential informants may be in danger. Sure enough, he was the lead detective on the case. He was grateful for the information.

In August, some more information came my way. Christopher's friend, Linda Tappan, had convinced Kevin McCarthy to meet with me at her house in Sylmar while she was at work. McCarthy had been friends with Christopher and also knew Steinberg and Weaver. Linda said he denied having any knowledge of the murder other than what he had heard through the grapevine.

McCarthy was slightly built with shoulder-length, copper-colored hair. He led me and Johnny Rio to his room. He sat down on a worn couch and motioned for me to sit on a chair adjacent to a desk. Instead, I sat down next to him and nodded to Johnny Rio, who promptly hopped onto the sofa on the other side of McCarthy. At 110 pounds, my Akita–wolfdog could look pretty intimidating.

"Is he gonna be okay?" McCarthy nervously asked.

"Sure, he'll be fine. He just hates liars," I answered.

"You've got Chris's sense of humor," he replied while scooting across the room to take a seat at the desk.

I wanted to know more about Steinberg and Weaver.

He gave me an earful. "I do pyrotechnics for the studios, you know, explosives," he said. "Steinberg and Weaver wanted me to make them some explosives with remote control devices so they could attach them to cars and detonate them with people inside the cars. I mean, what kind of shit is that? I didn't want to do it, but I was afraid to say no. I wasn't so worried about Jeff, but I was so scared Steinberg might kill me, I skipped bail on my case and went to jail. Steinberg is one dangerous son of a bitch."

I stopped McCarthy from going any further. He said it was all right to give Detective Fleming his number, which I did.

Later that month, DDA Stephanie Sparagna informed me that the District Attorney's Office had decided not to seek the death penalty. The news was disheartening, but I understood the rationale.

"Most of my witnesses are jailbirds and dopers, Dennis," Stephanie explained. "The star witness is an ex–Nazi Low Rider who is testifying in exchange for a deal. Even though the physical evidence is strong, we can't take the chance that jurors might choose not to send these defendants to their deaths based on that type of testimony."

I didn't like it, but I could live with it. My family was not too happy with the news, but they trusted me and they knew I trusted Stephanie Sparagna.

"Whatever you say, Dennis," Tim had said upon hearing of the DA's decision, "but if either of those motherfuckers ever hits the street, there's gonna be a death penalty whether the DA likes it or not."

It didn't take long for Steinberg to start manipulating the system. His attorney had filed a motion to dismiss the charges. Steinberg insisted on withdrawing the motion over the objection of his attorney. At the next hearing, Steinberg did not come to court. In county jail, an inmate does not have to voluntarily leave his cell and get on the bus for court appearances until a judge orders the sheriff's department to remove him. Judge Pastor issued a removal order, and Steinberg was brought to court on August 4. His motion was continued, but Steinberg informed the court he was refusing to appear at the next hearing. His attorney convinced him to appear on the next court date. Later that month, Steinberg complained of being denied access to the telephone for court-ordered phone calls. Judge Pastor ordered the sheriff's department to provide jail telephone records. DDA Sparagna filed a motion to remove all materials concerning the case from Steinberg's cell. There were rumors that Steinberg had been circulating copies of transcripts and police reports on the streets. Addresses and telephone numbers of witnesses were supposed to be redacted prior to furnishing a defendant with such paperwork. A thug had gone to the house of a former roommate of Shane Wilson's and threatened her son. There was no doubt in my mind that the messenger was acting at the behest of Steinberg, but the authorities weren't telling me anything.

On September 17, which would have been Christopher's thirty-ninth birthday, Steinberg filed a motion to proceed in pro per, without counsel. Pro pers were always a nightmare. Their lack of knowledge regarding procedural and substantive law created pure chaos in the court, causing the case to crawl along at a snail's pace. I believed Steinberg's motive was far more sinister. Pro per status allowed Steinberg to have copies of all court documents and also afforded him expanded telephone and law-library privileges, ultimately resulting in greater access to the hoodlums on the streets. Judge Pastor had no choice but to grant the motion. Frank DiSabatino was appointed as standby counsel.

On October 1, the judge ordered Steinberg to appear in court on October 4 to provide a handwriting exemplar. Weaver pleaded guilty to the robbery in which his crime partner had been shot in exchange for a sentence of fifteen years. His sentencing was put off until after the trial. The fact that he wouldn't be on the streets anytime soon was welcome news.

On Sunday, October 3, at around 9 P.M., I received a telephone message from an inmate in county jail: "Dennis Walsh, my name is Jason Donaldson. I've been sentenced to death. I'm in the county jail and my cell is two doors over from Steinberg—uh, 2-B, I think. You need to come and see me. I think we can do some business on your brother's case. My booking number is, uh, 6738851, Jason Donaldson."

The Internet provided a wealth of information on Jason Donaldson. He had been out of prison on parole for only two weeks in 1998 when he kidnapped a young Vietnamese woman, brutally raping and beating her, then locking her in the trunk of his car, which he lit on fire. Twelve years passed before California's new DNA database matched DNA evidence to Donaldson, who was already serving a sentence of over two hundred years for murder and carjacking on another case. The DA's office filed charges in 2000, touting it as one of Los Angeles County's first "cold hit" filings. A jury found him guilty of first-degree murder with special circumstances and was sufficiently horrified to unanimously recommend the death penalty. He had been removed from death row at San Quentin for a hearing on his motion to reduce his sentence to life without parole.

There was no way I was going down to see this depraved monster. I played the voice mail for Detective Fleming. All inmate calls are collect.

Someone has to accept the charges. Donaldson's message was left on my voice mail. It must have been a three-way call, probably arranged by Steinberg for as little as a pack of cigarettes.

"Do some business," Donaldson had said. If this wasn't a setup on a murder-for-hire plan hatched by Steinberg, I'd eat my Tribe cap. Steinberg was banking on me running down to see Donaldson, who would then claim I had attempted to solicit his services to kill Steinberg. He obviously thought I was reckless.

"I ran into Steinberg's buddy, Tim Miller, at the gym," Christopher's lifelong friend Andy Zakanych had told me. "Steinberg told him you fucked up the case, Dennis, and he was gonna beat the charges. Steinberg said to ask you where you were when Chris was alive. Miller wanted me to ask you to ease up on Steinberg. I couldn't believe it. I told him you're already out of your mind over Chris's murder and if I ask you that, you'll really go ape shit."

I didn't go ape shit, but the news galled me to no end. I hated to let Steinberg get under my skin, but the thought of possibly having helped him or Weaver in the slightest constantly weighed on my mind.

"The next time you see that shitbag, Miller, tell him Steinberg should have killed someone else's brother. We'll see who has the last laugh," I told Andy.

On October 5, Judge Michael Rosenblatt confirmed the jury's recommendation and sentenced Jason Donaldson to death. He was shipped back to San Quentin's death row.

On October 21, Steinberg's motion to receive the names of potential prosecution witnesses was denied. The prosecution was, however, ordered to turn over names and identifying information to Steinberg's court-appointed investigator, who was ordered not to divulge the information to Steinberg. Judge Pastor informed Steinberg that he would eventually receive the names of witnesses but not at this time "due to security reasons."

On November 4, a trial was set for a date in January 2005. I had no illusions that trial would commence that soon. I had learned long ago that the wheels of justice grind slowly, but they do grind. Sure enough, on Steinberg's birthday, December 17, the trial date was continued to February 25, 2005.

And so the year 2004 played out. Like I said, I was biding my time, waiting for trial, no matter how long it took. An old Gaelic quote had become my motto. It hung next to Christopher's prayer card, Steinberg's jail photo, and the five-dollar bill I had found. It read:

COIMHEAD FEARG FHEAR NA FOIGHDE

My father had brought the quote to my attention years ago. My sister Laura's husband had beaten her up. It had happened once before, but no one informed me, and he was merely sentenced to probation. I couldn't believe that he would lay a hand on her, seeing as how she had five brothers and a father with organized crime connections. I offered to ride along with my father and Bobby after they had located the motel where Laura's husband was hiding out.

"You're not going anywhere, Counselor," my father said. "You don't need to lose your ticket. Just bide your time and see to it that this little cocksucker gets locked up for a while."

After he and Bobby left, my mother handed me a piece of paper with the quote my father had printed out. "Your father said for you to look it up, Dennis. It's in Gaelic," my mother said.

My father and Bobby finally caught up with Laura's husband. Bobby beat him senseless in the motel lobby while my father watched from the car. He was on parole and risked being violated if he got involved. The temptation proved to be too great, however.

After Bobby had laid him out, my father walked in and kicked his erstwhile son-in-law in the face. "The next time you touch my daughter, I'll kill you," he warned.

It took me several days to decipher the meaning of the quote, which was "Beware the patience of an angry man."

I patiently followed the case until Laura's husband pleaded to the charges and was sentenced to two years in state prison, which was even more satisfying than the beating. After the sentencing at the Van Nuys Courthouse, I ran over and barely caught the elevator that his father and brother had just entered.

I held the door open with one hand and pointed with the other. "Tell him if he ever gets within fifty feet of my sister again, he'll never see a courtroom. Understand?" I said in a very calm voice.

Both of them looked at the elevator floor without answering. Two other people hurriedly exited the elevator.

"I asked if you understand," I said again without raising my voice.

They finally answered, "Yes." We've never heard from Laura's husband since.

12

BACK IN THE SADDLE AGAIN

I<small>T WAS ONLY THREE DAYS</small> into the new year before the drama resumed, one year to the day that Tim had lumped up Weaver on Kimmi's front lawn. Kimmi told Jeannie that Weaver had called. Steinberg's alibi would be that he was in Las Vegas when Christopher went missing. Weaver whined that Steinberg would probably walk. He also confided that Steinberg had tried to stab him, but only managed to cut his arm. Still, he refused to flip and take a deal, although if Diane Stewart was cooperating, any chance of a deal had probably gone down the drain.

"I can't be like Shane Wilson," he told Kimmi.

Steinberg was a busy man despite being behind bars. It worried me that if Weaver or Wilson turned up dead, Steinberg could pin the murder on one of them. I spoke with scores of inmates and hoodlums on the street. If they heard even the slightest hint of any retaliation aimed at either Wilson or Weaver, I wanted to know about it.

"Why don't you just let some of us in here take care of Steinberg for you?" Irish Mike offered.

"I want a jury to convict that bastard. Besides, when it's all over, I want to know how it really went down," I said.

News of Steinberg's alibi really yanked my chain. Maybe I had been asleep at the switch. I couldn't risk leaving any stone unturned, and that stone was Talking Tina's friend Linda Pallares. Dusty said she claimed not to have any relevant information, but I remembered Tina saying that Linda had attended the L.A. Erotica porn convention with Christopher days before he went missing. He was supposed to meet her on her birthday and never showed up. Call me crazy, but that seemed potentially relevant to me.

My pitch to everyone had been an appeal to come forward and let the homicide cops decide what was relevant. Some trivial fact that might otherwise seem irrelevant just might be evidentiary.

A case in point was Scary Sherry. Shortly after the murder, I met her around midnight in an alley behind the Safari Room. She was spun out on meth and yammered on without saying anything helpful. By the time I smoked an entire cigar, I was ready to dig out my own brain with a dull spoon.

"Hey, dude, what's your name again? Can I have some money to get a hamburger?" she asked.

I wasn't about to give her any money for dope. On the way to Jack in the Box, her endless stream of consciousness continued while I resisted the urge to drive into oncoming traffic. She was upset over a friend who had "abscounded." She meant absconded, but *abscounded* was a mispronunciation that every doper in the Valley used to describe someone on the run for violating the terms of their parole or probation.

"Good evening, may I help you?" the voice from the Jack in the Box speaker crackled.

Before I could respond, Scary Sherry crawled across me, knelt on my lap, and stuck her head out the window. "What do you have?" she asked.

I couldn't believe it when the kid on the other end of the speakerphone began to recite the entire Jack in the Box menu.

"What the fuck? She'll have a cheeseburger, fries, and a Coke," I said while pushing Scary Sherry back over to the passenger seat.

On the ride back to the Safari Room, Scary Sherry continued her monologue while intently inspecting each french fry before putting it into her mouth, completely oblivious of my lack of interest.

"My friend who abscounded knows Cloud Pierson, who helped clean up the apartment where your brother was murdered," she finally related.

"Bingo," I said out loud.

I had heard rumors of Cloud Pierson assisting Steinberg with the cleanup. It wasn't much, but it was something. My patience had been stretched to its limit, but it paid off, like the barn swallow that laboriously picks through piles of horse manure until it finds an undigested bit of grain.

Linda Pallares was frightened, and I was enjoined from contacting her. It was time to go to the bullpen and trot out my mother. I helped her draft a letter, which I hoped would play on Linda's sympathies. It read in part:

All I ask is that you answer the detective's questions truthfully. . . . This tragedy has been, and continues to be, a devastating ordeal for myself and my family. I enclose a prayer card from Christopher's funeral Mass. Thank you and God bless you. . . .

A few weeks later, Dusty called. "Hey, bro, Linda got your mother's letter. Tina said she broke down and cried. She went to Devonshire Division to talk to Detective Fleming," he said. "You just pulled a rabbit out of your ass, bro, 'cause she's scared shitless of Steinberg and Weaver."

It wasn't until the trial that I eventually learned that Linda Pallares and Tina Arnone provided details essential in establishing a time line leading up to the murder.

Did I violate the court order by having my mother contact a witness? To paraphrase Rhett Butler, frankly, my dear, I didn't give a shit.

In early March, I was happy to read in the *Los Angeles Times* that Detective Avila and his SIS partners had been cleared in the Northridge Beauty Club shooting. In April, I was even happier to hear that Diane Stewart had been arrested and booked into the Ventura County Jail for violating probation on a 2002 drug case. I didn't know that she had invited

Detective Fleming to come see her in custody. What Diane Purdie Stew-art, aka porn star Alexandra Quinn, told Detective Fleming during that jailhouse interview would wind up playing out like a cheap melodrama at trial, but nobody was telling me anything.

I got a clue when in June she was transferred to L.A. county jail and was being held on a $100,000 bail as a material witness. When I asked Detective Fleming if she was cooperating, he was noncommittal, as usual. His faint smile, however, spoke volumes. I worried that without her tes-timony, Weaver might walk. "If they get Diane Stewart, they might as well execute me," Weaver had said. If she did cooperate, Weaver would certainly be up shit creek without a paddle.

I was feeling more confident that both Steinberg and Weaver would be convicted at trial, causing my stress level to subside considerably. In May, I took a trip to the Smokey Mountains in Tennessee to play golf with a group of boyhood friends from Cleveland. Insulting my buddies relentlessly for a few days was just what the doctor ordered, but as soon as I got home, the excitement resumed. I was visiting an inmate at Lan-caster prison when another inmate was fatally stabbed. Sirens blared as the entire compound was placed on lockdown. A prison guard grabbed me by the arm and led me to a van. Inmates across the yard were face-down on the ground, spread-eagled. The guards at the gate searched my vehicle before permitting me to exit the prison grounds.

Since Christopher's murder, I had been in an almost constant state of high anxiety. The practice of law was stressful enough without all these stabbings. I definitely needed a diversion. The golf trip was only a tem-porary fix. In June, I purchased a little fourteen-month-old sorrel and white paint colt, with a splash of white down his right foreleg that re-minded me of an Apache pony. One of his brown eyes was half blue, an oddity that appealed to me. It made him just a little different, kind of like myself. I named him Rowdy.

The pretrial machinations continued while I kept busy with my prac-tice and my young stud colt. I put up a round pen and built a three-sided structure with a fenced enclosure running off it. Every morning, I stuck my head out the window and whistled for Rowdy. He came to know that whistle and always responded with a loud whinny. I started some ground training with him in the round pen. That, along with daily brushings and manure shoveling proved to be quite cathartic.

Steinberg, still pro per, was permitted to review documents and tapes with his investigator, but prohibited from keeping the materials in his cell. There were over six thousand pages of wiretap transcripts. Steinberg's motion to sever the shooting-at-the-deputy case from the murder case was denied. Both Steinberg and Weaver continued to complain of not having telephone access to contact their attorneys. Steinberg groused that he was being denied law-library privileges. The judge issued orders for the sheriff's department to accommodate the defendants. Counsel for the County of Los Angeles had to appear to rebut allegations that the sheriff's department had failed to comply with the court orders. These issues would become a running battle between the defendants and the sheriff's department up to and throughout trial.

The court denied Steinberg's motion to dismiss the charges on the grounds that the prosecution had failed to turn over Brady materials to the defense. That was a relief, in light of the federal case that had been kicked after the U.S. Attorney failed to turn over Brady materials, allowing Steinberg to be released after only five years of a twenty-year sentence.

One of many things that irritated me about Steinberg was the perception of him as some sort of genius. After his appellate attorney had his federal case reversed on the Brady issue, Steinberg credited himself. The lamebrains on the street bought into it lock, stock, and barrel. Even Andy Zakanych was caught in his spell.

"He's real smart, Dennis. He beat that federal case and he even taught himself to play guitar in jail," Andy had told me.

It pleased me immensely that DDA Sparagna had just figuratively shoved *People v. Brady* right up Steinberg's ass. Having a female DA prosecuting his case had to grate on him. Two ex-girlfriends commented on his lack of respect toward women. I welcomed most any information, but sometimes I unearthed just a little too much dirt.

"He used to have me shave his balls," one ex-girlfriend volunteered.

"Thanks for sharing that," I replied, "but the only time I need to hear about Steinberg's balls is if they're hanging from a meat cleaver."

The mother of Steinberg's daughter was one ex-girlfriend I was unable to locate. Her friend told me that she was so terrified of Steinberg that she and her daughter had relocated to another state. It was poetic justice that it was a female prosecutor who was now goring his ox.

Steinberg's motion to dismiss the charges for lack of due process was also denied. Next he claimed to have a conflict of interest with his stand-by counsel and attempted to have him removed, but Judge Pastor denied his request. He was permitted telephone calls only to his attorney and his investigator. After three stabbings, a kite note containing a hit list, and threats to witnesses, security was top priority in this case.

By the time October rolled around, trial appeared unlikely anytime soon. I jumped on the chance to take a float fishing trip down the Rogue River with some friends. The fishing was good and the scenery was spectacular, but sure enough, as soon as I returned, the soap opera continued.

Irish Mike called from county jail. An inmate named Danny Timms said that Steinberg was arranging to have me killed. I told Mike to have Timms call me as soon as possible. I accepted his collect call later that evening.

"Dude, you need to be careful. Steinberg's still doing business on the streets and is trying to have you hit," Timms said. "I'll talk to the cops, but only if I see you first."

I was concerned for my own safety and didn't have time to determine whether or not Timms was a witness. One thing I did know, if anyone was going to protect me, it would be me. The LAPD did not have the resources to offer 24/7 protection. I headed down to the county jail. Timms was housed in the 3100 A Row, the same cell block as Steinberg and Weaver.

"Steinberg is trying to get you hit through the Nazi Low Riders, 'cause you caused him a shitload of problems. He already contacted an NLR shot caller up in Pelican Bay about killing you. They have you targeted in Santa Clarita. That's where you live, right?" he asked.

I was careful not to bat an eye. I didn't live in Santa Clarita, but it was close enough. Pelican Bay State Prison was reserved for high-level gang members, the worst of the worst. They had the ability to reach out to the streets. I wondered if Timms was trying to elicit information from me.

He immediately picked up on my reticence to answer. "That's cool, dude, you don't have to answer. You know if it's true or not. Steinberg wants to have Kimmi Balmes, Diane Stewart, and a DA named Mike Kraut smoked, too," he continued. "Weaver says he hated your brother, and Steinberg is saying your brother was a rat."

I stopped him and told him I would ask Detective Fleming to come see him. Detective Fleming and DDA Kraut interviewed him, but unfortunately, Timms had previously been discredited and was not considered a reliable informant. I didn't care. He knew too many details not to be telling the truth. I moved a poker game that was scheduled at my place to Gary Valeriano's house. I couldn't risk having any of my friends getting caught in a cross fire.

In November, Steinberg had no choice but to withdraw his pro per status and have Frank DiSabatino reappointed to represent him. After getting slapped down on the Brady motion, he needed a competent response to the prosecution's motion for authorization to use wiretap information at trial and also needed to prepare a motion to suppress evidence seized from his Moorpark apartment. Judge Pastor later authorized the use of the tapes. During the middle of the suppression hearing, Steinberg demanded a Marsden hearing to have his attorney removed and another appointed in his place. The judge denied that motion and then in December denied his suppression motion. I didn't know what evidence had been recovered from the apartment, but I knew it was a big victory for the prosecution.

After my visit with Danny Timms, I stopped bringing women up to my house for a few months until the holidays rolled around. Months earlier, I had invited a vivacious woman from Philadelphia whom I had met at a wedding to visit me over New Year's. I explained that it might be dangerous at my place.

"Let's take a ride up to Lake Tahoe," I suggested.

"Are you kidding?" she replied. "You're taking me to Musso and

Frank's in Hollywood and to Universal Studios to see the *Desperate Housewives* set just like you promised. I want a picture of you and me on Wisteria Lane. Then I'm going to cook for you all week. All that gangster stuff doesn't scare me. This is going to be like being on *The Sopranos.*"

So stay at my place we did. I savored every moment of that week, knowing that while I enjoyed the company of an attractive woman, excellent Italian cooking, and plenty to drink, every second crawled by for Steinberg and Weaver inside the cold, dank, concrete confines of the dilapidated L.A. County Men's Central Jail.

Steinberg was right back at it in 2006. On January 20, he moved the court to reinstate his pro per status. The court denied his request. Without assistance of counsel, Steinberg filed a writ of habeas corpus to challenge the denial of his motion. The matter was heard down the hallway in Department 100. Judge David Wesley noted that the proper vehicle to challenge the denial was a writ of mandamus and very charitably deemed Steinberg's motion as such. He then promptly denied it as untimely filed. Steinberg had filed the motion after the filing deadline. The self-proclaimed jailhouse lawyer, who boasted of having single-handedly prevailed upon the Ninth Circuit of the U.S. District Court of Appeals to reverse his conviction, was in way over his head. The Emperor Who Had No Clothes would have been a more apropos nickname than Silent Thunder.

On March 9, Frank DiSabatino filed a motion to withdraw as Steinberg's counsel and was relieved. Steinberg had made the situation between himself and his attorney so untenable that DiSabatino had no choice but to resign. The Machiavellian Steinberg knew exactly what he was doing. Trial had been set for June 22. He wanted to put off judgment day as long as he could. A newly appointed attorney would have to review over thirty thousand pages of documents and hundreds of tapes. Trial would probably be delayed for another year. Steinberg might have been unable to put a bullet in me, but news of this setback took the wind out of my sails. I had no choice but to sit tight, believing that someday he would rue the patience of this angry man.

On March 15, Steve Hauser was appointed to represent Steinberg. Apparently, the two did not exactly hit it off. On May 1, Steinberg filed yet another motion to proceed in pro per, which was promptly denied.

In the meantime, in February, I had trailered Rowdy over to a local ranch to be broken and trained. It was only ten miles from my house. Johnny Rio and I made the trek over there just about every day. Hanging out at the ranch and enjoying a cold beer in the company of my trusty dog and rambunctious horse helped maintain my sanity while it seemed like the case would never get to trial.

In April, I read in the paper that Jimmy Bray's boss had been sentenced to life in federal prison for drug trafficking. A week later, I was rummaging through the accordion file I had taken from Steinberg's apartment. I came across an undated handwritten letter Steinberg had sent to Christopher. I wasn't sure if it had originally been in the file or if I had found it in the storage facility. The letter was written on BOARD TO PIECES, LLC letterhead. The LLC was a company formed by George Jassick, who had been charged as an accessory to the murder and was testifying against Steinberg.

It started off *Dear Finny* and ended with *I love you Bro. DMS,* followed by two lightning bolts, a Nazi Low Rider insignia. The content was a rambling hodgepodge of lofty platitudes purporting to advise Christopher how to better his life. The writing clearly evidenced the methodical nature of Steinberg's calculating mind:

> *. . . then plan, prep & lay the ground work—then begin to make sacrifices, saving money, reading, researching, improving your inner-self, shaping social skills, improving behavior patterns, etc . . . You must surround yourself with healthy people who will only positively assist you in accomplishing your goals/dreams.*

I had read the letter before and simply dismissed it as megalomaniacal delusions of grandeur. Upon rereading the letter, the underlined *only* struck me. Christopher had begun to disrespect Steinberg by challenging his authority in front of others. Steinberg was not about to let that happen. His express policy was to surround himself with people who would "only positively assist" him, not those who would dare to challenge him. I thought DDA Sparagna might find the letter provided some insight into the psyche of David Michael Steinberg, so I sent it to Detective Fleming.

Out of the blue, DDA Stephanie Sparagna called in July. "Dennis, I'm thinking about asking the judge to lift the court order and allow you back into the courtroom. You have to promise me not to disrupt the proceedings. You can't communicate with either Steinberg or Weaver. I'm serious, Dennis, if you pull anything in the courtroom again, you're going to wind up in contempt of court," she said.

Christmas had come early. I was so elated that Stephanie's manner of chastising me like a wayward schoolchild didn't even bother me. I almost replied, *Yes, Miss Sparagna.* Instead I thanked her profusely and promised to be on my best behavior. I hadn't been this happy since Detective Holmes called to say Weaver had been arrested.

I called my mother to deliver the good news.

"Oh, that's great, Dennis. You better behave in there, though, or this woman will have you thrown out again. It sounds like she's all business and doesn't tolerate any nonsense," my mother advised me.

I might as well have stayed on the phone to be lectured by Stephanie. This was déjà vu. Miss Morelli, my seventh-grade teacher, had written on my report card, *Dennis needs to improve his classroom behavior and conduct. He tends to consider the classroom as a playground.*

My mother had written back, *Dennis was told to improve his conduct.*

I got off the phone and made a few calls. The first person I could reach was Marta Wilson. The civil case I was representing her in had just been settled.

"I'm back, baby. I'm back in the saddle again. Stephanie is letting me back in the courtroom," I gloated. "I have to lay low, though. I can't come a ridin' and a whoopin' and a whoopin' and a ridin' no more."

"Good for you. Ride 'em, cowboy." Marta laughed.

It wasn't too long after that, though, that Marta got subpoenaed. I had come to really enjoy talking with Marta and would miss her company.

The next hearing was set for July 21. I could barely sleep the night before and rose at 4:30 A.M. The trip downtown to CCB was a little over sixty miles. If I left by 5:45, I could beat the traffic. I arrived by 7 A.M. and drank coffee and read the paper in the courthouse cafeteria until the ninth floor opened at 8 A.M. I paced the length of the hallway again and again, as I would do countless times over the next year and a half.

Finally, Detective Fleming arrived. "I see you're finally out of the dog-house," he said while shaking my hand.

A few minutes later, I spotted DDA Sparagna marching down the hallway, clutching her file with a big smile on her face. "Hi, John," she said to Detective Fleming. "Good morning, Dennis."

This time I could not resist. "Good morning, Miss Sparagna," I said.

I took a seat, but one too many cups of coffee caused me to pace about the back of the courtroom. Stephanie had been busy at the counsel table, but suddenly turned around as if she sensed something was not right.

"Dennis, will you please sit down?" she asked in her own inimitable way of making a question sound like anything but a question, while simultaneously shaking her head for emphasis.

"Yes, Miss Sparagna," I muttered under my breath.

I took a seat on one of the benches, positioning myself so that I would be in the direct line of sight of Steinberg and Weaver when the deputies brought them out from the lockup. It seemed like forever before the two defendants were led out. The wait was worth it. The looks on their faces were priceless as they zeroed in on my grinning visage. Both hurriedly whispered to their attorneys, who promptly voiced their objections over my presence to the judge. Judge Pastor explained that the court order had been lifted and that I was permitted to stay. He then denied Steinberg's motion to remove the judge for prejudice as untimely filed. Some other motions were argued and trial was set for August 26.

I walked with Stephanie to the elevators. "Stephanie, you know this egomaniacal little creep Steinberg is going to testify at trial, don't you?" I asked.

"I agree. He's like a puppeteer pulling the strings. He'll never be able to sit through trial without taking the stand," she answered. "Have you noticed how his attorney sometimes reads directly from Steinberg's handwritten notes when he's addressing the judge? Don't you worry, Dennis, I'll be ready for him."

That's what I loved about her. She understood what made the puppeteer tick. There was no question in my mind that she would indeed be ready for the likes of David Michael Steinberg.

The rest of the year trudged slowly by. Both Steinberg and Weaver continued to complain to the court about various issues. Trial dates were set and reset. I made the long haul down to CCB for every hearing, some of which lasted no more than two or three minutes. I didn't care. I wanted the killers to see my face every time that lockup door opened. My own caseload, my physical regimen, and my animals kept me busy. My faith in Stephanie Sparagna allowed me to remain resolute, no matter how many times the trial was continued. I would have followed her to hell and back.

On January 3, 2007, a hearing was held on Steinberg's complaints about posted signs in the Master Control area of the high-power unit, denial of telephone access, and one deputy allegedly ripping out the telephone wiring. One of the signs allegedly read DO NOT FEED THE ANIMALS. Judge Pastor took the complaints seriously and personally drove over to the Men's Central Jail to inspect the 3100 block. Not too many judges would have taken the time to do that.

The delays continued. One day, Weaver would refuse to come to court. The next hearing, Steinberg would refuse to come to court. Judge Pastor could only continue the matter and order them removed for the next hearing.

"Hey, Detective," I said to Detective Fleming one morning when Steinberg failed to appear in court. "Why don't you let me go get Steinberg. If I walk into his cell, that's the last place he'll want to be."

Detective Fleming just smiled.

Jury selection in the murder trial of music mogul Phil Spector commenced in March. The case was being heard across the hallway in Department 106. More than once, I had to elbow my way through a throng of media and court watchers to get to Department 107, and that was just during pretrial hearings. Judge Larry Fidler had allowed the trial to be televised. When the trial commenced in April, jurors and even more reporters filled the congested hallway.

In June, I made the mistake of using spurs on Rowdy. He had been a little defiant and was not responding to my cues. That plan went haywire when Rowdy shot straight up into the air with all four feet off the ground. One second I was atop a bucking bronco; the next second I was flat on my back. When I hoisted myself back into the saddle, it felt as if I had been stabbed with an ice pick. I didn't realize it, but I had broken my right femur at the neck where it goes into the hip. I finally went to the hospital on July 2, four years to the day that Christopher's body had been recovered. I underwent surgery, during which three long screws were inserted in the femur and into the hip. Then I began the painful process of recovery.

Finally, it looked like the case was going to trial in September, and here I was all banged up. I soon progressed from walking with crutches to walking with a cane. I went to physical therapy for a few weeks and then religiously performed the exercises at home. I was determined to be physically and mentally fit for the trial.

At one point, DDA Sparagna asked me to go over to her office on a Saturday morning to discuss my testimony. By now, Stephanie had the assistance of Deputy DA Ann Ambrose, whose task it was to deal with the forensic evidence, and senior law clerk Patrick Ball. Patrick could not have caught a better case to cut his teeth on.

Boxes of transcripts and documents lined the hallway outside Stephanie's office, which was crammed full with even more boxes, binders, documents, and stacks of files. A rack on the wall contained hundreds of cassette tapes labeled with names, dates, and times. A bunch of tapes under the heading DENNIS WALSH caught my eye.

I recalled Patrick Ball's comment on my involvement in the case. "We have meetings where the topics are 402 motions, witnesses, jury instructions, and what to do with Dennis Walsh," he had said.

"Come on, Stephanie," I said over a cup of coffee while seated across from her at her desk. "You must have had other cases where the family members were pretty upset," I said, causing her to roll her eyes.

"Dennis, I've never had anything like you and your brothers," she replied.

As late as August 8, Weaver was attempting to have his attorney removed. I believed it was the puppeteer Steinberg who was pulling the strings. At the end of August, Judge Pastor instructed the clerk to order the sheriff's department to arrange for haircuts and daily showers for the defendants during jury selection and trial. This case was proceeding to trial.

During the hearings, I usually pinned my eyes on the defendants. If either of them turned and caught my eye, I would glare straight at him. I didn't think anyone but the three of us noticed, until DDA Sparagna and the defense attorneys came out of the judge's chambers one morning.

"Dennis, Judge Pastor wants you to stop mad-dogging the defendants," Stephanie said.

"How does he want me to look at these jerks?" I asked.

Stephanie just shook her head and walked away.

At the next hearing, instead of glaring at Steinberg, I smiled at him. He cocked his head to the side like a dog that had just seen something for the first time. He probably lay awake all night, wondering what the hell I was so happy about.

I was exiting the courtroom after one hearing when Steinberg turned in his seat and mouthed *Fuck you* to me. I stopped in my tracks, smiled, and tapped my index finger on my wristwatch three times. He flipped me the bird and then whispered into his attorney's ear.

"Your Honor, my client has just informed me that Mr. Walsh was just tapping his wristwatch to indicate Mr. Steinberg's time is up," Steve Hauser said.

"I saw the defendant flip off Mr. Walsh, Your Honor," Deputy Jones interjected.

Judge Pastor instructed me to leave. Out in the hallway, Stephanie informed me that Judge Pastor had admonished Steinberg. It chapped my hide that Steinberg could put four bullets in the back of my brother's head and then cry to the judge like a little schoolgirl because I had tapped my wristwatch. The case was finally proceeding to trial, and the "evil genius" was running scared.

There would be two juries packed into one courtroom. Weaver's jury was deemed the "red jury" and Steinberg's the "green jury." Each jury comprised twelve jurors and six alternate jurors. Each day, a sign on the courtroom door would announce which jury was sitting in the jury box. The other jury would sit in the first two rows of the gallery. The time estimate for the length of the trial was three months. Jury selection for the red jury began on September 6 and for the green jury on September 11.

DDA Sparagna had requested a meeting with my family before the trial. My mother, Tim, Kathy, Dan, Laura, Bobby, and myself met with her at the DA's office in a conference room on the eighteenth floor of the CCB.

Stephanie explained the prosecution's theory of the murder, mainly addressing my mother. "Mrs. Walsh, we believe that David Steinberg shot Christopher in the back of the head from behind. He may have even been sleeping," she said.

"Well, Stephanie, that's exactly how I thought it must have been because if anybody pointed a gun at any of my boys, they would have hell to pay."

I winced. *Jesus Christ, Mom,* I thought to myself, *do you have to sound like Ma Barker?*

Tim, Dan, and myself would be barred from the trial as potential witnesses. Stephanie cautioned that grisly autopsy photographs would be introduced at trial and recommended that family members either avert their eyes or leave the courtroom. She discussed my involvement in the case and the inherent dangers of tainting witnesses. I could feel my family's eyes boring through me like laser beams.

After they left, I was alone with Stephanie. "Geez, Stephanie, thanks for laying me out in front of my family," I kidded.

"Don't worry, Dennis, we're going to get these fuckers," she replied.

Opening statements were set for September 18. Four years, two months, two weeks, and two days from the date Christopher's body had been recovered at the Van Nuys storage facility. It was finally showtime.

THE WHEELS OF JUSTICE

13

A TALE OF DARK HEARTS

O<small>N THE EVE OF OPENING</small> statements, I was watching the Cleveland Indians battle the Detroit Tigers on television. The Tribe was in the thick of a pennant race. It was Christopher's birthday. He would have been forty-two years old. At the end of nine, the game was tied and went into extra innings. Third baseman Casey Blake homered in the bottom of the eleventh to win it for the Tribe. I took the home run to be a good omen. I whooped and hollered, raising my bottle of Heineken in a toast to my kid brother. Later, I would look back on how our hometown team had gone into extra innings to get it done that evening as a metaphor for the trial.

Jim Cavanaugh accompanied my sister Kathy on the first day of trial. Being a witness, I was excluded. I caught a news report that the Phil Spector jury was ordered to continue deliberations after the jury foreman informed the judge they were deadlocked. The mere thought of a mistrial sent shivers up my spine.

I met Kathy and Cavanaugh for dinner that evening for a firsthand report of the trial.

"You're right, Dennis. Stephanie's good, real good," Kathy said.

My sister and Cavanaugh alternately related how DDA Sparagna skillfully wove the underlying story of the shooting at the deputy into the very fabric of the murder tale during her opening statement.

"I'm going to tell you a story," DDA Sparagna had begun. "It is somewhat of a long story, about people who were affected by greed and drugs. People with fairly dark hearts. Felons and thieves. You are also going to hear testimony from drug users, from porno queens, and from various people who know Defendant Steinberg and Defendant Weaver."

The veteran prosecutor succinctly yet dramatically previewed the prosecution's case, telling the two juries what they could expect to see and hear from a colorful cast of miscreants who were the prosecution's witnesses.

"All of them, their whole sense of time is so skewed because of drug use. Their daytime is our nighttime, and vice versa. You will learn their memories are questionable, and their sense of timing is off," she explained to the juries.

As Kathy began to relate what DDA Sparagna told the juries about the testimony of Diane Stewart, Cavanaugh interrupted with information that damn near knocked the wind out of me.

"What's with that porno whore, Diane Stewart? Stephanie told the juries that she doesn't know what that bitch is gonna say. She confessed that Weaver fired the final shot to put Chris out of his misery and now she's changing her story," he said.

"You gotta be shittin' me," I replied.

My entire evening was ruined with that revelation.

"Well, then you're gonna love this," Kathy said. "Steinberg's attorney said you told all these witnesses what to say, and then he blamed the murder on that creep, Shane Wilson."

I hadn't expected anything less from Steinberg's attorney. Steve Hauser's calm demeanor and clean-cut looks reminded me of the actor Fred MacMurray. He was nothing less than the consummate professional, but definitely had his work cut out for him. I worried that the green jury might like him just a bit too much.

"Besides the police trying to solve the case," Hauser had said, "the brother of the victim, Dennis Walsh, a criminal defense lawyer, also made every effort to gather evidence against David Steinberg. He spoke to almost every witness in the case. Some were in jail. Others were on the streets, but he got to all the witnesses before the police. He somehow motivated the many felons and drug addicts to come forward to tell the police bits and pieces that seemed to fit into the scenario that my client is guilty. Some of the witnesses in jail on their own crimes were more than anxious to tell police something to try and better their own situations. They were looking to deal."

Hauser claimed that the prosecution granted immunity to Shane Wilson, the only person to whom Steinberg had allegedly confessed, only because they couldn't establish a case against his client.

"Mr. Wilson has a most colorful past. With swastikas tattooed on his earlobes, he will make a most colorful witness here in this courtroom. The real issue in this case is not did David Steinberg kill Christopher Walsh, but rather did Tony Shane Wilson get away with murder," Hauser stated.

Seymour Amster, Weaver's attorney, had waived making an opening statement. Either he thought he had a good case and was holding his cards close to his vest, or he knew he was piloting a turd boat to shit town and was in no rush to get there. We would just have to wait and see.

The prosecution called its first witness, Marta Wilson. The day before the shooting-at-the-deputy incident, Steinberg had shown up at her house. She knew him only as Frankie. He waited in her living room for Moises Tovar, whom she knew as Joey. When Tovar arrived, Steinberg pulled a pistol from a book that had been hollowed out in the shape of a gun and pointed it at him. He held Tovar at gunpoint until her husband, Irish Mike, came home.

She stated that I never asked her to lie, never threatened to kill her, and never told her what to say to the police.

During cross-examination by Steinberg's attorney, she was asked if she knew Joey to be involved in any type of crime.

"All my husband's friends were," she answered matter-of-factly.

When Marta was asked why she did not report the incident to the police if she was so frightened, her answer foreshadowed the state of mind of many witnesses who would sit in that very seat.

"I wasn't going to rat these guys out. Are you kidding me?" she asked. Marta was asked about speaking with me.

"He asked if I knew anything about his brother's murder. I told him, 'No.' He said if he found out that my husband or I knew anything about the planning, the carrying out, or covering up of the murder, he would walk us straight through the gates of hell," she said.

"When he said he would walk you through the gates of hell, did you think that was an endearing remark?" Seymour Amster asked.

Marta replied that she did not take the remark as a threat.

"Well, I don't know about you, but I don't have too many people saying they will walk me through the gates of hell," Amster editorialized.

"Then maybe he should get out more," I sarcastically told Cavanaugh when he related Amster's comment.

DDA Sparagna called Deputy Alex Dixon as her next witness. He had retired from the sheriff's department shortly after the shoot-out for a career in music. I later learned that his grandfather was the legendary blues musician William James "Willie" Dixon, a Grammy Award–winning member of the Rock and Roll Hall of Fame. In his soft-spoken manner, the retired deputy recounted the harrowing events of the shoot-out. He was speaking with Christopher in the alley behind the Chatsworth town house when Steinberg walked out with a crazy look on his face, yelled, "Freeze!" and started shooting. The deputy returned fire while back-pedaling and falling against the condominium wall, losing a flip-flop in the process.

Christopher yelled at Steinberg, "Why would you shoot at a deputy? You're crazy!"

"Were you upset?" DDA Sparagna inquired.

"Well, yeah, I wasn't expecting to get shot at or anything. It was my day off," the deputy answered.

Michelle O'Halloran, the mother of Christopher's children, took the witness stand at the end of the day. She was the first of many witnesses to identify People's Exhibit No. 44, a photograph of the large sectional couch that ultimately became Christopher's deathbed. She had paid five thousand dollars for it. She also identified a side-by-side refrigerator freezer that had been in the Chatsworth town house. The particular significance of that appliance would not be revealed until later in the trial.

The opening day of trial in the corner courtroom on the ninth floor of the Criminal Courts Building had been a barnburner. A trial is like a roller coaster ride, fraught with exhilarating highs and devastating lows, and this one would be no exception. There was no guarantee that this trial would end on a high note. It was just down the hallway that a jury had acquitted O. J. Simpson. There was no way I could rest easy until the day I actually heard each defendant pronounced "Guilty."

The next morning the L.A. *Daily News* page-three headline blared, FRIENDSHIP ALLEGEDLY ENDED WITH BODY IN TRASH—TRIAL OPENS IN CASE WITH "SHANKSTER GANGSTER" WITNESS. Reporter Brent Hopkins wrote:

> Somewhere between the time David Steinberg helped Chris Walsh move out of his apartment and the day Walsh ended up shot five times and stuffed in a trash can, their relationship went south. Or so went the dramatic tale that opened Steinberg's murder trial Tuesday. . . . The 39-year-old Granada Hills man is now balding in a rumpled gray suit, accused of executing Walsh, his former housemate. The Deputy District Attorney populated her case with a cast of characters with such names as Mouse and Irish Mike, building to a chilling scene in which Steinberg's girlfriend found a blue, city-issued trash can in her Van Nuys storage unit. Encased in bubble wrap, duct tape, and plastic, the trash can gave off a foul odor. The girlfriend called the authorities, who cut it open to discover its grisly cargo—a decomposed Walsh.

I poured myself a cup of coffee and finished reading the article before making the long drive downtown. I cooled my heels in the hallway while Pat Murphy listened to the testimony.

The prosecution's case started off slowly. An L.A. City Sanitation clerk testified that on June 25, 2003, a resident on Bellaire Street called to report a missing ninety-gallon blue trash barrel. The missing container that would become Christopher's coffin could not be linked to a specific residence, but Steinberg's apartment was on the corner of Moorpark Street and Bellaire Street. It didn't take a giant leap of faith to conclude that Steinberg had stolen the barrel. Brick by painstaking brick, DDA Sparagna was laying the foundation for her case.

The prosecution then kicked it into high gear by calling Robert "Mouse" Hayes to the stand. I peeked into the courtroom to try to get Pat Murphy's attention. Mouse was not hard to miss, sitting on the witness stand in his orange jailhouse jumpsuit. I quickly closed the door. His tattooed neck and arms, shaven head, goatee, and cuffed hands must have stood in startling contrast to the prior witnesses.

Mouse admitted to eight felony convictions and having spent about twenty-five years in state prison during his forty-five years. He related having been attacked by an inmate known as Buddy Feathers in the 1750 block of the high-power unit in county jail the night before testifying against Steinberg at the preliminary hearing. DDA Sparagna asked him what 1750 block was.

"High power is for very unusual cases of violence. Also, prison gang members, Mexican Mafia, Brotherhood, and Nazi Low Riders. Also, violence on peace officers would be there," he answered.

DDA Sparagna then asked him to describe the attack.

"I was coming out from my evening shower and the man next to me—I was in Cell Twelve. The man next to me in Cell Thirteen reached out of the bars. He was trying to cut my throat. I ducked down, and he lacerated my head from here down to my eye with a homemade knife," he explained. "He tried to slice me again and he said, 'That's for giving testimony against David.'"

His chilling testimony continued.

"I called him a coward. I told him I would have tied up with him through the bars," he said.

"Can you explain what that means?" DDA Sparagna asked.

"We would tie one of our hands together to a cell bar with a piece of sheet or whatever, and we would have our shanks in the other hand and handle our business against each other," he replied.

The image of Mouse and his would-be assassin separated by the bars of their cells, lashed together at the wrists, and locked in mortal combat to settle their differences contradicted the drama playing out in the courtroom, where it was the rule of law that prevailed.

Mouse told how Amy Sheeley had brought Steinberg with her after the shooting at the deputy. He then drove Steinberg to George Jassick's apartment in North Hollywood.

"Turn on the TV. I just shot a cop," Steinberg had told Jassick.

DDA Sparagna explored the politics of jail protocol regarding having a snitch killed by asking Mouse to explain the term *paperwork*.

"Paperwork means that you have someone's court hearings, witness statements, evidence of any kind. In prison, if you don't have the legal documents explaining exactly what was said and what was done, it doesn't hold no water," he explained.

"When you are in the prison system, is it important to affiliate with a group?" DDA Sparagna asked.

"If you walk into a prison yard and you have no affiliations, it'll be rough on you. The groups in there are power hungry to control everything in the prison population. It's drugs and also extortion. They can get your family to send money by holding your life in their hand as collateral," he responded.

"Holy shit," Pat told me during a recess, "the jurors were riveted on every word Mouse said. I've never been in jail, and now I guarantee you, I never will be."

During cross-examination by Steinberg's attorney, Mouse discussed Desiree Manthe. She had a daughter that was one-quarter African American. Their relationship caused him to drop out of the Nazi Low Riders.

"I can't be a Nazi Low Rider, having the feelings I had for a part-black child. I still walked the yard with all the fellas and everybody knew."

Most inmates ignored the situation. A Nazi Low Rider called Popeye mentioned the biracial child at Chino state prison, with dire consequences.

"In 2000, I was in Delano state prison, in the hole," Mouse said. "I waited, moved him in my cell. I showed him a picture of the child and told him, 'Call her that in front of me.' He said she doesn't look like no nigger. I punched him in his mouth. I went to Pelican Bay. He went to Corcoran state prison, which are SHUs, Security Housing Units. They killed him for talking about me and doing nothing about it."

Steve Hauser asked him whether he cared about getting killed for testifying.

"Oh, I care, but I'm not having wackos coming into my neighborhood when I got kids and they are shooting at the cops that are going to put their life on the line for them."

"So you are testifying for the kids in the San Fernando Valley?" Hauser asked.

"I am testifying to keep this wacko out of my neighborhood," Mouse answered with a straight face.

When Pat Murphy recounted his testimony, I couldn't help but picture Mouse at the Neighborhood Watch meetings.

My brother Dan was called as the next witness.

"Steinberg said he saw that guy with Chris and just started shooting. He mentioned that it was kind of cool because it was a nigger with a badge that he was shooting at," he related.

"Christopher had a copy of a police report that he pulled out of his briefcase. The highlighted section was where he was refusing to cooperate. He said he had been accused of being a rat and was being threatened by Steinberg, but that all was cool at that point," Dan stated.

"Your brother is getting a little crazy arguing with me," Steinberg had told Dan in a telephone conversation.

"I thought it was just leading to a fight between friends," Dan testified.

I had warned Dan to expect some fireworks. The action commenced during a re-cross-examination by Weaver's attorney after Dan mentioned that our brother Tim lived in Las Vegas. Amster fired off a series of ridiculous questions obviously designed to insinuate my family's connections with organized crime.

"You remember a place called the Mounds Club outside Cleveland? Never remember driving there and seeing two guard towers with armed guys? Never knew it was a place for illegal gambling that the Mafia, the old Cleveland crew, hung out? That it was the same crew that went out to Las Vegas and took over the Desert Inn? Your family had absolutely nothing to do with them?"

The Mounds Club opened in 1930 and by 1950 the proprietor, Black Jack McGinty, had sold his interest in the club and invested in the fledgling Desert Inn. At that time, my father was a Cleveland detective. Dan was not born until 1957. Amster might as well have inquired about the St. Valentine's Day Massacre.

DDA Sparagna was forced to counter the spurious allegations on redirect examination.

"Mr. Walsh, are you in the Mafia?" she asked.

"No, ma'am, I'm Irish," Dan responded.

"Are you involved in illegal activity with some organized crime syndicate?" DDA Sparagna inquired.

"No, I'm not," Dan responded emphatically. "I'm a working Irishman. I work for the fifth-largest home builder in the nation. My brother Tim is a concrete superintendent, probably fifteen years."

During an interview, Detective Cochran had asked whether Dan knew Steinberg intended to kill Christopher.

Dan answered, "You know our history. We won't tolerate that."

At a sidebar conference, Weaver's attorney argued that he should be permitted to explore that issue.

"Any number of witnesses contact Dennis Walsh and they change their statements. Dennis Walsh's footprints are all over here. He threatened witnesses. He talked in a tough tone. He brought up the history of the family. The threat is out there because what this family was involved in. They have influenced the witnesses. Even Detective Fleming said to one of the witnesses, 'You know this family. If you don't come in, they will take care of this like they would twenty years ago.'"

Judge Pastor allowed further inquiry for the defense attorneys to attempt to impeach Dan's testimony. Dan denied that our father had any connections with the Mafia. It was a matter of semantics. My father did associate with known organized crime figures. Had Seymour Amster done his homework, he might have been able to effectively make his point.

Dan was furious after his testimony. "This goofy little hump asking me about the Mounds Club, like I was even around during Prohibition. What the fuck does the old man have to do with our brother getting murdered?" he asked me.

"I told you they would try to muddy us up," I replied. "Don't worry, I'll answer all their questions about the old man when I'm on the stand."

DDA Sparagna moved her case along at a brisk pace. Next in order was Mouse's ex-girlfriend, Desiree Manthe. She testified to being with Amy Sheeley and picking up Steinberg, whom she knew as Frankie, after the shoot-out with the deputy.

"He looked really pale and scared and had no shirt on. He was rocking back and forth in the car and said, 'I thought it was a big fat nigger,'" she recounted.

"Did Frankie show you something unusual?" the prosecutor asked.

"Just a gun being put into a Bible, which I thought was funny because it reminded me of *The Sopranos,*" she answered.

Later in the afternoon Cowboy, Marlon Grueskin, took the stand. He was in custody on a drug charge and was testifying under court order pursuant to a grant of immunity. His testimony would stretch over four days, with some interruptions for other witnesses called out of order.

Cowboy testified that after Steinberg got released from jail, he "became pretty much the brains and leader of our crew." DDA Sparagna asked about the crew's operations.

"Each of us had anywhere from five to ten people underneath us. It was supposed to be like somewhat of a Mafia," he replied.

DDA Sparagna asked if he thought Steinberg was intelligent.

"Beyond intelligent, a genius. I'm pretty intelligent myself, and I considered him to be far superior in knowledge than I am," Cowboy answered.

Cowboy confirmed that Jeff Weaver had been extremely jealous of

Christopher. Weaver had become Steinberg's best friend and "right-hand man."

Cowboy confirmed that Christopher carried a copy of the police report indicating he was not cooperating with the police.

During cross-examination, Cowboy recited a list of the crew's illegal activities and ticked off the cast of nefarious characters who had inhabited Christopher's world. He told of meeting an escort named Brandi at a party where she was paid to perform oral sex on the crew members.

Pat Murphy related the episode to me in the hallway during a break.

"A blow job party? Great, just what this trial needs, more sensationalism." I sighed.

After DDA Sparagna resumed her direct examination, Cowboy dropped a bombshell. In December 2003, at Kimmi Balmes's house, Weaver had confronted Cowboy in the presence of Ivan Masabanda.

"Jeff said, 'Fuck you, fuck Chris, Chris deserved what he got.' He proceeded to tell me, yeah, he *did* Chris. He said to me, 'You better stop talking to the Walshes or I will do the same thing to you,' " he testified.

"What does *did* mean?" DDA Sparagna asked.

"It means kill," Cowboy responded.

Cowboy admitted to asking Detective Fleming for a deal during an interview at Parker Center. Detective Fleming was rewinding the tape when Cowboy first mentioned Weaver admitting that he *did* Christopher. Cowboy repeated his statement when the tape was restarted. Weaver's attorney, Seymour Amster, hammered away at Cowboy's motive, implying that the detective had fed him information in exchange for a deal while the tape was being rewound.

Amster then bore in on my family's alleged organized crime connections. Cowboy described the Walshes as "tough brothers, connected to the Gambino crime family."

"Why did you feel it was important to provide information to Dennis Walsh when you were already providing information to law enforcement?" Amster probed.

"Put it like this," Cowboy replied, "the reputation the Walsh brothers had, you didn't want to cross them. If I didn't provide the information they wanted, I had fear for my life."

"But who are you in fear of, the Walsh brothers or Mr. Weaver?" Amster inquired.

"The Walsh brothers," Cowboy answered.

Amster's line of questioning was proving to be fertile ground, and he knew it.

Amster may have been making some hay with his questions, but sometimes an attorney commits the mistake of asking one too many questions. This was one of those times.

"And as long as you are in more fear of the Walsh brothers, you will not do what Jeff Weaver wants and stop talking to the Walshes?" Amster continued.

"I know the Walsh brothers weren't committing murder at the time, but he was," Cowboy shot back.

DDA Sparagna wasted no time rehabilitating her witness on redirect examination:

"Knowing the Walshes could potentially whack you, did you lie to them?" she asked.

"Why would I want to get whacked? I told everything I knew," he replied.

"What did Dennis Walsh want from you?" she asked.

"To go and be honest with the police, tell them what I knew," he responded.

"The issue is whether you are telling this jury what you have told them the last couple of days in order to get a deal," she stated.

"I didn't get a deal. You gave me a hamburger. That was about it, ma'am," Cowboy replied.

I was about sixty-five miles away at the time, but swear I could hear the air escaping from Seymour Amster's ass.

There had been some excitement behind the scenes during Cowboy's four days on the witness stand. He had been mistakenly placed in a holding cell next to Weaver in the lockup just off the courtroom. After Judge Pastor was informed of the gaffe, he admonished the deputies to keep witnesses away from the two defendants. Two witnesses had already been stabbed in this case. Nevertheless, the very next morning, Cowboy and Weaver were placed on the same bus on the short ride from Men's Central Jail to the courthouse.

Judge Pastor was quick to act. "I am livid. There is a major breakdown in terms of sheriff's security. I directed Deputy Jones to have his superiors meet me at noon to discuss this matter," he said for the record.

Judge Pastor had his hands full on this case since day one.

The next day, I was jarred by a news report that a mistrial had been declared in the Phil Spector case. Short of outright acquittals, a mistrial was what I feared most. Retrying either Steinberg or Weaver would probably take another year. The testimony of all the jailbird and tweaker witnesses, already rife with inconsistencies, would be even more vulnerable to attack. It had been only a week, but every day there seemed to be something that caused me to wonder whether the day would ever come when Steinberg and Weaver would be convicted.

As the sun slowly set that evening, I lay back in a feed trough and drank a few cold Heinekens while Rowdy munched on a flake of alfalfa and Johnny Rio lay contentedly between piles of dried manure.

"Well, boys, that's what they call the vicissitudes of trial, but these bastards are going down, no matter how many trials it takes," I said.

Neither Rowdy nor Johnny Rio knew what the hell I was talking about, but their quiet composure steadily eased my mind as the autumn dusk faded to darkness.

Like the vast majority of murder cases, this was a case of circumstantial evidence. There would be no direct evidence. No witness had actually seen either Steinberg or Weaver pull the trigger. The prosecution would have to lay out its case brick by brick.

DDA Sparagna was assisted by DDA Ann Ambrose, who was assigned the task of questioning witnesses regarding physical evidence, such as fingerprint and ballistics experts, as well as the coroner. The parade of witnesses marched on as the prosecution methodically laid the foundation of its case like journeymen bricklayers troweling mortar.

Alan Sarkin, a criminal defense attorney who had represented Michelle O'Halloran, testified that he had met with Christopher and David Steinberg at Uncle Chen's Chinese restaurant to discuss her case while she was in county jail. Steinberg hijacked the meeting and attempted to tell the lawyer how to handle her case. Sarkin described Steinberg as "cocky" and "self-assured."

"He was upset that the owner of the restaurant didn't come down to see him," he stated.

"Did you tell Detective Fleming that he was actually annoying and telling you how to practice law?" DDA Sparagna asked.

"He was suggesting certain motions. I don't like people telling me how to conduct my case any more than you probably do," Sarkin answered.

He was on the stand less than ten minutes, but DDA Sparagna had subtly landed a major blow in establishing Steinberg's controlling nature. David Michael Steinberg, someone with no formal education, had the temerity to dictate orders to an attorney. If the two defense attorneys had yet to realize they were up against a consummate professional in DDA Stephanie Sparagna, they certainly knew it now.

The general manager from the North Hollywood U-Haul center took the stand and identified a fourteen-foot U-Haul truck, service dolly, and appliance dolly depicted in photographs. A charge of $614.80 had been charged to the credit card of George Jassick, Steinberg's "lackey."

Talking Tina Arnone and Rosalinda Pallares were on deck. Tina was first up.

She testified that Christopher was "like a big brother to me." She identified the large sectional couch depicted in People's Exhibit 44. She had seen two blue trash bins on the patio at the Moorpark Street apartment. When she returned, the two barrels were in the kitchen. She watched Steinberg put a pistol in his waistband before they went out to Club 66 in Hollywood. On the way home, she could sense something was wrong.

"I was so shocked about the way Chris was squeezing my hand. I was going, 'What is wrong? Something is wrong.'"

Tina testified that over the last few months, Cowboy had been Christopher's constant companion. "He just followed Christopher around like a puppy dog."

Upon hearing of her comment, I recalled Dan telling me how Steinberg had cleverly waited until Cowboy, Christopher's "right-hand man," had taken his girlfriend to Magic Mountain before making his move to commit murder.

Tina related that she called Christopher on Sunday. She was short on cash and asked him to pick up some articles for her at the store. Because she was retiring early that evening, she told him to just throw the items over the balcony.

"He said, 'No problem, kid, I'll be there.' He was always there. When he said he'd be there, he showed," she testified.

When she awoke and the articles were not on the balcony, she called Christopher and left messages. She called Steinberg, who claimed that he did not know where Christopher was.

"He had a very sarcastic, evil voice saying that he did not know where Chris was, nobody had seen him. It was very eerie," she said.

She never saw Christopher again.

On cross-examination, Steinberg's attorney quizzed her about contacting me before she spoke to the police.

"Did you call the police department and say, 'I have information'?" Steve Hauser inquired.

"No. Kenny Williams put me in touch with Dennis," Tina replied. "He drove me to Devonshire Division."

"Did you know anything about his family's reputation?" Hauser asked.

"Just that his father was in prison. I knew his mother was grieving and that his children would be grieving. I knew that his brothers were, everybody was hurt. Everybody was sad. That is all the reputation that I know of them," she responded.

Step by step, DDA Sparagna was establishing the time line from the point Christopher went missing up until his body was discovered.

Next up was Rosalinda Pallares, who was known simply as Linda. She testified to having received a letter from my mother asking her to speak with the homicide detectives.

"After reading the letter, how did it affect you?" DDA Sparagna asked.

"I started to cry uncontrollably," she answered.

She described how Christopher introduced Steinberg to her.

"He is the one who shot at the cop," Christopher had said.

"What did Steinberg say?" DDA Sparagna asked.

"He specifically told Chris, 'Shut the fuck up, you stupid idiot.' He was very upset that he told me that," Linda responded.

She testified that they went to the L.A. Erotica porn convention the evening of June 21, and that Christopher made plans to meet her on her birthday the following Wednesday, June 25.

"What happened on your birthday?" DDA Sparagna inquired.

"Nothing happened," she answered. "I couldn't get ahold of him. It wasn't like him not to call me."

She called Steinberg, looking for Christopher. "I specifically recall him being kind of smart-assey, like kind of chuckling. 'No. If you talk to him, let him know I am looking for him, too,'" she said.

Linda stated that she was not sure she had any relevant information when she first spoke to Detective Fleming. Playing on her emotions by having my mother write to her appeared to have worked in spades.

Perhaps Stephanie was right. Maybe I had tainted all these witnesses by speaking with them before they contacted the police. Tainted or not, at least they spoke to the homicide detectives. Having these witnesses tell their stories in a court of law, instead of whispering them on street corners, was almost too good to be true. After hearing reports of the testimony of Tina and Linda, I felt especially like that patient little barn swallow, and I was chirping like I had just seen the first signs of spring.

I was well aware, however, that my time was coming. If I didn't acquit myself well on the witness stand, it would all be for naught.

14

THE COWARD THAT ROARED

I T WAS SEPTEMBER 27, NINE days since opening statements had been made. The stage was set for the prosecution's star witness, Tony Shane Wilson, the former Shankster Gangster. Everyone had eagerly anticipated his testimony. Wilson had been released from custody earlier in the year. Pursuant to his plea bargain, he had served three years and one week for accessory to murder after the fact. I didn't like it, but that's the way it was.

He had been appearing pursuant to a subpoena for a few days prior to his testimony. Tensions were running high. Out of the presence of the jury, Weaver's attorney complained about the uniformed LAPD officer who was assigned to accompany Wilson for his protection. He requested the judge to order a plainclothes officer instead, to make it less conspicuous in front of the jury members.

"We are short on staff, I'm going to allow it to remain," Judge Pastor ruled. "We can't ignore the threat to Tony Shane Wilson's life."

DDA Sparagna wasted no time eliciting testimony that Wilson was formerly a high-ranking member of the Nazi Low Rider white supremacist prison gang. She intended to muddy up her own witness before the defense attorneys had their shot at him.

"I was a shot caller, I had the keys," he stated.

"When you say the *keys,* is that a term of art?" DDA Sparagna inquired.

"Just a term of who had the power," he replied.

The ex–Nazi Low Rider was obviously nervous. Judge Pastor had positioned a bailiff near the witness stand to watch both defendants after he had noticed Steinberg mad-dogging some prior witnesses. Wilson admitted that testifying was difficult for him.

"It puts a big fat target on me. I already got cut. I got to watch my back everywhere I go. I can't be in certain areas and I can't associate with certain people. It has been real hard to testify because I have done things against people who have testified," he said.

DDA Sparagna elicited testimony concerning a kite note dated March 16, 2004, in Steinberg's handwriting, which had been passed down the 3100 A Row tier by a trustee along with a transcript of Mouse's interview with Detective Fleming.

Dear Shane and Jeff, the kite read, *I hope and pray you are not saying intimate details about our case over the tier.*

The kite was ominously signed *Silent Thunder.*

"I knew what it meant because there was talk between the top tier and the bottom tier," Wilson explained. "David was concerned that I was talking to those guys because they were placed there to get information. They are PC and they would turn state's evidence pretty quick," he elaborated, referring to the protective-custody tier.

He expressed his understanding of the implication of receiving Mouse's transcript.

"I thought Mouse is going to get hit," he testified.

Wilson was housed on the same tier with Steinberg, Weaver, and George Jassick—3100 A Row.

"That row is locked down. It is an active tier, everybody is participating in gang activity. It is locked down because we have been ordered by the courts for no phone calls, so it is basically no communication," he said.

He explained how they went "fishing" with inmates on the floor above to have them make their phone calls.

"Fish means if you want to get a note to somebody upstairs, they would get it out over their bars and over the rails down into the tier below, and then we would shoot out something that will be hooked to a line. They would pull it up to their cell," he said.

All twenty-four jurors and twelve alternates listened with rapt attention as Wilson described getting stabbed in custody after testifying at the preliminary hearing. DDA Sparagna had him stand to exhibit the garish five-inch scar for both juries. The drama continued as Wilson described a sinister encounter with Steinberg on 3100 A Row while Weaver was still on the run.

"David was in Cell Block Three, next to the shower. When you go down to the shower, you could talk to him. I would pose questions like, 'What if Jeff rolls?' David said, 'Just find out where he's at. I can have him hit in jail or out.' I realized he's going to have him hit not even knowing if he will testify."

He described accompanying Steinberg and Weaver to a dry cleaner's on a $100,000 debt collection for the Russian mob. Steinberg did not appreciate the tone of the young guy behind the counter and punched him to the floor. After that, the dazed dry cleaner called Steinberg "sir."

DDA Sparagna was showing the jury another instance where David Michael Steinberg demanded respect, believing he was entitled to it.

Wilson told of a phone conversation Steinberg had with Christopher, where Steinberg appeared "perturbed."

"After Mr. Steinberg hung up, what did he say to you?" she asked.

"He said, 'This guy is going to make me kill him,'" he replied.

Wilson recounted the events of the evening Steinberg had summoned him and Weaver to the Moorpark Street apartment.

"I had to shoot Chris," he quoted Steinberg as saying.

"He said he shot him three times from across the room, and stabbed him in the neck three times," Wilson said.

Steinberg claimed he and Christopher had argued over missing ecstasy tablets, Christopher threatened to kill him while searching for his gun, and that he shot him in self-defense. Steinberg was holding some small-caliber shells, .22s or .25s.

Wilson was asked whether he inquired if anyone else may have heard the gunshot.

"He said he turned the radio up real loud," he replied.

DDA Sparagna's line of questioning allowed Wilson to paint the grisly scene for the two juries.

"I seen Chris laying on his back, half on, half off the couch," Wilson related in grim detail. "His legs were off the couch. It looked to me he was bleeding around his neck. He was breathing. It sounded like loud snoring, but it was actually gurgling. His mouth was closed, but he was still trying to breathe. I think it was coming out of his neck."

While Christopher struggled for his life, the three of them discussed whether Christopher would take it as a "check." DDA Sparagna asked Wilson to explain the term.

"Reprimand. Like you do something wrong and you get spanked for it as a kid, and that is a check. So I was saying would Chris accept what he just received as a check," he explained.

He and Weaver "split" after Steinberg assured them Christopher would not live through it anyway. Wilson tried to justify leaving the scene with Weaver, abandoning Christopher to die.

"I felt bad for him, but I also believed what David was saying, that it was self-defense. So it was kind of between them two," he said.

That didn't surprise me. I had heard that Shane Wilson did not stick his neck out for anyone.

"When you left, did you say anything to Jeff?" DDA Sparagna asked.

"That is some crazy shit," Wilson responded.

Wilson described the scene after Steinberg called him to return to the apartment "the next day or the day after." The trash can was lying on its side on the floor.

"He said his back was out. He couldn't lift the trash can, upright it. I saw Chris Walsh's body lying headfirst in the trash can with his legs sticking out. He had his pants and his socks on. No shoes," he said as casually as he might discuss what he just had for lunch.

After they righted the trash barrel, Steinberg assured him their fingerprints would not be left on the can.

"He said he was going to spray it down with WD-40 and wrap it up," Wilson stated. "As I was leaving, he put his hands on top of Chris's feet and was trying to push them down into the trash can."

According to Wilson, the large sectional couch Christopher had been lying on as he was mortally wounded was gone, having been replaced by a different couch.

Later that day, Wilson returned the U-Haul truck Steinberg had lent him to move some of his own furniture. By that time, Steinberg had sealed the body in a blue ninety-gallon trash barrel. He took Wilson out onto the patio to exhibit his handiwork.

"Chris was in the trash can all wrapped up with stuff, cellophane, cardboard," Wilson related.

Later he had a conversation with Steinberg pertaining to getting rid of the body with Red Devil Lye, commonly used in the manufacture of crystal meth.

"Tell the jurors what Red Devil Lye is," DDA Sparagna instructed him.

"Red Devil Lye eats tissue, bone, and everything," he answered.

Wilson told of taking Steinberg to a Laundromat in Granada Hills to meet a "drug chemist," someone he knew to be running a methamphetamine lab.

During the following week, prior to Steinberg's arrest on June 30, 2003, Wilson testified to seeing Christopher's girlfriend, Christina Karath.

"I would go over to her house with Jeff and then I was going over by myself. She was selling drugs, dealing ounces. We partied and stuff," he stated. "She knew something happened to Chris, and she knew I had to keep my mouth shut."

On cross-examination late in the day, Steinberg's attorney, Steve Hauser, had no trouble painting Shane Wilson as a racist who had already served four prison terms. Wilson freely admitted to still having a swastika tattoo. He agreed that being a racist was a prerequisite for joining the Nazi Low Riders. Hauser's attempt at proving some animus toward his Jewish client fell flat, however.

"One of the ideas of the Nazis is anti-Jewish, is that correct?" Hauser asked.

"The Nazi Low Riders are a prison gang," Wilson replied. "It's not against Jews. There is not a lot of Jews in prison."

Wilson testified he had been trying to disassociate himself from the

Nazi Low Riders. Christopher had helped make it easy for him to assimilate with the new crew.

"Chris was, as soon as you met him, the guy was really outgoing. He would talk your ear off about things and really get into stories, a pretty animated guy. I liked him," he said.

"He liked him enough to leave him to die," I said when my sister Kathy related his comment.

The trial recessed for the day. I had driven downtown in the afternoon with Johnny Rio to pick up Kathy. Hundreds of court interpreters had been on strike for weeks. They were parading in front of the courthouse, banging drums, blowing whistles, and playing loud music. It was pure pandemonium. The chaos caused Johnny Rio to pace back and forth on his leash, low to the ground as wolves are prone to do when stressed. We waited on the courthouse steps until my sister, DDA Sparagna, and Detective Fleming emerged from the courthouse. Kathy was dabbing at her eyes with Kleenex.

"Hello, Dennis!" Stephanie shouted over the clamor. "It was a rough day for your sister. We put Shane Wilson up. I think it went well, so far. The juries were absolutely spellbound.

"I'm sorry, Kathy!" she yelled. "I know it's pretty rough stuff. Are you going to be okay? It'll be even worse when the coroner testifies."

"I'm all right, Stephanie. I need to be in there for Chris as much as I can," Kathy responded.

During the drive home, while my sister recounted Wilson's testimony, her tears turned to anger. "I don't know why that weasel Shane Wilson is out walking around and not in jail," she complained.

"It's better that coward is walking around than having that animal Steinberg out on the streets," I said.

In between portions of Shane Wilson's testimony, the prosecution had ducked in testimony from a forensic locksmith regarding the Chateau padlock from Carolyn Vasquez's storage unit. DDA Ann Ambrose took over the questioning. She was a sharp dresser with reddish hair and just the right amount of makeup. I thought she looked more like a Madison Avenue advertising executive than a lawyer, but she was a more-than-capable prosecutor.

Although the padlock had been drilled through its tumbler, the expert witness concluded that the Chateau key that had been on a lanyard around Steinberg's neck at the time of his arrest was more likely than not a match for that particular padlock. It was dry, mundane testimony, but nevertheless highly incriminating. One more brick in a foundation of circumstantial evidence.

Before Wilson took the stand the next day, DDA Ambrose called an LAPD crime lab criminalist who had examined the Moorpark Street apartment crime scene and observed a large stain on the carpet with a reddish tint, red stains on the wall, and a red stain on a mattress in the upstairs bedroom. During presumptive testing for blood, the "hot pink" color of the cotton swab indicated a positive finding. Later he noticed a foul odor coming from the patio.

"It's an odor which we commonly refer to as decomp, a type of odor you commonly smell with a decomposing body or flesh," he explained.

He followed the foul smell to a wet-dry Shop-Vac on the patio.

"We opened it up and I could really smell that decomp smell," he said.

Oddly enough, a strange odor arose, causing Judge Pastor to clear the courtroom. It turned out that Deputy Jason Jones's pepper spray container had sprung a leak. Before the two juries returned after a thirty-five-minute delay, the judge asked Weaver, who was seated at the counsel table closest to Deputy Jones's desk, if he was okay.

"I'm fine. I live at the county jail. I smell it all day long," he replied nonchalantly.

When the criminalist resumed his testimony, he stated that he observed biological tissue in some of the bloodstains.

"Biological tissue can be anything from skin tissue to muscle tissue to brain tissue," he explained.

Sections of the bloodstained carpet, mattress, and swabs from the wall stains were collected and booked into evidence along with the Shop-Vac and its contents.

Another LAPD criminalist testified that the bloodstains on the couch were fairly large—"eight inches to a foot across."

Steinberg's attorney then resumed his cross-examination of Shane Wilson, painting him as a racist and a liar. The former shot caller readily admitted that he initially lied to me and lied again to detectives when he claimed he knew nothing about the murder. He was on the stand all afternoon until court adjourned for the weekend.

The next day, I read an L.A. *Daily News* blog on the Internet titled IRISH MIKE DIDN'T SNITCH, written by Brent Hopkins. Earlier that week, Marta Wilson had called and said that Mike had caught some grief in county jail over Hopkins's article at the start of the trial. I suggested that she call the reporter to ask him to write a retraction.

"I would like to set this straight," Hopkins wrote,

> Irish Mike didn't testify against Steinberg. His wife described an incident . . . but Irish Mike wasn't called as a witness, nor did her testimony have anything to do with the actual murder charge. I hope things get straightened out and he's not roughed up just because the DA mentioned his name in her opening statement.

I mailed a copy to Mike in county jail. I didn't want anyone else getting stabbed on this case.

Monday morning, October 1, could not have rolled around quickly enough. Shane Wilson was scheduled to resume his testimony at 9 A.M., but it was 11:05 before he sauntered into the courtroom. Judge Pastor was fairly apoplectic, while the jurors milled about the hallway.

"Mr. Wilson, why are you two hours late, sir?" the judge inquired.

"I overslept," Wilson casually replied.

"Do you have an alarm clock? You have inconvenienced this whole courtroom. I'm going to see about sanctions after your testimony, including up to five days in county jail and a fifteen-hundred-dollar fine," the exasperated judge spat out.

When Steinberg's attorney resumed his cross-examination, he hammered Wilson hard. Wilson admitted that he had not told law enforcement about the blue trash barrel on the apartment patio until after almost three years in custody. Then he acknowledged that someone removed a 9 mm pistol and a .22- or .25-caliber pistol from his car while he was in custody.

Weaver's attorney then commenced his cross-examination. Wilson admitted that while Christopher lay gurgling on the couch, there was a discussion between Steinberg, Weaver, and himself about putting the body in a refrigerator. After he and Weaver left, they went to Wilson's apartment and "smoked a bowl," which he explained as "a little methamphetamine in a pipe." Seymour Amster then homed in on the Walsh brothers.

"Who do you know Chris's brothers to be?" he asked.

"I know one is a lawyer, and one lives in Arizona. I thought they had connections," Wilson responded.

He proceeded to describe the altercation in front of Kimmi Balmes's house.

"I was in my car with a girl. Jeff was at my window. They came screeching up and stopped right beside us, and jumped out of their car. They were fighting, Jeff Weaver and one of those guys. The other had his hand behind his back like he had a gun. I spun the car around and started to get out. They pulled up to my car and said I better testify to the gurgling. I told them I didn't know nothing," he said.

"Were you afraid of what the Walsh brothers could do to you?" Amster inquired.

"Sure, I was afraid they could put a hit on me," he replied.

"Did you ever receive any telephone messages from any Walsh brothers?" Weaver's counsel asked.

"My ex-wife called me from her bar she was working at and told me that the Walsh brothers were there, that they were packing, and they were surrounding the bar, threatening that I should come down there," he answered.

Wilson claimed that he had been driving to the bar in defense of his ex-wife when he had a phone conversation with "them."

"I took it as them being drunk and wanting to, you know, if your brother got killed, you would want to do the same thing. I think they probably wanted to kick my ass," he stated.

On redirect examination, DDA Sparagna read from a transcript of Wilson's interview with Detective Fleming regarding the conversation while Christopher gasped for breath on the couch.

"Steinberg would go, 'Come on, Jeff, you know,' and Jeff would say, 'Yeah, Chris is like that. Chris has got a bad attitude. They called him I'm Going to Kill You. He is always treating David bad. He tries to punk Dave all the time,'" she quoted Wilson.

He said Steinberg had planned to dismiss his attorney and go pro per to obtain paperwork on additional witnesses.

"Did the Walsh brothers ever ask you to lie, and make sure you lay out David Steinberg?" DDA Sparagna asked.

"No, they told me to tell the truth," he answered. "They wanted the truth to come out."

The vainglorious ex–Nazi Low Rider could not, however, resist the temptation to redeem his reputation.

"I was willing to take them both on," he boasted, "but the one guy acted like he had a gun, and Jeff was already up by the house."

As I said, Shane Wilson doesn't stick his neck out for anyone.

Wilson returned to testify on October 2. The defense attorneys continued their relentless assault on his credibility. They focused on Wilson's initial mistaken belief that he was looking at a third-strike offense and possibly a life sentence. He was finally excused after almost four days on the witness stand. How credible he had been only the two juries knew. The repugnant sea cucumber had publicly spewed his guts, effectively trading his notorious reputation as Shot Caller Shankster Gangster for a plain old rat jacket and the freedom to slither back into the cesspool whence he had emerged.

15

BRICK BY BRICK

THE PEOPLE OF THE STATE of California's star witness may have been done testifying, but their case was far from over. The prosecution shouldered the twin burden of not only proving guilt beyond a reasonable doubt, the highest standard of proof in American jurisprudence, but also proving it unanimously to twelve jurors. In this case, the prosecution had two juries to convince: twenty-four different people from all walks of life. Every day, the prosecution team of DDAs Sparagna, Ambrose, and senior law clerk Patrick Ball, and lead investigator Detective Fleming flanked the right side of the counsel table nearest the jury box. As soon as one witness was excused, another took his place on the stand.

On October 2, Carolyn Vasquez was next in order. She admitted to having an affair with Steinberg while living with her son's father. Her testimony must have hit Steinberg like a swift kick to the groin. She told of Steinberg bragging of being a "high-ranking leader" in the Nazi Low Riders.

"What did he tell you about Jews?" DDA Sparagna inquired.

"That he was not Jewish, that he didn't like Jews," she answered.

Steinberg had introduced her to his friend Finny, Chris Walsh, who had recently moved in with him at his Moorpark Street apartment. She joined the list of witnesses who identified Christopher's large "brownish U-shaped couch."

Steinberg told her he believed Christopher had stolen ecstacy, a "boatful of E-tabs," from him.

Carolyn had given him the only key to her storage unit along with the security gate access code to retrieve furniture she no longer wanted. She visited Steinberg at his apartment on Wednesday, June 25, after Christopher had gone missing.

"It was very dark in there. David was sitting at the dining room table having a drink of alcohol," she stated.

She noticed that Christopher's sectional couch and most of the furniture was missing. She had seen the couch still there the day before. Steinberg said he "gave it away." DDA Sparagna was patiently establishing more evidence of the time line.

Carolyn recalled a Shop-Vac being in the living room. Steinberg refused to allow her into the kitchen to put bottled water in the refrigerator, claiming it was broken. She tried but could not reach him by telephone later that evening and most of the next day. She was driving on the 405 when he finally called her after just waking up around 3 or 4 P.M.

She had noticed a sudden change in his personality all that week.

"He screamed that if I didn't do whatever he asked, he was going to come to my house and beat the shit out of me or kill me, and that he was going to drag me across the pool table and do the same thing with my son's father, or he would bust the door down and come after us," she exclaimed.

Steinberg called her the next day, to tell her that he had gone to her storage unit and moved the furniture she said he could have into his apartment. He needed to purchase a throw rug for the apartment.

"I told him wait, I could probably get a less expensive one downtown," she testified, "but he said no. He needed it immediately," she said.

At this point, every juror had to be thinking about the section of bloodstained carpet the LAPD criminalist had cut out and booked into evidence. There was indeed a method to DDA Sparagna's madness. She was not calling her witnesses in any haphazard order.

When Carolyn arrived at the apartment later that day, she noticed a U-Haul truck parked out front. Inside, she saw her furniture arrayed about the apartment. A brand-new throw rug lay in the center of the living room.

Carolyn told of a phone conversation she overheard that day between Steinberg and an unidentified female, whom I believe to be Christina Karath.

"It was a female saying, 'Where is he?' They were referring to Chris Walsh. She says, 'Are you going to do to me what you did to him?'"

After he hung up, Carolyn asked him where Chris Walsh was.

"He's not here. I don't know," Steinberg had responded. "I don't want to talk about him. He's not my friend anymore, and he is no longer my roommate."

She drove to her storage facility while Steinberg followed in the U-Haul truck. She left him there after he agreed to take the dinette set and remaining items to her house. She intended to vacate the unit by July 1. On the following Monday, June 30, Steinberg called to ask if he could pay for the unit for one more month.

"I asked David why. He said, 'I need to put my couch in there.' I said, 'I thought it was Chris's couch.' He said, 'I just need to put it in there.' That was strange. Initially, it was Chris's couch, then all of a sudden it's David's couch," she said.

She refused Steinberg's request. Steinberg was arrested later that evening. On July 1, George Jassick called and said her dinette set was at the North Hollywood U-Haul. She drove there and found her dinette set still inside the U-Haul truck along with a refrigerator. She took the dinette and paid a fee to dispose of the refrigerator. Carolyn had no idea that the refrigerator was something more than an appliance: it was evidence.

The next morning, July 2, she went to her storage unit and had the padlock drilled. The only key was in Steinberg's property bag in county jail.

"I opened the storage. It was dark. I saw papers belonging to Chris Walsh, a notebook, a phone book. I saw what looked like a big blue petroleum drum. There was trash bags and duct tape around it. I smelled it and I thought it was Chris Walsh," she testified.

She drove to the FBI office on Wilshire Boulevard to meet her handler, Special Agent Robert Harris. She admitted to being a confidential informant. He contacted Devonshire Division detectives.

Bit by bit, Steinberg's erstwhile paramour was helping to seal his fate just as he had sealed Christopher's lifeless body in the blue trash barrel.

Trial was recessed for eight days until October 10. Although Carolyn Vasquez's testimony certainly seemed fatal to Steinberg's case, it was way too early in the game to get my hopes up.

On October 10, the prosecution called its next witness, LAPD Detective Orlando Martinez. He testified that he executed a search warrant on July 2, 2003, at a residence rented by George Jassick, where he recovered a "huge five-piece L-shaped sectional couch." He identified what appeared to be two bloodstains on the couch in People's Exhibit 44. The couch was transported to Devonshire Division for analysis by crime lab criminalists.

Later that evening, he accompanied Detective Fleming to serve a search warrant at Steinberg's apartment. He observed the inside of the apartment to be in complete disarray with clothing, luggage, and boxes strewn about. DDA Ambrose asked what the detectives were searching for.

"Evidence that a murder had happened there, specifically blood evidence," Detective Martinez replied.

He told the juries what he discovered.

"I moved the couch and there was a throw rug on top of the carpet. We lifted up the throw rug, there was a big dried puddle of blood on the carpet," he stated.

While searching for evidence that could be connected to the Erwin Street storage unit, they recovered a dolly with an attached U-Haul key, duct tape, plastic trash bags, dark plastic tarps, clear drop cloths, a can of WD-40, and numerous sets of keys. None of the keys were marked with the Chateau brand, which was consistent with Carolyn Vasquez's testimony that only one key to her storage unit existed.

He confirmed the criminalist's observations of bloodstains and the foul smell emitting from the wet-dry vac on the patio.

"Inside the wet-dry vac there was apparent blood," he said. "It smelled like rotted, rotting meat."

Next up was Detective Fleming's partner, Detective Brad Cochran, a thirty-six-year veteran who had retired in 2005. On January 29, 2003, he accompanied his partner to investigate the assault against Deputy Alex Dixon. A two-block area around Topanga Boulevard and Lassen Street had been cordoned off with yellow tape. Metropolitan SWAT officers, uniformed officers, and detectives were already on the scene.

"Alex was very scared, second-guessing himself," Detective Cochran stated. "He was sweating profusely. This was approximately three hours after the incident."

He testified to recovering two spent .40-caliber brass Fiocchi cartridge casings in the alleyway. He located an impact from a bullet in the drain spout of the building. Later he located a second point of impact in the stucco. The fact that no bullets were recovered did not concern him, as they sometimes disintegrate upon impact. Inside the town house, he recovered a loaded semiautomatic .40-caliber Glock handgun. A day planner was recovered bearing the name Frank Levy, Steinberg's alias.

He went to the coroner's office on September 17, 2003, to obtain a bone sample that had been retrieved from Christopher's remains. The date of the detective's errand did not escape my sister Kathy's attention as she related the incident to me during a recess.

"It was Chris's birthday, Dennis. He would have been thirty-eight that day," she said.

Christopher's ashes had already been scattered and interred by that time. Instead of a birthday celebration that day, all that remained of our youngest brother, a single bone fragment, was bagged, tagged, and booked into evidence.

An LAPD criminalist told DDA Ambrose that a DNA test of the swabs from the wet-dry vac was unsuccessful, probably due to degradation.

An expert in DNA identification testified that a blood sample from the sectional couch came from Christopher Walsh with a statistical frequency of 1 in 280 trillion. The carpet sample contained DNA from at least three individuals, one of whom was Christopher. Other samples were determined to match Steinberg's DNA sample with a statistical probability of 1 in 780 trillion.

DDA Sparagna took over the questioning and called the assistant manager of the Sherman Oaks MiniStorage to the stand. He confirmed much of Carolyn Vasquez's testimony. Surveillance cameras were not in operation on dates in question. Computerized records for Unit 2420 indicated various entries for the period of June 27 through June 30.

More dry, mundane testimony, but DDA Sparagna was filling in the time line in painstaking detail.

Detective John Fleming, a thirty-two-year veteran of the LAPD, was next up. He had arrested Christopher after the January 29, 2003, shooting involving Deputy Dixon for making a misdemeanor threat against a neighbor. He confirmed that criminal charges for the assault on Deputy Dixon were not filed until June 24, 2003. Christopher had been charged as an accessory.

Six days after charges were filed, he arrived at the Moorpark Street apartment, where other detectives, officers from the Gang Unit, Vice Squad, Metropolitan SWAT Division, and Bomb Squad were already assembled. David Steinberg was placed under arrest for the assault on Deputy Dixon.

A night scope and a laser sight were recovered from a hutch in the living room. At that time, Detective Fleming had no reason to believe the apartment was a crime scene. Christopher's body would not be discovered for two more days. It never occurred to him to lift up the brand-new throw rug that Steinberg had placed over the bloodstained carpet.

One can only imagine what thoughts must have been racing through Steinberg's mind as he stood handcuffed, only a few feet from evidence of bloody murder while LAPD detectives searched his apartment. Christopher's body was sealed in a trash barrel entombed inside a storage unit only six miles away. Material evidence that could warrant the death penalty or life in prison lay merely a few feet away, yet Steinberg remained composed while Detective Fleming took possession of the keys to the U-Haul truck parked outside.

Neither the vehicle nor the side-by-side refrigerator freezer it housed, with its shelves stacked nearby, had any particular significance at that time to Detective Fleming.

Once Christopher's body was recovered, the relevance of that evidence became manifestly apparent to the veteran detective, but his hands were full at the other crime scene, the Sherman Oaks MiniStorage. He sent Officer Mehrdad Fard to retrieve the rental truck and refrigerator from the U-Haul agency on Riverside Boulevard. By the time Officer Fard hustled over there, the truck had already been rented out. He doggedly tracked it down and confiscated it from people who were in the process of moving furniture. U-Haul employees directed Officer Fard to a Dumpster, where he recovered the side-by-side refrigerator and booked it and its shelves into evidence.

Back at the storage facility, the ink was barely dry on the search warrant when Bomb Squad officers carefully opened Unit 2420 with the new key delivered by Carolyn Vasquez's FBI handler. Storage facility personnel provided an extension cord and lighting so the detectives and LAPD crime lab criminalists could examine the darkened crime scene.

A large trash barrel encased in several layers of Bubble Wrap and plastic drop cloth wrapped in duct tape and masking tape dominated the scene. The rim of its lid was sealed with a green foam material. Lying on the concrete floor surrounding the trash container were Christopher's high school yearbook—with his name and *51,* his football jersey number, inscribed on the corner—along with his Blockbuster Video card and a parking citation issued to him. The original Chateau lock and drilled-out tumbler lay nearby. An aerosol can of green foam labeled SPACE IN-VADER EXPANDING FOAM, masking tape, latex gloves, plastic bags, Bubble Wrap, clear plastic wrap, plastic drop cloths, and yellow gloves (one bearing traces of green foam), were also recovered from Unit 2420, which had quietly and without ceremony become Christopher's tomb.

Detective Fleming testified that he returned to the storage unit sixteen days later with Detective Cochran and me. He noticed a black briefcase that contained a copy of the arrest report he had written, with an underlined portion of the report indicating that Christopher was not cooperating in the investigation. It not only corroborated Dan's testimony, but it was identical to another copy recovered from the apartment of Steinberg's "lackey," Gary Schimmel.

Detective Fleming also identified the two keys attached to a lanyard recovered from Steinberg's personal property bag at the county jail, one of which bore the brand name CHATEAU. The keys had been hanging from the lanyard around Steinberg's neck at the time of his arrest.

Detective Fleming's testimony had been extremely compelling. When he routinely rattled off a list of jewelry—"a ring, a watch, a bracelet, a Rolex watch"—that had been recovered from a jewelry box on the nightstand beside Steinberg's bed, it paled in comparison to most of his prior testimony. No one could have possibly imagined the particular significance of one of those items, People's Exhibit 40. Detective Fleming had described the exhibit as simply "a men's watch, the name of this is Rolex."

Like the dirty, dusty stepsister who was transformed into a princess in the fairy tale "Cinderella," that otherwise nondescript Rolex watch was soon to shine as brilliantly as the Hope Diamond.

On October 15, an LAPD Forensic Print Specialist testified that fingerprints collected from a window of George Jassick's Cadillac, Bubble Wrap that had encased the blue trash barrel, and three plastic bags and a black lacquered table recovered from storage Unit 2420 were all identified as matching the fingerprints of David Michael Steinberg.

No latent fingerprints were recovered from the trash barrel, however. The lack of prints on the blue barrel was due to the "oily, slimy" substance that coated the barrel, probably WD-40.

"Quite often, a bottle of WD-40 is left behind by car thieves," the expert witness explained.

DDA Ambrose astutely introduced a photograph of a can of WD-40 that had been recovered from the storage unit.

Brick by brick, the walls of the prosecution's case were closing around David Michael Steinberg.

The following week, another fingerprint expert would testify to matching a fingerprint lifted from the U-Haul sideview mirror to Steinberg.

LAPD Homicide Detective Craig Sacha testified to having witnessed the autopsy on July 3, 2003. The trash barrel was wrapped in six layers of materials that the coroner sliced open. A hammer and chisel were necessary to break the green foam seal around the lid and another brown puttylike seal inside the rim. As the lid was opened, the detective noticed several maggots on the inside of the rim. He observed two feet, one wearing a white sock. A forklift hoisted the barrel onto the autopsy table. Christopher's body, in a fetal position with a blue moving blanket loosely wrapped around his torso, was removed from the barrel. He wore tan Levi's, both pockets pulled out, and a white undershirt. His hands were inside a white plastic kitchen bag, tied tightly with a red plastic strap. DDA Ambrose produced pictures of similar white plastic bags in the apartment kitchen and on top of the toilet in Steinberg's bathroom.

"Does that appear to be consistent with the white plastic bag with the red trim that you saw wrapped around the victim's hands?" DDA Ambrose inquired.

"Yes, identical," Detective Sacha replied.

If I hadn't already hated Steinberg and Weaver with every fiber of my being, I certainly did after hearing of Detective Sacha's testimony.

Detective Sacha testified to observing a green clover tattoo on the upper right arm of the body. A deputy medical examiner would later identify the tattoo of a wolf on the right shoulder.

The clover was a testament to Christopher's Irish heritage. The wolf was in honor of his beloved wolfdog, Jake.

A senior criminalist from the coroner's office testified that the body was in an advanced state of decomposition. In his opinion, death had occurred at least a week prior to the autopsy. The prosecution's time line was getting filled in, day by day.

On October 16, Steinberg's other "lackey," George Jassick, was next up. He had pleaded to the charge of accessory after the fact and had been released after serving over a year in county jail. He testified to having been gainfully employed, prepping locations for television shoots.

Choosing to associate with David Michael Steinberg had landed him smack-dab in the middle of a couple of real shoots. One witness had described him as looking like Grateful Dead lead guitarist Jerry Garcia. His long gray hair, tied in a ponytail, gave him the appearance of a burnt-out hippie.

Initially, Jassick had denied that Steinberg admitted to shooting at Deputy Dixon.

"Did you lie to the police?" the prosecutor inquired.

"Yes," he admitted.

Steinberg had admitted to shooting at a cop, but told Jassick it was in "total self-defense."

"What did David Steinberg tell you about the case?" DDA Sparagna asked.

"He said they don't have a case. There wasn't any witnesses. They had to drop it," he responded.

If DDA Sparagna could have foreseen the rest of his testimony, she probably would have hauled him to the witness stand trussed up like a Christmas goose. He hedged on quite a few of the statements he had made to the detectives. He claimed he didn't know who left his Cadillac in the alley after the shooting at Deputy Dixon.

He had gone to the Moorpark Street apartment days before Christopher went missing.

"There was a bunch of scary white guys there. It looked like a big old pizza thing going on," he testified.

He was referring to the "pizza party" after the crew had burglarized a bunch of tools. Both Cowboy and Shane had mentioned it during their testimony.

A few days later, after Christopher went missing, Steinberg had called him and asked to borrow a steam cleaner. Jasssick brought over his Shop-Vac, and left it at the door when Steinberg would not let him in. Jassick said when he had first seen the large sectional couch in Steinberg's apartment, he offered to buy it for a thousand dollars. At that time, there were no stains on the couch. A few hours after he delivered the Shop-Vac, Steinberg called him.

"He said he had a surprise for me," Jassick stated. "He said, 'The couch is yours if you want it.'"

"He told you he was just going to give it to you?" DDA Sparagna asked with just a hint of incredulity.

"Yes," the lackey answered.

"When I went over there and saw the couch, I said, 'What happened? The thing is all fucked up.' It had a stain on it," he stated.

"What kind of stain?" DDA Sparagna asked.

"I asked David what the stain was. He said it was probably Kool-Aid. I think it looked like wine. Then he said, 'Okay, probably wine.' I thought it was a wine stain," Jassick replied.

The lackey Jassick had no idea where the skilled prosecutor was headed with her next line of questioning, but the relevance could not have been lost on the two juries. Shane Wilson had testified that Steinberg need help to lift the trash barrel, claiming that his back was out.

"Is that a heavy couch to move?" she inquired.

"Yes," Jassick answered.

"Who helped you?" she continued.

"David helped me," Jassick responded.

"Did you have to turn the sections sideways to get it out the door?" she asked.

"I think we had to try a few times, different ways to shove it in, shove it out," he replied.

She then moved on to the matter of the carpet.

"When you moved that couch, did you notice anything about the rug in that apartment?" the prosecutor queried.

"There was a stain on the rug. Sticky, like there was a pizza dropped on there," he answered.

"In fact, you told the detectives that it looked like there was chunky stuff on the rug," she stated.

"Yes, chunky stuff on the rug," he agreed.

Jassick admitted that Steinberg called him a day or two later.

"He said, 'Rent me a U-Haul,'" Jassick related.

"He actually ordered you, correct, Mr. Jassick?" DDA Sparagna asked in her own inimitable way of telling and not asking.

"He was pretty firm about it. Get him a U-Haul," Jassick answered.

He testified to renting the U-Haul truck along with an appliance dolly on June 27, 2003.

"Did you ask David Steinberg," DDA Sparagna inquired, "'Why do you need an appliance dolly if the truck already comes with a utility dolly?'"

"I think he needed a refrigerator dolly," he answered.

Jassick tried to soft-pedal his statement to detectives regarding seeing a gun in Steinberg's bedroom.

"It looked like a BB gun. It was bluish or polished blue, and then it had a laser sight on top of it," he stated.

"In fact, when you were arrested, did you describe to detectives that it looked like a German Luger, that it had a laser sight on it?" she asked.

"Yeah, I might have said that."

Jassick had just described the .22 Colt Challenger that Kenny Williams gave to Steinberg.

"Did you tell Detective Martinez that you were scared of David Steinberg, that he was a scary motherfucker?" DDA Sparagna inquired.

"I might have, yes," he responded.

"Is David Steinberg a smart guy?" DDA Sparagna inquired.

"I believe he is very intelligent, yes," Jassick answered.

"Would you call him brilliant?" she continued.

"No, if he was brilliant, none of us would be sitting here," he responded.

That comment, from his own lackey, must have been especially sting-
ing to the mastermind who had dubbed himself Silent Thunder.

On October 17, Deputy Medical Examiner Stephen Scholtz testified that
Christopher had sustained five gunshot wounds and a "sharp force or
cutting-type injury on the face, a slicing-type injury." He observed no
defensive wounds that would indicate he was "trying to ward off either a
blow or a knife." Because of the advanced state of decomposition, he was
not able to form an opinion as to how close the gun was when it was fired
or in which order the five bullets were fired. He did conclude that all five
wounds were consistent with a small-caliber firearm.

Four of the five gunshots were consistent with Christopher being
seated or reclining on a couch and the shooter shooting from behind.
All four were fired from the same location and direction, with minimal
movement, if any, by the victim, indicating rapid fire. One bullet entered
his left lower jawbone and came to rest on the inner surface of his lip. A
second shot entered at the left ear, traveled along the jawbone, and wound
up near the breastbone. The third and fourth bullets of the group entered
at the left shoulder and came to rest in the armpit area. None of the four
shots pierced any vital organs or could be considered immediately life
threatening.

The trajectory of the other bullet was horizontal and downward, different from the other four shots, indicating that either Christopher or
the shooter, or shooters, changed positions between the volley of four
shots and the single shot. It had lodged in Christopher's brain, the only
shot having pierced a vital organ. Nonetheless, in Dr. Scholtz's expert
medical opinion, the shot was not immediately fatal. Christopher could
possibly have survived for a few days.

"Now, hypothetically, if a witness testified to seeing Christopher Walsh
lying on his back on a couch making gurgling noises, if someone is shot
through the cheek and into the jaw, and if there was bleeding in the
mouth, could that cause the victim to aspirate or breathe in that blood?"
DDA Ambrose asked.

"Yes," the doctor answered.

The term "gurgling," which had haunted me since I first heard it from Kimmi Balmes, quoting Shane Wilson, had become an integral part of the prosecution's case.

"And what did you determine to be the manner of Christopher Walsh's death?" DDA Ambrose inquired.

"Homicide," the deputy medical examiner succinctly replied.

It was October 18. The People's case was in full steam. The next prosecution witness was Glenn Hartley. He testified that he had employed Steinberg to assist him in remodeling a residential property owned by actor Ving Rhames in La Cañada. He described an uncomfortable incident on the job.

"We were working on one of the houses that wasn't the main house. There was a laser from a pistol that David shined on the wall where I was working," he related.

Next up was Magic Mark Prines. He stated that Christopher had been managing his career as a magician.

In his statement to homicide detectives, he had said that Steinberg called him on Wednesday evening, the week Christopher was missing, and asked for a ride to the La Cañada remodel job to pick up a paycheck. The next day he and his niece drove him to the job site. Although it was in the dead of summer, Steinberg had been bundled in a heavy jacket. During the drive there, Steinberg seemed "very nervous," but seemed "relieved" on the ride home.

The following day, Friday, June 27, Steinberg had tried to recruit him to rent a U-Haul truck. He was able to beg off after getting into a fender bender. He told detectives that later that day he went to the apartment to help Steinberg move furniture from the storage facility. These dates were important to the prosecution's time line.

To characterize Magic Mark as a reluctant witness would be a gross understatement. If DDA Sparagna felt frustrated with George Jassick's testimony, she probably felt like horsewhipping this witness.

After he described Steinberg's demeanor and odd attire during the
trip to La Cañada, he testified that he had no further contact with Steinberg after getting into the traffic accident.

DDA Sparagna could hardly mask her frustration. "Do you consider
yourself to be a fairly intelligent man?" she asked.

"Average intelligence, sure," the magician answered.

"The questions I'm asking you. Are you having trouble understanding me?" she continued.

"No," he replied.

"Well, did you tell the detectives that you had several contacts with
David Steinberg during the week when Chris Walsh was missing?" she
asked.

"I don't recall whether I said I had several or one or two," he hedged.

It was like pulling teeth, but DDA Sparagna was able to elicit some
telling testimony. After he and his niece drove to the Moorpark Street
apartment to pick up Steinberg for the trip to La Cañada, Magic Mark
had walked in unannounced.

"I caught David by surprise. He seemed sort of startled. He was angry that I just walked in. He turned me around and told me not to come
back in. 'Don't just come right in,' you know," he explained.

Magic Mark admitted that Steinberg had been "pissed off" when he
was unable to rent the U-Haul truck for him.

When the prosecutor asked him about the duct tape and speaker wire
he told detectives Steinberg had requested him to bring to the apartment, his memory suddenly took a turn for the worse.

"Did you get another phone call from David Steinberg where he
asked you to bring something to the Moorpark apartment?" DDA Sparagna inquired.

"No, it wasn't from him. I'm sorry. Yes, it wasn't from him. No. No, I
didn't," he stammered. "I think it was Cowboy, I think. Yeah, it was, Cowboy, I think. Yes."

On the witness stand, in front of two juries, Magic Mark had inexpli-
cably disavowed his prior statement to police. Pat Murphy told me that he
thought DDA Sparagna's head was going to spin right off her shoulders.

"Did you tell Detective Fleming that it was David Steinberg who asked you to bring duct tape and speaker wire?" she asked, obviously irritated.

"Yes, I did, but now that I recall, it wasn't David at that point," he countered.

"When did you have the epiphany that it was Cowboy that called rather than David?" she asked icily.

"Just now," he replied.

On redirect examination, DDA Sparagna questioned the magician with regard to his contact with me.

"Well, he was angry at first," Magic Mark said.

He stated that I had asked him to cooperate with the police, that I never threatened him, and that I just wanted him to tell the truth. I was thankful at least that he didn't get squirrelly over that issue.

When I caught up with Stephanie in the hallway after Pat Murphy related the gist of the confrontational exchange, she was still fuming.

"Stephanie, what happened?" I asked. "I heard Magic Mark went sideways on you."

DDA Sparagna was not about to discuss any testimony with me. "I don't care what he says, Dennis, Mark Prines was no friend of your brother's," was all she would say as she marched away.

I couldn't help but love Stephanie's passion for her case.

Court was in recess for four days until October 23. In the meantime, wildfires, fueled by dry brush and hot Santa Ana winds, had been raging across Southern California from Santa Barbara to San Diego. The Buckweed Fire in Agua Dulce had been burning since the twenty-first. It was fairly close to my house and the ranch where I kept Rowdy. A slight change in the wind could spell disaster at a moment's notice.

Detective Fleming had served me with subpoenas to appear in court to testify on October 15 and 16. I was on stand-by, waiting for his call as well as waiting to determine if I might have to evacuate my house or whether the horses would have to be trailered from the ranch. The fires would continue throughout November, burning over half a million acres and destroying more than fifteen hundred houses.

I let Detective Fleming know that I intended to be there whenever Stephanie wanted me, come hell or high water, but if the canyon roads got shut down, I might be delayed.

Ain't this a kick in the slats, I thought to myself. *I'll be there if I have to shoot myself out of a cannon.*

I had been waiting four and a half years to get on that witness stand to avenge my brother's death and vindicate myself. Now I was in the middle of an inferno. Maybe it was payback for telling Marta Wilson I would walk her and Irish Mike straight through the gates of hell.

The trial continued while flames engulfed Southern California. Kenny Williams was next to take the stand. He had served twenty-six months in county jail after the night Agent Barker informed me of Kenny's arrest. He admitted that his expertise in firearms had earned him the nickname Mr. Gadget. He confirmed that a .22-caliber weapon was one of the quieter firearms. He discussed giving a .22 Colt Challenger to Steinberg at Christopher's direction after he had cleaned and repaired it. He removed the laser sight at Steinberg's request.

"I'm not going to be shooting anybody from across the range. If anything, I'm going to be sticking this thing right in their ear to get their attention," Steinberg had told Kenny.

Could any jury member possibly not have recalled the coroner testifying that one of the gunshots entered behind Christopher's left ear? I hoped not.

Kenny discussed teaching Steinberg how to make a silencer. Then came some blockbuster testimony that was news to me. Kenny had a signature habit of loading his firearms with alternate types of rounds.

"When you loaded the magazine, how did you load it?" the prosecutor asked.

"I would alternate rounds, depending on what I had. One round might be a full metal jacket. Another might be a jacket hollow point after that. The next one would be just a hollow point no jacket, and I would alternate them all the way down," he explained.

"Did you alternate the types of rounds that you put in the .22 Colt Challenger you gave to David Steinberg?" she asked.

"Yes, that is what I'm saying," he replied.

The juries would not understand the full impact of that particular testimony until the next day, when an LAPD criminalist would testify that of the five bullets recovered from Christopher's body, some were brass jacketed and some were copper jacketed.

Kenny's testimony regarding a conversation with me helped to counter the defense's theme that I had provided witnesses with pertinent details.

"I asked him plainly, 'Was Chris killed with a .22?' He said, 'I can't tell you that.' I said, 'Well, what do you want me to do?' He said, 'You have to go to the police.' I said, 'You are aware of what I'm doing for a living, aren't you?' He is like, 'Yeah,'" Kenny stated.

According to Kenny, he had last spoken with Christopher around midnight on June 23, the night before he went missing. One more bit of crucial time line evidence.

The prosecutor proceeded to bring out testimony about the deteriorating relationship between Christopher and Steinberg. Kenny had overheard a telephone conversation between the two.

"What did you hear Chris say to Steinberg?" DDA Sparagna asked.

"'You fucking son of a bitch. I'm coming for you. I'm coming heavy and I'm not coming alone,'" he stated.

"Later, what did Steinberg say to you?" DDA Sparagna inquired.

"He said, 'Kenny, it's not just like two friends arguing. If Chris Walsh calls you on the phone and says he is coming armed and not coming alone, you better take him at his word. I was in prison. If somebody said they are coming to kill you, you don't wait for them to come kill you,'" Kenny related.

Kenny stated that he spoke with Steinberg to dissuade him from taking any preemptive action.

"What did David Steinberg say to you?" the prosecutor asked.

"He said he would do that. He also said, 'If this happens again, I have to do something about it,'" Kenny testified.

Jim Cavanaugh and Pat Murphy had been reporting back to me. Their impressions were that both juries seemed to be on the edge of their seats, hanging on every word of the very compelling prosecution witnesses. There had been no letdown after star witness Shane Wilson stepped down, and there was still a lot more to come.

It was time for the prosecution to train the crosshairs on Jeffrey Lawrence Weaver. LAPD Sergeant David Harrison testified that he had arrested Weaver after he fled the Saharan Motor Hotel in Hollywood when U.S. Marshals crashed another room he was believed to be in. A citizen had held Weaver at gunpoint in the 1400 block of N. Fuller until the sergeant and his partner arrived.

"He was trying to get out of the country to get away from a pending case," the sergeant stated. "He said he just completed getting everything he needed to get out of the country other than getting the money to make his flight successful. He didn't want to go to Mexico, because he knew he would be extradited."

Detective David Holmes testified to searching room 119 at the Saharan Motor Hotel after Weaver's arrest. Several letters in Weaver's handwriting mentioned his intention to flee the country because he was looking at two life sentences. The letters, along with a falsified birth certificate and driver's license, were introduced into evidence.

DDA Sparagna then called my old nemesis, the old crystal meth cook, Don Mercatoris. She had subpoenaed him from state prison. He had been friends with Weaver for "fifteen to twenty years." He was not happy to be called as a prosecution witness.

"Did you tell Detective Fleming that Jeff Weaver wanted to tell you about the case, but you didn't want to talk to him?" she inquired.

"No," he responded while his old friend Jeff Weaver watched from his seat at the counsel table.

DDA Sparagna handed Mercatoris a copy of his interview transcript to refresh his memory. He read it over as if it were the small print in a credit card application.

"Did you tell Detective Fleming, 'Jeff didn't tell me nothing. He wanted to tell me all about it just to get it off his chest, and I didn't want to listen to it. I told him don't tell me.' Did you say that?" DDA Sparagna asked.

"I guess I did. It's right there on the paper, but yeah," he admitted.

Mercatoris was champing at the bit to lay me out in front of the jury.

"I told the detective what I knew was nothing except for what Dennis Walsh told me about," he claimed.

"Okay, we are going to get to Dennis Walsh in a second," she assured him.

Mercatoris had told detectives that Steinberg had plans to "take over the San Fernando Valley" and had tried to recruit him into his crew. When he denied making the statement, DDA Sparagna read from the transcript.

"Are you sure you didn't tell Detective Fleming, ''Cause I had one meeting with him and I thought he was a fucking clown'?" she inquired.

"I don't remember saying that to him, because I've never really had a meeting with Steinberg," he replied.

The wily prosecutor was effectively impeaching his credibility before he had the opportunity to lie about his meeting with me at the Sundown bar. Before she addressed that topic, she had him describe his first encounter with me.

"When I got arrested, he was standing on the side of the road waving and jumping up and down making all kinds of noise. I thought it was just some nut on the street."

Mercatoris then explained how Jimmy Bray had arranged our meeting at the notorious Sundown bar in Tujunga.

"He said Dennis Walsh wanted to talk to me about his brother and why he called the cops on me," he declared.

"What did you say to Jimmy Bray?" DDA Sparagna asked.

"I told him I'd go see him, but I don't know what's going to keep me from whipping his ass," he boasted.

"Why did you go to meet Dennis Walsh?" she continued.

"Truthfully? I wanted to knock him in the mouth," he replied.

"Tell us what happened," the clever prosecutor invited.

"We went in the bar. We started shooting pool and drinking beer, and then Dennis came in. I told him, 'Hey, what's up.' He told me, 'I want to talk to you.' I said, 'Truthfully, I don't want to talk to you. I just want to take you out back.' Jimmy told me, 'No, you can't do that.' Blah, blah, blah. He started telling me about the murder of his brother. I told him I really didn't care about it," he said.

"He's the one who got you busted with how much dope?" she questioned.

"It was a little over three and a half pounds of dope," he admitted.

"He's the guy that basically got you ten years in state prison, correct?" she asked, her voice laden with sarcasm.

"Yes, he did," he answered meekly.

"Now, when you saw Dennis Walsh in that bar, the guy that got you busted and got you ten years in state prison, you didn't take him outside and beat him up, did you?" she asked in her almost patented manner of turning a question into a statement.

"No, I didn't," he replied even more meekly.

"You sat down with him in a booth, correct?" she asked.

"Yes," he admitted.

"Was he yelling and screaming at you?" she asked.

"No, he was trying to be real cool and calm. I was doing the yelling," he ventured. "I called him a rat and a punk. I told him, 'I really don't appreciate what you did to me.'"

"Tell the jury what Dennis Walsh said to you," she said.

"He wanted me to help him catch Jeff Weaver and the other guys," he answered.

"Did you tell him that Jeff Weaver was the one who took the last shot," she asked.

"No, I didn't. Dennis Walsh told me that," he answered. "He said he knows Jeff Weaver took the last shot. I told him, 'Hey, maybe you owe him a thank-you now that you are not stuck wiping your brother's ass for the rest of his life.'"

"Actually, did you tell the detectives what you told Dennis Walsh was 'If that's what he did, he took your brother out of his misery'?" she challenged.

"Pretty much like what I just said," he responded.

Mercatoris had just unwittingly confirmed what porn actress Diane Stewart finally confessed, that Weaver said he fired the final shot to put Christopher out of his misery.

DDA Sparagna had just effectively eviscerated and skinned the hapless Don Lee Mercatoris with the skill of a professional taxidermist. She should have had been awarded the privilege of nailing his worn-out hide to the courtroom wall.

Mercatoris had been serving his time at a fire camp in Jamestown, nestled in the foothills of the high Sierras. The opportunity to spend time outdoors in the fresh air instead of in a fetid jail cell made it a much-coveted designation among prison inmates. Instead of being returned to the fire camp, however, Mercatoris was somehow shipped to Mule Creek State Prison to serve out the rest of his time. I heard it's a real shithole. Some say it was a little barn swallow that arranged for his new accommodations. As I tried to tell him, nobody walks.

When Kathy informed me of Mercatoris's testimony, I was already in a foul mood. The Cleveland Indians had just been knocked out of the playoffs after being up on the Boston Red Sox three games to one in the American League Championship series. The meth cook's recollection of our paths crossing differed markedly from mine.

"He said he was going to kick my ass?" I asked incredulously.

Kathy neglected to mention the part about me not having to care for my brother the rest of his life. I wouldn't learn that until closing arguments. It was just as well. I had other matters to be concerned with.

Detective Fleming called later that evening. "Fleming here," he said as usual. "The DA wants you in Department 107 at eight thirty sharp. You're going to be testifying, Dennis, so get a good night's sleep."

16

A TROUT IN THE MILK

I T WAS TIME TO PUT up or shut up. I made a tactical decision not to review my notes prior to testifying. After I had surrendered my "journal" to DDA Sparagna, Detective Fleming had returned a copy of it to me. The detective may have been a crackerjack investigator, but his secretarial skills were wanting. The file was a complete mess. Hundreds of pages were out of order. Legal-size pages were overlapped onto two letter-size pages. I had been able to rifle through my file to retrieve a phone number or review notes from a particular day. Now I might as well be skimming through the children's book *Where's Waldo?*

I had lived and breathed this case for four and a half years. I had nothing to hide. Both sides had my notes to refresh my memory, if necessary. I went into this thing on a wing and a prayer. I might as well go out that way.

The Buckweed wildfire was still burning out of control. The fire would lie down at night when the temperature cooled and flame up in the early morning with renewed vigor. Just in case the fire jumped the canyon and headed my way, I made arrangements for Dave and Sharon Bullard to evacuate Johnny Rio and Frank the Cat. As I drove down the canyon at 5:45 A.M., miles of smoldering embers lighting up the mountain ridge did nothing to ease my concern.

I dialed Stephanie's number as I was exiting the freeway on Temple Street at around 7 A.M. She was already in her office and answered the phone. I had previously offered to discuss my father's organized crime connections, if necessary, during my testimony.

"Hey, Stephanie, it's me, Dennis," I said. "I thought you might need some theme music."

I cranked up the CD player and put my cell phone near the speaker. *Wah, wah, wah, wah—wah, wah, wah,* wailed the signature bars from the theme song of *The Godfather,* causing Stephanie to laugh heartily.

"Thanks, Dennis," she said, "I needed that. See you in the courtroom."

I drank coffee and read the newspaper in the first-floor cafeteria until the ninth floor opened at 8 A.M. I paced the hallway for half an hour until I spotted DDAs Sparagna, Ambrose, and Ball heading toward Department 107.

"Good morning, Dennis," Stephanie said with a big grin.

"Good morning, Miss Sparagna. Hi, Ann. Hi, Patrick," I replied.

Stephanie had a few more witnesses to call before me. I wound up not taking the stand until around 3 P.M.

In the meantime, an LAPD criminalist gave testimony regarding the side-by-side refrigerator freezer. The prosecution theorized that Steinberg had removed the shelves to stuff Christopher's body inside the refrigerator while he cleaned the apartment and stole a trash barrel from a neighbor.

"The shelves were missing, and it appeared to be very clean. It smelled like it had just been cleaned with a cleanser," the criminalist testified. "If I had to compare it with my refrigerator at home, I think that one was cleaner."

The electrical cord to the refrigerator had been cut, as clearly evident in a photograph. The implication was clear: Who, but the killer, would have bothered to scrub the refrigerator squeaky clean before discarding it?

Next up was an LAPD criminalist from the Firearms Analysis Unit.

She testified that the five bullets extracted from Christopher's body were .22-caliber rimfire, some copper jacketed and some brass jacketed, matching Kenny Williams's signature habit.

"You're going to follow the bug guy," Detective Fleming informed me in the hallway while I was on my cell phone, checking to see if my house had burned down.

Next at bat was David Faulkner, an entomologist. His testimony, based on an analysis of maggots recovered from Christopher's body, served to complete the prosecution's time line, although the time of death could not be conclusively established.

After a recess, I took a seat on the witness stand. Mrs. Benson, the clerk of the court, ushered in Steinberg's green jury and Weaver's red jury. As the jurors filled the jury box to my immediate left and the first two rows of the gallery, it occurred to me that I had not testified as a witness since my father's trial when I was in high school.

Some jurors fiddled with their notebooks, some placed personal items on the floor in front of them, and some looked at me, probably wondering who I was and what I would be telling them. I was wearing a suit and tie and could have been any type of professional.

DDA Sparagna stood up and announced, "The People call Dennis Walsh."

I wouldn't say a hush fell over the crowd, but all twenty-four jurors and twelve alternates stopped what they were doing and directed their attention toward me. They had been hearing my name day after day, almost every day of the trial, and now here I was, in the flesh.

My sister Kathy was seated in the back of the courtroom. I glanced at Steinberg and Weaver, seated in front of me at the counsel table to my right. Steinberg had shaved off his goatee and let his hair grow out just a bit to avoid the skinhead look. He wore the same gray rumpled suit the *Daily News* reporter had commented on. He looked more like an accountant than like a hoodlum, except for the soulless eyes. Those could not be hidden from the jury. Weaver wore a white dress shirt with no tie. He had let his hair grow long and affected the look of a grunge band member rather than a skinhead supremacist. Out of the corner of my right eye, I gave a quick wink to Steinberg.

Here's where I bury you, you gutless prick, I thought to myself.

Seeing him bite down on the corner of his lip told me he got the message.

DDA Sparagna began with some questions to establish that I had been estranged from my brother Christopher since I had bailed him out of jail.

"You still loved your brother?" she asked.

"Absolutely," I answered.

It was the first time I had ever admitted that, even to myself. Since the day I had paced back and forth in front of that dark, cavernous storage facility where my brother's cold, lifeless body lay sealed in a trash barrel, my actions seemed born out of nothing but rage and vengeance. One simple question in front of a roomful of strangers triggered the sudden realization that all I had done over the past four and a half years I had done out of love.

I had to catch myself—I did not intend to give Steinberg and Weaver the satisfaction of seeing me shed a tear. Maybe I wasn't as ready for this as I thought I would be.

DDA Sparagna had me confirm that I had never seen my brother's body nor had I received any details of his injuries from either the coroner's office or the LAPD. One by one, she had me recount my dealings with the cast of characters I had encountered during my odyssey through a netherworld I had never dreamed of visiting.

"You are sitting here today, talking very calmly. Was this the way you spoke to potential witnesses?" she continued.

"No," I replied. "Anybody that I spoke to would tell you I was angry."

"Describe how you spoke to them, generally speaking," she said.

"When they told me they were afraid of these people," I said, pointing at the defendants, "I said, 'These people are nothing to be afraid of, they are gutless back shooters.'"

"Now your voice is rising. Were you upset just talking about your brother?" the prosecutor asked.

"I'm upset to this day. I'm every bit as enraged as when I first heard about it," I answered.

There were several young guys on both juries. I thought maybe they, at least, would get my point.

"What were you worried about with respect to the prosecution of the case involving the death of your brother?" she asked.

"My concern was, I mean no disrespect to the DA's Office or LAPD, but that no one cared," I replied, barely able to hold back my emotions.

"Why did you think nobody would care about the death of your brother?" she continued.

"Because my brother was involved in the same things they are," I answered, nodding toward Steinberg and Weaver.

I noticed my sister wiping her eyes in the back of the courtroom, and it got to me.

"I didn't think anybody would care about his death," I managed to get out, but not without a catch in my voice, ". . . but we cared."

I attempted to explain my intentions and my conduct as best I could as DDA Sparagna questioned me concerning my involvement in the case.

Steinberg's attorney had the first shot at cross-examining me. The thrust of his questioning implied that my initial belief that Steinberg was the killer caused me to gather only that information and those witnesses that supported that contention.

"Information that you were looking for, information that you got, concerned David Steinberg as a suspect?" Steve Hauser asked.

"Some of it concerned David Steinberg, some of it concerned Jeffrey Weaver. I frankly didn't care who it concerned," I responded.

Seymour Amster, Weaver's attorney, followed up with a line of questions that implied my brothers and I could not accept that Christopher was killed by just one man and therefore dragged his client into the mix.

"Was it hard in your mind to believe that one person alone could have killed your brother?" he probed.

"Not when they shot him in the back of the head," I answered sharply.

"Was it hard for you to believe that one person could take out your brother with a gun?" Amster continued.

The implication that I somehow believed that Christopher could not have been slain by a single gunman annoyed me.

"If you were to point a gun at any one of my brothers, you better pull the trigger in a heartbeat. They didn't face him and pull the trigger," I responded.

I could see DDA Sparagna wince slightly, putting her hand to her face to shield her reaction from the jury. When my mother had said basically the same thing to Stephanie prior to the trial, I had likened her to Ma Barker. Perhaps I had taken Amster's bait, but it was difficult to contain my disdain for the two cowardly killers who sat only about fifteen feet away.

Amster was obsessed with the notion that I had violated the court order against talking to witnesses and absolutely incensed that I had not been charged with contempt of court. He was like a butcher's dog with a shoulder bone.

"Did you abide by that order after it was issued?" he asked.

"To the best of my knowledge. I never had a witness list," I answered. "I thought it was void for vagueness, because I didn't know who was a witness and who wasn't. People I thought were witnesses—Cowboy, Kenny Williams, Tina—I never talked to again. I'm sure they've been up here. Ask them. They haven't had any contact with me all that time," I replied.

The void for vagueness doctrine basically means that criminal liability should not attach if it relies on vague, ambiguous, or conflicting legal requirements.

Court was recessed for the day, but Amster continued his rant at a sidebar conference with the DDAs and the judge.

"I believe that law enforcement was aware Dennis Walsh was still having contact with witnesses and they never brought an order to show cause for contempt," he railed.

"Maybe you can give us more specificity," Judge Pastor said. "We will deal with it tomorrow morning."

The next morning, I made the long drive downtown only to find that the trial had been recessed until the next day. Weaver had complained of being moved from his module at county jail during the middle of the night and placed "in the hole," where all inmates were "green-lighted." He said it was payback for having caused Judge Pastor to personally inspect the 3100 row. He claimed that he was now in the hat and feared for his life. He slept for only forty-five minutes, had not been allowed to shower or shave, and was not ready for trial.

Judge Pastor subsequently contacted the jail and learned that a search of Weaver's cell had uncovered a loose razor blade and a makeshift handcuff key, hence the transfer to the hole.

"I will be honest, there is a razor blade," Weaver admitted. "Everybody in the module has razor blades, but I did not have no handcuff key. I will take my time in the hole in 3301 or 4500, not in 3300 or 2300, the green-light hole."

"Mr. Weaver, you are not renting a room at a hotel where you can choose what room you want," Judge Pastor admonished him.

"You don't put somebody where they are going to get hit, get whacked. You are putting me in a position of having me killed or I got to do something to somebody," Weaver pleaded.

Judge Pastor cautioned Weaver that his statements were being recorded by the court reporter and said he would notify the sheriff's department of his safety concerns.

I was ordered to return the next morning. I wondered if Judge Pastor had ever presided over a case with so many headaches.

I got a late start the next morning and hit heavy traffic on the 5. By the time I arrived at the courthouse, it was almost 9 A.M. and the sign at the entrance to the courthouse parking lot read FULL. I drove around the sign, threw my truck into park, left the engine running, and handed the surprised attendant the parking fee along with an extra twenty-dollar bill.

"I'm a witness in a murder trial and I'm late," I explained over my shoulder as I hurriedly limped away, still suffering the effects of my surgery.

When I got upstairs, I was immediately taken aside by DDA Sparagna. "'Void for vagueness,' Dennis? Did you have to say you thought the court order was void for vagueness? Both these juries seem to like you. Just be Chris's big brother. Don't sound like a lawyer," she said. "And by the way, Patrick noticed you almost choked up on the stand yesterday. It's okay to cry, Dennis. You don't have to be a tough guy."

Stephanie omitted telling me that during a sidebar she had just argued that the court order was "vague" by failing to clearly define who was a witness. The judge allowed Seymour Amster to inquire into my contacts with witnesses, but would not allow him to discuss contempt of court in front of the juries.

Less than a minute later, I took the stand. I would be in that seat all day long. Right off the bat, Weaver's attorney approached and handed me my original journal, marked as Defendant's Exhibit D. Holding it reminded me of being a kid when I had finally found the misplaced baseball mitt that I had dutifully oiled and kneaded for months. That file had been my bible.

Amster had me explain various notes detailing conversations with a variety of characters, some who had testified and others who had not been called.

He directed my attention to a notation made on February 7, 2004, after my meeting with Don Mercatoris at the Sundown bar.

I had written, *Don said Weaver put the final shot in CJW's head!*

The exclamation mark became a point of contention. Amster characterized it as a question mark. I was quick to correct his error. He had the page marked as an exhibit. It was obvious that he intended to argue that the notation was in the form of a question and not a declarative statement. During a recess, I told Stephanie that there should be numerous examples of my style of both exclamation points and question marks throughout my notebook. She was way ahead of me and already had them circled. During redirect examination, it was clarified for the juries.

The defense attorneys would later argue that my failure to tell the detectives about Don Mercatoris's comment proved I was lying.

Amster focused on my harsh demeanor with many of the witnesses.

"If you felt somebody was not being truthful or helping you, then you got hot with them to get them to be more helpful?" he queried.

"I didn't want to get hot with anybody," I replied. "If I did, it was a natural reaction when I felt I was being run around the block about information that was pertinent to this case."

"This was a very important investigation to you, correct?" Amster asked.

"My brother was shot in the back of the head, and his body was stuffed in a trash can like a piece of garbage. Okay? So, yeah, it was personal to me, real personal," I retorted emphatically. "For four years, I feel like I have been swimming in a septic tank dealing with these people."

"You sometimes got results when you got mad or hot?" he asked.

"I don't recall getting results from losing my temper, no," I answered.

"When Shane Wilson told you the Walsh family should handle this without the police and you told him, 'You're lucky that is not the case, because you would be dead,' what did you mean?" he inquired.

"That the case was going through the system. That the DA and the LAPD were handling it. That we weren't on the streets killing people. That was the point from the beginning, to make sure that it went through the system," I replied.

At Amster's urging, I related the incident where I threatened to duct-tape a cell phone to Dusty Urban's forehead. I noticed a few jurors smiling. Kathy lowered her head and tried to stifle her laughter. I was certainly not trying to be amusing.

"Did you ever say to anybody, 'How'd you like me to drag you out of that house, you piece of shit. I know you're talking to Weaver. Tell him I'm out there'?" he asked.

"I said that to Little Ricky, Ricky Veloz," I answered.

On redirect, DDA Sparagna asked me to explain my understanding of the court order regarding contacting witnesses.

"I was always in a dilemma as to who was and who wasn't a witness because I didn't know. You didn't share anything with me. The LAPD didn't share any information, so I was kind of operating in the dark," I explained.

"Why did you even speak to anybody about this case?" she asked.

This would probably be my last shot at defending myself in front of the juries.

"From the beginning, I was told that people won't cooperate because they are afraid of these two," I said, nodding in the direction of Steinberg and Weaver. "Or they don't want to be rats. I knew there was evidence out there. I hoped that I could talk to them, tell them about my mother and my family. If they loved Christopher, to please do the right thing, which some of them did. I'll always be indebted to those people who put their own safety at risk."

Finally, I was excused at the end of a long day. I had no clue how the juries had received my testimony.

Stephanie attempted to ease my mind. "The juries loved you, Dennis," she said.

I still didn't know how well I had done. One thing I did know, however, I liked asking questions a hell of a lot better than answering them.

On October 30, when Diane Stewart, aka porn actress Alexandra Quinn, took the stand, the old adage "Truth is stranger than fiction" may never have been more apropos.

It was Kimmi Balmes who first told me of Weaver's prophetic remark, "If they get Diane Stewart, they might as well execute me." Weaver figuratively signed his own death warrant with those eleven words. If he had merely witnessed Christopher gasping and gurgling on the couch, he would hardly have feared catching a ticket to the San Quentin death chamber for a hot shot in the arm. The highly incriminating statement was the reason I had pursued him so relentlessly.

Diane Stewart had always denied that Weaver confessed to pulling the trigger. That is, until she caught a probation violation that landed her in the Ventura County Jail. Suddenly she was frantic to speak with Detective Fleming. On June 1, 2004, Detective Fleming drove to Ventura and interviewed Diane at the jail. She had a change of heart, admitting that Weaver had shown up at her motel room around 6 A.M. and confessed to firing the final shot.

"I don't think I've ever seen anybody so white as a ghost in my life," she told the detective. "He said he shot him. Chris was sitting there for days. He helped him, he helped Chris. Chris was dead, and he wasn't coming back. Jeff said, 'You can never tell anybody.'"

No wonder Detective Fleming had been smiling when I asked him about her being held as a material witness. They finally did get Diane Stewart, but as they say, "It ain't over until it's over."

Three years later, on September 8, 2007, while the prosecutors were busy selecting Weaver's jury, Diane told the detective and DDA Sparagna that she was recanting her jailhouse statement, claiming it had all been a lie. The beleaguered prosecutor had no choice but to impeach her in front of Weaver's jury at trial.

After eliciting testimony that Diane was a porn actress, a nude dancer, and an escort, who loved Weaver "like a brother," DDA Sparagna began to subtly discredit her witness.

"What did you tell the guards in the Ventura County jail?" the deputy DA inquired.

"I woke up in the hole after they put me on lithium. I was in a lithium haze," Diane responded. "I was screaming, 'I'm a witness on a homicide. I need to talk to Detective Fleming out of Devonshire Division.'"

"Despite being on a lithium high, you were able to give the jailers sufficient information to contact this detective in another county. Am I correct?" the prosecutor asked with evident skepticism.

"Yes," Diane replied.

"Tell us about the dream you had in jail," the prosecutor said.

"I dreamed the police put blinders on my eyes and shut me in a room, where I specifically recall seeing a little Asian girl that was cut in half. You could see her whole insides, the meat of her body. All around, people were being sliced up and slaughtered. Then I noticed a porn photographer I knew. He said he had to do this to me because I wasn't telling him what Dennis Walsh wanted me to say. I just remember waking up and pounding on the door, screaming for the police so I could talk to the detectives," she shared.

Jim Cavanaugh said it was difficult to tell which was more remarkable, her alleged dream or the fact that the porn "actress" had managed to finish the dream sequence without someone yelling *"Cut."*

"This dream you had regarding Dennis Walsh, did it make you want to speak to the police?" DDA Sparagna inquired.

"Yes, the fact that he sent this guy after me. I was about to be slaughtered. It was very vivid, very real to me. I was on lithium. I believed it to be true," she answered. "By the time Detective Fleming came to see me, which was a period of time later, I realized that the dream must not have been real. I was afraid, so I proceeded to say what I thought the person that was going to kill me in my dream wanted."

"Did you ever talk to Dennis Walsh?" DDA Sparagna asked.

"No, I just got very threatening messages from Dennis Walsh. 'You two-bit whore, you're hiding Jeff. You need to talk to the police. I'm calling Immigration. If it's the last thing I do, you will never work in the U.S. again.' He would call me every time somebody got arrested. It seemed that he had a lot of pull. When I was living with Kimmi, she had about twenty people coming in and out, half staying there. All of a sudden, everybody was in jail but the two of us," she responded.

She forgot to mention that whenever I called to tell her who had just gotten collared, I would end the call by playing the *Dragnet* theme: *dum-duh-dum-dum.*

"Did you believe Dennis Walsh could cause bodily injury to you if you didn't do what he wanted?" DDA Sparagna rejoined.

"Yes. I wasn't sure that he hadn't put an okay out to have his brother killed. I heard the Walsh family collected for the porn industry. They were feared," she stated.

"Dennis Walsh didn't say, 'Go down to the police and lie, tell them Jeff Weaver fired the last shot at my brother,' did he?" the Deputy DA asked.

"No, I made the decision to say that on my own," she answered.

"What did you tell Detective Fleming that you are now telling the jury is a lie?" DDA Sparagna inquired.

"I told him that Jeff had told me he shot the last shot," she answered.

"Why would you say that if it were a lie?" the prosecutor asked.

"Because I thought it would get me out of jail," the porn actress/nude dancer/escort replied.

"Did you tell Detective Fleming that Jeff told you he was helping Chris when he shot him and put him out of his misery?" DDA Sparagna continued.

"Uhm, I could have. Like I said, that whole statement was a lie," Diane replied.

"Did you tell Detective Fleming that Jeff said that before he shot Chris, he was like a vegetable?" she inquired.

"Possibly, I don't recall," the witness answered.

"Did you tell Detective Fleming that Jeff Weaver said, 'You are going to get me executed'?" the prosecutor asked.

"I possibly did. I'm not sure exactly," she replied.

DDA Sparagna asked, "Did you tell Detective Fleming, that 'after reading the Bible, every day I'm bugged by the fact that I didn't come forward earlier. Whenever he fell asleep, I should have called'?"

"That is possible, but how many times can I tell you I was lying?" Diane responded.

"Jeff was concerned you had ratted him out. Correct, Miss Stewart?" DDA Sparagna asked.

"Yes," she answered. "He told me to go to Canada so I could be out of this. I said, 'I don't have anything to live for. I'm all tweaked out. My business is gone. I'm living in hotels. I'm afraid all the time, so why don't you just kill me?' I wanted him to shoot me up with heroin. So he got some heroin. I checked into a hotel under Kimmi Balmes's name. He had his chance to kill me, but he didn't."

"Did you tell Detective Fleming it was Jeff Weaver who said he was going to kill you because you were the main witness?" the prosecutor asked.

When she could not recall, DDA Sparagna quoted from the interview transcript to further impeach the witness.

"Did Jeff Weaver tell you he took Christopher's sunglasses off his head?" she asked.

"Yes, he did," Diane responded.

When Diane Stewart decided to recant her testimony, she made one crucial mistake: while reviewing a transcript of her prior testimony, in anticipation of her comments regarding Don Mercatoris, she mispronounced the name as *Rikitoris* before they had even reached the portion of the transcript where a typographical error read "Rickitoros." The veteran detective immediately realized that she must have been provided with a copy of the transcript by someone on behalf of Weaver.

During her testimony, Diane inadvertently raised the issue when she repeated the mispronunciation in response to DDA Sparagna's question of whether she felt threatened by me.

"Yes. Especially since I heard that one of the detectives on the case had gotten in trouble because they had brought Dennis Walsh on one of the arrests of Don Rickitoros," she had replied.

DDA Sparagna seized the opportunity to impeach the witness.

"Isn't it true his name is Mercatoris?" she asked.

"I always heard it as *Rickitoros*. It could be," Diane steadfastly insisted.

"Isn't it true that there was a misprint in the transcripts that had the word *Rickitoros* rather than Mercatoris?" DDA Sparagna quickly countered.

"No. I've never seen any transcripts except for the ones you've showed me. You know, I know what you are trying to get at. No. I don't know. Maybe, possibly. I have no idea because I haven't seen any, but I've always said *Rickitoros*," the clearly flustered witness replied.

The jury was already aware that transcripts had been floating in and out of county jail. The damage was already done. The jurors had front-row seats to a seasoned prosecutor doing battle with a ham actress. Detective Fleming testified later that not only did Diane refer to Mercatoris as Rickitoros during her interview after recanting shortly before trial, but also that she made reference to exact phrases or terms before they came up on the audiotape they were reviewing. His testimony supported the inference that Diane must have had access to the transcripts.

Like Don Mercatoris, Diane Stewart had taken the witness stand with a specific agenda, to cover for Jeffrey Weaver by vilifying Dennis Walsh. While it appeared that DDA Sparagna had successfully impeached them both, ultimately it would hinge on how the juries had assessed my credibility.

Although judgment day in the case of *The People v. David Michael Steinberg and Jeffrey Lawrence Weaver* would arrive soon enough, it couldn't be soon enough for me.

Deputy William Gilbert testified to having searched the cells of Steinberg and Weaver on September 17, 2004, which would have been Christopher's thirty-ninth birthday. The search provided a posthumous birthday gift. A kite note recovered from Weaver's cell, addressed to *Jeff*, ending with a lightning bolt and Branch *W/S,* signifying the Branch of David and Weaver/Steinberg. The kite was signed, *As always, Silent Thunder.* It read:

> *I'm against anyone who was or is in the gang then rolls over. Shane, Troy, all the guys upstairs, they are my enemies. My job is to turn them around when I can or put them down if I cannot. I don't like explaining my tactics or my strategy. Are you familiar with the word "stratagem"? It is a cunning plan or scheme especially for deceiving an enemy. I can be quite clever, and one thing I have learned is that the less people know about your plan, the more likely you will succeed. Anyhow, Shane is the enemy now. He can smile, send his love, and tell you he is sorry, but if he is truly sorry he won't take the stand.*

It was now November 2, six weeks into the trial. Out of the presence of the juries and prosecutors, Steinberg once again attempted to have his attorney removed. The judge denied the request. Judge Pastor had been like a juggler juggling live grenades. He was masterfully issuing limiting instructions to either jury regarding evidence they should not consider in their particular case, excluding one jury from hearing certain testimony, making sidebar rulings, and dealing with the defendants' complaints regarding mistreatment at the county jail.

"Miss Sparagna, do the People have any additional witnesses to call at this time?" Judge Pastor inquired.

"No, Your Honor," the prosecutor replied. "At this time, the People rest."

Defense motions to dismiss the charges were denied.

Now Steinberg and Weaver would have the opportunity to defend themselves, something Christopher never had a chance to do. My money said Steinberg would take the stand. Weaver was as dumb as a fence post. Amster would have to be out of his mind to let him testify. All the cards would be on the table soon enough.

On November 5, a member of the red jury was excused after failing to report to court due to an emergency appendectomy. He was promptly replaced by an alternate juror.

Steinberg's attorney called his first witness to the stand, Robert "Bigfoot" Dragusica. His testimony mainly concerned having thrown a couple of Shane Wilson's pistols off the Malibu pier while Wilson was in custody, characterizing Robert "Mouse" Hayes as a liar, and stating that Shane Wilson said he believed it was the Mexican Mafia, not Steinberg, that had him stabbed.

Next up was Detective Cochran. He admitted that Shane Wilson had initially denied any involvement in the murder. He conceded to pressuring Wilson.

"You can be a witness or you can be a suspect. What you say to us is going to determine whether the DA files charges or not," he had told Wilson.

Jennifer Hull took the stand and hedged on her statement to police that she had slept with both Weaver and Shane Wilson, and that both had confessed to the murder.

"Like I told you, Steven Hauser, I was telling these cops pretty much what they wanted to hear," she testified.

Later in the afternoon, Mrs. Benson herded the two juries into the courtroom, where they were greeted by the sight of Steinberg perched on the witness stand. Career criminal David Michael Steinberg would have to deliver the performance of a lifetime, or spend the rest of his natural life in the custody of the California Department of Corrections.

After first admitting to some prior felony convictions, Steinberg took a swipe at Christopher, characterizing him as a "kind of the school bully" in high school. They rekindled their friendship in late 2002 and began to engage in credit card fraud. He admitted to confronting Moises "Joey" Tovar at Marta Wilson's house with a .40-caliber Glock he carried in a hollowed-out book. He claimed to have disarmed Tovar after Tovar lifted his shirt and exposed his weapon.

"Why did you do that?" Hauser asked.

"I didn't want him to shoot me," Steinberg replied.

He was pleading self-defense to the assault on Tovar.

Hauser moved on to the assault on Deputy Dixon. Steinberg claimed he had driven George Jassick's Cadillac to Christopher's town house to pick up a new refrigerator from Kevin McCarthy. He had come down the stairs into the garage and "observed" Alex Dixon.

"What did you see?" his attorney asked.

"I saw Alex Dixon really gesticulating with the gun or gesturing with the gun. I didn't know who he was. He was saying, 'Who the fuck do you think you are? You don't own this fucking place,'" Steinberg answered.

Pat Murphy later described Steinberg's comment to me.

"This arrogant bastard couldn't just say *pointing*. It had to be *gesticulating*," Pat groused. "Is there even such a word as gesticulating? Den, I can't believe these juries are buying any of his bullshit."

As far as which of my buddies was most indignant over the testimony of various witnesses, Pat and Jim Cavanaugh were running neck and neck. It didn't take much to set their Irish blood aboil.

"What were you thinking at the time?" Hauser asked.

"I thought this guy was going to kill Chris. I grabbed the gun and put a bullet in the pipe and pointed it at Alex Dixon. I told him to freeze," he responded. "He moved the gun towards me and started running backwards. I fired into the air," he explained.

Steinberg said he fired twice, but did not intend to shoot Dixon.

"And your intent was to?" Hauser asked.

"Dissuade him," Steinberg responded.

Self-defense again. He was merely protecting himself and Christopher. Surely the jury would understand.

He was asked about being shirtless when Amy Sheeley and Desiree Manthe picked him up.

"I took off my sweater and a sweatshirt as I hopped the fence, for no other reason. I was just burning up."

His description of what happened next rivaled Diane Stewart's Fellini-like dream sequence.

"I ran down to my friend's metal fabricating shop. He had a rottweiler named Gus, but I hadn't seen him in years. It was wagging its tail. I put my face up to him. I saw the tag and it wasn't Gus. I don't remember the name, but it clearly wasn't Gus. The dog went for, really, my throat. It got my arm, pulled my arm down and regrabbed my throat. It was on a chain, and as I was backing up, his mouth was closing, and, oh well, it didn't—fortunately it didn't get me. I took my T-shirt off and tried to lead the dog away by throwing it so I could run up and knock on the door," he offered with a straight face.

Apparently, the all-purpose self-defense theory even covered his run-in with Gus's doppelgänger.

Trial was recessed for the day. After the jurors spilled out into the hall-way, Pat Murphy almost flew out of the courtroom. Two of Steinberg's friends, Tim Miller and Jeff Smith, had sat in on the proceedings as well.

Pat could barely contain his anger. "Den, you should have seen that weasel Steinberg after the juries left. He strutted off the stand with his chest stuck out like a peacock, smirking at his two idiot buddies like he just pulled one over," Pat fumed.

Steinberg clearly fancied himself as a Svengali who was going to sweet-talk his jury into an acquittal.

I glared at Steinberg's hoodlum pals as they walked past. Earlier in the trial, Jeff Smith had followed my sister Kathy to the restroom, waited until she came out, and then followed her outside. When Kathy told me about it, I was tempted to take matters into my own hands. Had I done that, I have no doubt Stephanie Sparagna would have gone into full cardiac arrest. If a juror witnessed any such altercation, it could cause a mistrial. Instead, I informed Detective Fleming. After that, Deputy Jason Jones was kind enough to escort Kathy to the Metro Rail whenever she was alone.

The next day, Silent Thunder resumed his testimony.

"Was there any truth to what Cowboy said about setting up some organization and having you lead this group?" his attorney questioned.

"Absolutely not. That is ridiculous," he denied.

"What did Chris say about the incident with Deputy Dixon?" Steve Hauser asked.

"He always said, 'This is the guy who saved my life,'" he replied.

He admitted to seeing a copy of the police report of the shoot-out.

"Chris was proud of not talking to the police. That is the way he was brought up with his dad. He wanted everybody to know he was a stand-up guy. It wasn't because anybody accused him of being a rat. No one would have done that to Chris, and not at least gotten a black eye," he responded.

He had no reason to kill Christopher. Chris wasn't going to rat him out, and the cops had to know he only fired in self-defense. Surely the jury would see that.

"I knew I was a suspect, but I thought Mr. Dixon was at fault. I thought maybe the cops came to the same conclusion or I would have been arrested already," he explained.

He denied buying Christopher a cell phone for any criminal purposes.

"It was so I could get ahold of him. He always had an excuse about his pager. I cared about him. He was my friend and I was getting his life straightened out," he explained.

He was no killer: he was a Good Samaritan. Surely the jury could see that.

It was Shane Wilson and Cowboy who moved furniture out of his apartment when Christopher was missing, not him. He admitted to possessing a key to Carolyn Vasquez's storage unit. He claimed he wanted to replace Christopher's sectional couch.

"Although I thought it was a very nice couch, it didn't fit the apartment. It was huge," he declared.

Steinberg alleged that Christopher gave him the large sectional couch as a gift after Steinberg's own sofa had mysteriously disappeared.

"So he just gave you the couch that Michelle O'Halloran purchased for five thousand dollars?" she asked.

He claimed not to have known the value of the couch at that time, and denied that George Jassick had offered to buy it for a thousand dollars.

"I don't remember ever bringing up the thousand dollars. I think he is confused on something else that transpired."

According to him, the stains on the carpet and couch were easily explained. He didn't notice them until Monday. The night before, Christopher, Cowboy, Shane Wilson, George Jassick, and others had been at the apartment, dividing up stolen burglar tools and eating pizzas that been delivered.

"The stain on the carpet appeared like somebody dropped a pizza. It seemed chunky, like tomato paste. The stain on the couch didn't look like blood. It appeared to be wine, wine cooler. It was pink. A stain by the sliding glass door looked like rust. Chris's friends were disrespecting my house. It was just par for the course, just more of the same," he exclaimed.

He said he borrowed George Jassick's Shop-Vac to clean up the mess.

The "pizza stain" came out, but the stains on the couch and near the patio door were more of a problem.

"The stains weren't coming out, and I sort of abandoned the project," he related.

He claimed he left the Shop-Vac on the patio for no particular reason.

"I just left it there and really didn't have any thoughts about it," he explained.

Steinberg denied ever having blue recycle bins in the apartment, ever summoning Weaver and Wilson to the apartment and saying he had to shoot Chris, and knowing if Christopher owned a .22-caliber pistol.

"Do you know how Chris died?" his attorney asked.

"I do now," he answered, perhaps a bit too eagerly.

"Personal knowledge?" Hauser inquired.

"Oh, no," Steinberg innocently proclaimed.

DDA Sparagna stood up and began her cross-examination. I was in the hallway climbing the walls, every bit as worried as Steinberg must have been sitting in county jail with a body stashed in a trash barrel. I still wasn't sure how things would shake out, but I had no doubt Stephanie Sparagna was locked and loaded, with Silent Thunder trained in her sights.

She started by having Steinberg admit that he was a liar and a "scam artist." Next she had Steinberg read aloud from a kite he had written. It offered the juries a telling insight into the psyche of David Michael Steinberg.

"I grew up in the martial arts. . . . As my talents developed, a new understanding was formed. . . . Eastern philosophy. This is where I developed my own understanding of truth. . . . Facts are not the same thing as the truth. The truth is the way something must be to satisfy your obligations. To me, it is a complete analysis and the will to do what you think is right. Almost any educated man could realize this sagacity, but is this a fact or truth? For me, it is both. My sincere beliefs in God as depicted in the Holy Bible give me the best kind of understanding," he read.

"Was the book in which you placed a gun the Holy Bible?" DDA Sparagna asked.

"No, it was a book of stories on the Bible," Steinberg clarified, as if that were less sacrilegious.

He admitted the pages were cut out in the shape of a gun, and that the book was used to conceal the .40-caliber Glock that he had fired at Deputy Dixon. He stated that Kenny Williams was "lying or mistaken" when he testified to having given him a .22-caliber Colt Challenger.

"Why did you go with Chris to talk to Michelle O'Halloran's attorney?" DDA Sparagna inquired.

"I felt I had insight into criminal law. I wanted to be helpful," he answered.

"Chris looked up to you. He thought you were very clever when it came to the law. Correct, Mr. Steinberg?" the prosecutor asked.

"Clever? I don't know what he thought, but I think he thought something similar to that," he replied.

He earnestly offered that he only meant to help out Michelle, despite not having seen her for twenty years.

"Was there a fear that she might have ratted on you and Christopher Walsh for the shooting at Deputy Dixon unless someone got her out of custody?" the clever prosecutor inquired.

"No," the self-proclaimed clever defendant answered.

Court was recessed for the day. Pat Murphy gave DDA Sparagna glowing reviews. Had we been in the theater, I would have waited at the stage door with a dozen roses.

The next morning, Steinberg was not transported to the courtroom until 10 A.M. due to a dispute with a new jailer who would not allow him to wear a long john shirt under his county jumpsuit. Defendants did not change into their trial clothing until they reached the courtroom lockup. Steinberg refused to board the bus. Finally a senior deputy okayed the long john.

Judge Pastor was not happy over the thirty-minute delay. "Deputy

Jones is going to find who I can speak to about this latest issue about underwear. That's what it's come to. I have thirty-five jurors who are being inconvenienced," the exasperated judge announced.

DDA Sparagna wasted no time when Steinberg resumed his testimony. He admitted to having a driver's license and a credit card in the name of Frank Levy. Silent Thunder was a name given to him by a friend in jail.

"What does it mean?" DDA Sparagna asked him.

"It means lightning," he said.

"Silent Thunder means lightning?" she asked with a hint of disbelief.

"Yes," he replied in tacit confirmation of his stated philosophy that facts are not the same thing as the truth.

He admitted that when he signs his name as Silent Thunder, he follows it with a lightning bolt "just for the heck of it."

He denied knowing how he got possession of actress Dana Delany's credit card or the twenty-thousand-dollar check payable to her that I had given to Detective Fleming. He admitted passing copies of transcripts to George Jassick and Shane Wilson and to receiving a kite from other inmates acknowledging receipt of transcripts of Shane Wilson and Jimmy Bray's statements. He admitted "cracking" the kid at the dry cleaners.

"Because I thought he was coming at me," he explained.

Steinberg had gone to the well one too many times.

DDA Sparagna seized the opportunity. "So you were only acting in self-defense, correct?" she asked.

"Yes," he responded.

"Self-defense with Deputy Dixon, correct?" she continued.

"Correct," he said.

"Self-defense with Joey, Moises Tovar?" she pressed further.

"Yes," he replied.

"Self-defense with Gus the dog, correct?"

"What?" Judge Pastor interjected.

"Yes, self-defense," Steinberg answered.

"Excuse me, Your Honor," Steinberg's attorney said. "It wasn't Gus. He thought it was Gus."

Later Pat Murphy cracked, "Thank God his attorney cleared Gus. The over/under in Vegas on how many times Steinberg will claim self-defense just went up to forty."

The prosecutor got Steinberg to admit that his study partner in the jail law library when he was pro per was Michael "Mosca" Torres, a reputed member of *Eme,* the Mexican Mafia. A deputy sheriff had pulled a kite signed by Mosca from Steinberg's pocket one day after he returned from court.

"How did you get in possession of that kite?" the Deputy DA asked.

"I don't know. It was a surprise. It was just pulled out of my pocket," he claimed.

David Michael Steinberg, always the victim. Surely the jury would see that.

"Did you attempt to start your own organization called the Branch?" DDA Sparagna inquired.

"Yes, he replied. "It's from Jeremiah 23:5. It talks about the raising of a cane from the branch of David that will unite all the tribes."

"Do you see yourself as a leader amongst men?" she asked.

"Sometimes. I hope that is the case," he responded.

DDA Sparagna had no idea she was about to hit the lotto when she directed Steinberg's attention to People's Exhibit 40.

"The Rolex watch found in your jewelry box belonged to Chris, correct?" the prosecutor asked.

"Yes, but it is a fake," he claimed. "A friend of mine had sold the watch to Chris. He took it back to get fixed and my friend wouldn't give it back because Chris still owed him money. I paid my friend off and that's how I ended up with the watch."

Steinberg had painted himself as the savior, while throwing Christopher under the bus as a deadbeat. Surely the jury would see what a good friend he was.

Trial was recessed for the day. Detective Fleming was grinning like he had just solved the infamous Black Dahlia murder case. Stephanie Sparagna and Ann Ambrose seemed downright gleeful as they hurried off, wheeling boxes of legal materials behind them. Something was going on, but as Don Mercatoris might have said, "Nobody told me nothing."

The next morning during redirect examination, Steinberg's attorney addressed the issue of Steinberg's fingerprints. He readily admitted going to Carolyn Vasquez's storage unit on June 27 only to discover that the ecstacy tabs were missing.

"I tore the storage unit apart," he claimed. "Quite frankly, I'm surprised that my fingerprints aren't on more of the items."

He claimed that the refrigerator that was moved from his apartment was an "over and under," not a side-by-side. It was "greenish tan," not white.

Steinberg was excused and Steve Hauser rested his case.

Seymour Amster told the court that Weaver had chosen to exercise his Fifth Amendment right not to testify, hardly a surprise. The surprise was when DDA Sparagna informed me that Jimmy Bray was in lockup. He was being called as a witness for Weaver.

I immediately called my brother Tim. "What the hell is Jimmy doing testifying for Weaver?" I asked.

"I don't know, Dennis. Jimmy ain't gonna fuck us over. Ask Stephanie if I can sit in the courtroom when he testifies," Tim said.

"Like the scene in *The Godfather*? That'll go over real big, Tim," I replied.

"What the hell could Jimmy Bray possibly say to help Weaver?" I wondered.

Weaver's attorney elected to deliver the opening statement he had waived at the beginning of the trial. He told the jury that Weaver's defense would be focused around Dr. Terrence McGee, an expert in methamphetamine use, who would show that witnesses who are meth users are not reliable. They didn't care about the truth; they cared only about getting their meth.

Dr. McGee took the stand and testified as advertised.

Next up, Seymour Amster called Detective Fleming. He grilled the detective all day long and into the next morning on his contacts with me and with Cowboy. Ivan Masabanda, Diane Stewart's boyfriend, testified while chained to the witness stand in his jailhouse jumpsuit. He denied hearing Weaver tell Cowboy that he *did* Chris. He denied that Jeff Weaver asked him to kill Diane Stewart.

"Did you tell Mr. Amster and his investigator that Jeff told you to get Diane out of the way?" DDA Ambrose cross-examined.

"Yeah, I probably recall that," Ivan replied.

"Did Jeffrey tell you to get Diane out of the way?" DDA Ambrose asked.

"No, they were the ones who told me that," he responded. "I heard it from the gentleman sitting next to Jeff Weaver, which happens to be his attorney, I believe."

"Have you ever beaten Diane Stewart?" DDA Ambrose asked.

"Yes, I have hit her. Beaten is a little bit strong. I bear-pawed her once, meaning I slapped her," he answered.

DDA Ambrose asked the ex-boxer to stand up and show the juries his hands.

It made for one of the more dramatic moments in the trial when Ivan attempted to stand while shackled to the chair.

"Well, I might bring up the chair with me," he said as he could only crouch above his chair, a few feet from the wide-eyed jury. A bailiff jumped to position himself between the burly inmate and the jury, as if to protect them. His chains were loosened so he could exhibit his fists, which resembled canned hams.

DDA Ambrose had made her point. Diane Stewart had testified to being afraid of Ivan Masabanda. It was evident that Ivan Masabanda was someone to be feared.

Weaver's next witness was Kevin McCarthy. He testified I had demanded that he meet with me. He said I told him that Weaver had fired the last shot, but also said he had already "heard it through the grapevine."

During cross-examination, he stated that I never asked him to go to the police and say that Weaver had fired the last shot.

"Why did you feel you had to go meet with Dennis Walsh in the first place?" DDA Sparagna asked.

"Because you don't say no to those guys. You go down to see them. They are the Walsh brothers, you know. They are friends of mine. They are like the tough guys in high school, guys who got in fights and things," he replied.

Weaver's own witness had just changed the perception of the Mafia-like Walsh brothers to the "tough guys in high school."

After McCarthy and the juries were excused, Weaver's attorney put up a ferocious battle to admit tapes of messages Dan and I had left for Christina Karath after she failed to produce cell phone records. Judge Pastor refused to admit the tapes, ruling that the highly inflammatory content of the message made the tapes more prejudicial than probative. Seymour Amster was fuming, but the real fireworks were just getting started.

Detective Fleming came out into the hallway and peered around until he spotted me sitting on bench against the wall. As he walked toward me, I could see the same broad grin he had flashed two days earlier.

"Don't go anywhere, Dennis. This is gonna be good," he promised before heading back into the courtroom.

Inside the courtroom, DDA Ambrose made a startling admission. During Steinberg's testimony, as he went to such great lengths to characterize Christopher's Rolex watch as a fake, she had picked up the plastic evidence bag to see just how obvious a knockoff it was. While examining the watch, she noticed a bright green material on the bottom of the watch, in the crevices and in the coils of the band.

"Oh, my God, John," she had whispered to Detective Fleming, "doesn't this green goo look like the foam that was used to seal the lid of the trash barrel?" she asked.

The significance of the find was staggering. The murderer clearly wore this watch when he sealed Christopher's body in the blue trash barrel that had become his coffin.

Detective Fleming told me later that as Ann made her revelation to the judge, Steinberg's jaw dropped and he mouthed the word *Fuck*. His attorney argued that it should be inadmissible since the Rolex had sat in the evidence locker for four and a half years and had not been scientifically analyzed. Ann Ambrose argued that the watch had been recovered from the Moorpark Street apartment and bagged and tagged accordingly. It was never in contact with items recovered from the storage facility, where it could have been contaminated with the Space Invader foam sealant.

The trial was into its second month. There would be no time for scientific testing. Judge Pastor ruled that the watch was admissible, but that the prosecution would be precluded from arguing that it was, in fact, the same substance. The jurors could examine the substance and decide whether the color, texture, and consistency matched the foam sealant.

"Holy shit, this stuff only happens on *Perry Mason*," I crowed when Detective Fleming related the good fortune.

On my drive home, I called as many friends and family members as I could contact to spread the good news. It wasn't until I lost cell phone reception in the canyon heading home that I had time to reflect on the situation. Clients would often downplay a case against them as "only circumstantial." I routinely quoted Henry David Thoreau while trying to explain the value of circumstantial evidence.

"Some circumstantial evidence is very strong, as when you find a trout in the milk," Thoreau had said.

"That ain't no Rolex, Christopher, it's the goddamned trout in the milk!" I bellowed out the window of my truck as I sped up the canyon.

17

"ALL IT TAKES FOR EVIL TO TRIUMPH IS FOR GOOD PEOPLE TO STAND BY AND DO NOTHING"

IT WAS NOW NOVEMBER 19. Weaver's attorney rested his case. The juries were excused for the Thanksgiving holiday. Steinberg's jury was ordered back on November 29 for closing arguments. The attorneys began the laborious process of dealing with exhibits and jury instructions. Jury instructions are guidelines instructing the jury how to apply the law to the facts of the case. Seymour Amster, ever the butcher's dog, proposed a special jury instruction dealing with judging my credibility on the basis of my having violated a court order. Judge Pastor declined to issue the instruction.

The next nine days crawled by almost as slowly as the seventy-eight days Weaver had been on the streets. DDA Sparagna had acquiesced to my request to sit in on the closing arguments.

Between the jurors and the Walsh family and friends, Department 107 was packed. Extra deputies were assigned to the courtroom as the now infamous Walsh brothers—Tim, Dan, Bobby, and myself—were present in full force. My sisters, Kathy and Laura, were on hand as well. Because of the gruesome details of the murder, we felt it best that our mother not attend. Barry "the Shooter" White and a group of Christopher's lifelong friends sat in anticipation of finally learning the facts of their friend's untimely demise. Pat Murphy and Jim Cavanaugh, who had been my eyes and ears throughout the trial, joined the crowd.

Over the last four and a half years, Cavanaugh, with his obviously Irish mug, had been mistaken as one of the Walsh brothers on several occasions.

A female sheriff's deputy took one look at Tim, clad in the same black leather coat he had worn while lumping up Weaver, leaned over, and whispered in Cavanaugh's ear. "He's your brother, if he tries to come over the railing, he's all yours."

I was returning from the men's room when Stephanie Sparagna caught me in the hallway.

She clearly had a lot on her mind. "Dennis, please talk to your brothers and all those other guys in there. I don't want anything happening in that courtroom. No faces, no comments, and no mad-dogging the defendants. Okay?" she asked without really asking.

"Yes, Miss Sparagna," I replied as Detective Fleming walked up.

Stephanie turned as she latched on to the handle of the courtroom door.

"John, you're in charge of the Walsh brothers," she said before ducking into Department 107.

"Great," the veteran detective muttered.

The entire morning session was devoted to reading the jury instructions to the green jury. A man and a woman sitting next to me had arrived late and squeezed into the pewlike court bench. During the lunch hour recess, I bumped into them in the cafeteria. It turned out they were Stephanie's parents. They had flown in from out of state. I complimented Stephanie's stellar work on the case.

"This case is all she has talked about over the last few years," her father told me.

"Did you know Stephanie didn't even go to law school until she was thirty and that she used to be a schoolteacher?" her mother interjected.

"No, but that sure explains a lot," I replied.

At 1:20 P.M., Steinberg's jury took their seats in the jury box for the afternoon session. DDA Sparagna approached the lectern while DDAs

Ambrose and Ball sat at the counsel table with Detectives Fleming and Cochran. Steinberg and Weaver sat with their lawyers on the left side of the counsel table.

"It's been a long time since I spoke to you," she began.

She proceeded to discuss the circumstantial nature of the prosecution's case and their duties as jurors in applying the law to the facts. She was hardly delicate in describing Christopher's chosen lifestyle.

"Christopher Walsh is what is referred to as the unpopular victim, but the laws are meant to protect even Christopher Walsh. Our laws don't judge the quality of life. Our laws give meaningfulness to life itself. Remember Dennis Walsh? He worried that nobody would care. Witnesses aren't going to care, the police aren't going to care, nobody is going to care about his kid brother. Well, the law cares," she said.

The facts of both cases, the assault on Deputy Dixon and the murder, were recounted by highlighting the testimony of the numerous witnesses and the voluminous physical evidence.

"This man was put in a trash can, dumped in that trash can headfirst. No care, no remorse, no accident, no mistake. A human being as disposable to the murderer as some piece of trash, maggot ridden and decomposing in a mausoleum-like catacomb. Gunshot wounds consistent with Chris having been shot by a coward," she said, emphasizing the word coward.

The ability of "the warrior king Silent Thunder" to get others to do his bidding was addressed with biting sarcasm.

"'I sign with a lightning bolt, my name is Silent Thunder. I have soldiers.' He's used to people paying homage. 'Carolyn, I need some furniture and clothes.' 'Gary, get me an apartment.' 'George, I need a U-Haul. How about a Shop-Vac?' There are people that get others to do for them, that suck them into their web.

"You also heard about the one guy who wasn't buying his gig," she pointed out. "The one guy nicknamed I Am Going to Fucking Kill You, Chris Walsh. Remember what Jeff said to Shane, 'Chris was disrespecting David.'"

The feisty prosecutor was unable to mask her disdain for Steinberg, dismissing the episode with Gus the dog as a "stupid story" fabricated to cover Steinberg's true intention of preventing witnesses from identifying him.

The cut to Christopher's face was emphasized in support of the special allegation of killing a witness.

"It's a signature, a very distinct, unique signature, consistent with the mark of a snitch," the Deputy DA proclaimed.

The issue of the credibility of the prosecution's witnesses was tackled head-on.

"I actually brought a neo-Nazi, a Nazi Low Rider—swastikas, lightning bolts, and all—into court. I am going to argue that he should be believed over the Jewish guy, David Steinberg. We didn't just bring in Tony Shane Wilson. We brought in a cast, a host of people who, each unbeknownst to the other, was corroborating one another. We brought you people as they are—liars, thieves, drug addicts, and felons. Boy, you got a real taste of some interesting characters. We watched you watching this case with equal parts horror and fascination, but this isn't *Pulp Fiction*. This is reality," she pleaded her case.

"When crimes are committed in hell, don't expect angels for witnesses," DDA Sparagna remarked with dramatic flair.

"Now, ladies and gentlemen," she continued, "I am conscious of who these people are. I didn't stand on the street corner and say, 'Oh, you, Mr. Butcher, Mr. Baker, Mr. Candlestick Maker, come and be a witness in this case.' You know who picked these witnesses? David Steinberg handpicked every one of these witnesses."

At 4:20 P.M., the green jury was excused for the day. DDA Sparagna estimated that she could conclude her argument in less than an hour. Judge Pastor asked Steinberg's attorney how long he thought his closing argument might be.

"It's going to be probably the longest argument I have ever made," Steve Hauser answered.

My family and friends were buoyed by Stephanie's powerful presentation. I didn't want to burst anybody's bubble, but this was merely the calm before the storm. From day one, I had expected the defense attorneys to savagely attack the prosecution's case, without sparing me. I kept my concerns to myself.

The next day, the proceedings were delayed for over an hour due to a thunderstorm. Even the slightest hint of rain usually paralyzed the L.A. freeways. A little after 10 A.M., DDA Sparagna stood in front of another packed courtroom to conclude the prosecution's closing argument. Due to the high hurdle of proving guilt beyond a reasonable doubt, the government would be afforded one final rebuttal argument following the defense's closing argument.

"The murderers in this case were clever and cunning, but not clever and cunning enough," Stephanie told the green jury. "Things went awry as they normally do. Every Napoléon has his Waterloo. They did not expect people to miss Chris and be looking for him. That was not supposed to happen."

She hammered away at Diane Stewart's recanted testimony.

"Once again it's the Walsh card, the evil Walsh brothers. 'I had a dream and Dennis was in it.' They kind of overplayed that card," she said.

DDA Sparagna ended her argument with the proverbial "trout in the milk."

"Take a real good look at that watch. You are going to see green goo on it. You are going to say to yourselves, 'The watch belongs to the murderer.' Amazing, amazing story. I stand here on behalf of the People of the State of California. I ask you to examine all of the evidence in this case and I ask you to find defendant David Steinberg guilty of the murder of Christopher Walsh," she pleaded.

I've heard a lot of closing arguments, but have to say that DDA Sparagna's heartfelt plea to the jury was nothing less than electrifying.

Steinberg's attorney then rose to address the jury. He wasted no time in painting his client as the innocent victim, wrongly accused of this horrible crime.

"A noted jurist once said, 'Our criminal justice system is always haunted by the ghosts of the innocent men convicted,'" Steve Hauser began.

He recited the biblical story of Joseph and the multicolored robe to counter the weight of the circumstantial evidence presented by the prosecution.

"So when you look at circumstantial evidence, you must reject it if there are two reasonable interpretations," he argued.

Hauser spent the next couple of hours attacking every shred of physical evidence and the testimony of every prosecution witness, presenting alternate theories for every prosecution theory.

"Chris was most likely killed by Shankster and put in that storage locker," Hauser contended.

Suprisingly enough, he barely mentioned my involvement, which was fine with me. He did such a capable job of planting the seed of reasonable doubt that my family and friends were noticeably glum.

"We shoulda just killed these no-good fuckers from the get-go," my brother Tim complained, standing next to me at the urinals.

"The prosecution has one more crack at it, Tim," I replied. "Just sit back and enjoy the show."

DDA Ann Ambrose stepped up to deliver the prosecution's rebuttal argument. She was more than up for the task.

"The defense attorney said the People's witnesses have no credibility, their case rests solely on the testimony of Tony Shane Wilson. If you don't believe him, then it's a big old not guilty. Well, not true. There is more than enough evidence to convict David Steinberg without calling a single meth-addicted convicted felon, porn star, or Nazi Low Rider. Let me pretend this is an episode of *Law and Order*," the redheaded prosecutor began.

A picture of the large blue trash barrel swathed in Bubble Wrap inside the dark storage locker was projected onto the large screen hanging from the ceiling across the court room.

"Da-doink," she said, echoing the iconic theme sound from the popular television crime series.

DDA Ambrose proceeded with her PowerPoint presentation. Pictures of the physical evidence from the storage unit followed. The Space Invader foam sealant can, the latex gloves, Christopher's high school yearbook, his Blockbuster card, pictures of Christopher's kids, all of which led detectives the Moorpark Street apartment. Pictures of bloody carpet and human tissue on the walls, the U-Haul truck and the refrigerator with its missing shelves were flashed onto the screen, evidence that connected Christopher Walsh to the apartment. On and on she went, linking the prominently displayed photos to both the victim and to David Steinberg.

"And finally, this would be towards the end of the *Law and Order* episode. Just when you think the defendant is going to get away with it, they come across the green goo. There is no evidence of green goo at the apartment. He was stuffed into the trash can there, but he was sealed inside at the storage unit," she said.

A close-up of the Rolex watch with the bright green "goo" clearly evident in its crevices jumped onto the screen.

She walked over to Steinberg and held the plastic evidence bag holding the Rolex watch and held it accusingly over his head.

"You be the criminalists. This green goo marks him like a highlighter would highlight your notes: 'This is the murderer. This is the murderer,'" she stated.

"Da-doink," DDA Ambrose added for emphasis.

"They may be liars, thieves, porn stars, Nazis, and white supremacists, but they were there. They saw it, and it's corroborated by the physical evidence. That's why you should believe them, because they were there," she continued.

Next she used Steinberg's own words to tighten the noose around his neck.

"Look at the letter from the defendant to Jeffrey Weaver in jail. Not once does he call Shane Wilson a liar. He says, 'Shane is the enemy,'" she pointed out. "He is against anyone who is 'in the game and rolls over,' not who lies."

DDA Ambrose was gathering steam, heading into her summation. Everybody in the courtroom had fallen under the spell of the fiery redhead.

"So, ladies and gentlemen, what are we left with? This was an ambush of an unsuspecting person sitting on the couch crashed out from drugs. This is a quote David Steinberg would truly appreciate. 'All it takes for evil to triumph is for good people to stand by and do nothing.' This is what he was counting on, because he didn't surround himself with good people. Shane Wilson is not a good person. He stood there while Christopher was bleeding and gasping and gurgling, and he did nothing. He left Christopher to die. That's what David Steinberg was counting on. It was all they talked about in prison and out of prison, in county jail, and they did nothing. It was the Walsh family who sought justice for their brother. His brothers cared. This was their baby brother. They weren't going to stand by and let these people do nothing. He was ambushed, executed, and shoved in the trash and the defense attorneys tried to paint them like some Mafia family because they used bad language. If this was a Mafia family, the scary, evil Walsh family the defense would paint them as, none of us would have had to spend the last three months of our life here. David Steinberg would have been shot in the back of the head and left to rot instead of sitting here in front of a jury seeking justice.

"On behalf of the People of the State of California, it has been my great honor. I thank you for your service in this matter," she told the jury.

DDA Ambrose had delivered a rebuttal argument every bit as powerful as DDA Sparagna's closing argument. Now the fate of David Michael Steinberg was handed over to the green jury.

It was late Friday afternoon. The green jury was ordered to return Monday morning at 9 A.M. to begin deliberations. Jury instructions and opening arguments in front of Weaver's red jury would commence at that time.

The die was cast; all I could do was wait.

Most of the morning of December 3 was taken up by Judge Pastor reading jury instructions to Weaver's jury while the green jury deliberated in the jury room. It was almost 11 A.M. when DDA Sparagna stood up to deliver her opening statement to the red jury. Her theme was basically the same as she had presented to Steinberg's jury, adjusted slightly to emphasize those facts that incriminated Weaver.

"This defense tried to put the Walsh family on trial. On a wiretap you will hear Troy Wilcox say to Jeff Weaver, 'I had the Walsh brothers in town this week fuckin' threatening me every day, "You know more than what you're telling us,"'" she stated.

"What Dennis Walsh was saying to people is 'You know more than you're telling,' not get in there and lie to the police," she explained.

She reminded the jury of Steinberg's kite instructing Weaver to remain silent, Weaver's wiretapped conversations with the Wilcoxes, and Weaver's confession to Diane Stewart.

"Jeff is totally incapable of shutting his mouth, and on behalf of the People of the State of California, we are very happy that Jeff couldn't shut his mouth," she said.

She told the jury that it would be Weaver's own words that would convict him.

The next morning, Seymour Amster rose to deliver his closing argument in front of a courtroom that had remained jam-packed.

"I want to try to make this entertaining. I'm going to reach back into my mom's side of the family and grab some of my old vaudeville genes," he told the jury.

He began by launching into a tortured dissertation of lessons he learned from his father and his father's service in World War II, followed by a rambling discussion of John Adams's service as the lawyer for a British military officer after the Boston Massacre.

Amster's point was completely lost on my brother Tim. "This asshole shoulda brought a case of Sam Adams if we gotta listen to this shit," Tim whispered.

"It gets better in the second act when his mother does her vaudeville routine," I replied.

I hoped Amster was irritating the jury as much as he irritated Tim. He proceeded to blame the murder solely on Steinberg.

"Nobody, with the exception of David Steinberg, is all bad or all good. David Steinberg is all bad," he proclaimed.

"It's not so much the Walshes are evil. Emotional? Yeah. Stubborn and see it one way? Yeah. Lived off a reputation? Yeah. Is that reputation true? I'm not sure. Chris Walsh made everybody think he was connected to the Mafia so he could be really bad. It's not that they are saying it, but it's out there. So these people, who want to buy and sell their meth, without having the police all over them, go to the police to get the Walshes off their back. They believed the Walsh family had a connection to the Mafia," he argued.

"Daniel Walsh tells police, 'You know our history. We won't tolerate that.' If I walk into the police station and say, 'You know my history, I won't tolerate that,' they are going to laugh at me," he told the red jury.

"Then we have this attack on Jeff Weaver by two brothers. They crossed the line. Did they feel they were immune from getting arrested?" he asked rhetorically.

"The police were investigating, but that's not good enough for the Walshes. They have to interview people themselves and feed them information for them to lie, not necessarily, but I can't eliminate that. The problem is that they are feeding them information. They are part of the grapevine. 'Dennis said Jeff fired the final shot because Jeff took the sunglasses.' That sounds like an emotionally involved individual who is saying whatever he can with his temper to let people know 'Don't mess around with me,'" Amster told the jury impassionedly.

Amster used a bench he had brought to demonstrate his convoluted theory that Christopher may have been shot while falling forward. The demonstration proved quite awkward in front of the jury.

"Do you believe this clown?" Tim asked.

"He would have been better off putting Stephanie in a box and sawing her in half," I whispered to Tim.

Amster finally finished his closing argument on December 5, reiterating that his client was wrongly accused, it was Steinberg who was the killer.

"Chris Walsh and David Steinberg. This was the classic confrontation of a gunslinger in the Old West versus the Prince of Darkness," he said in a mix of metaphors.

That afternoon, DDA Ambrose delivered the prosecution's rebuttal argument in much the same fashion as she had to the green jury. The red jury then retired to a different jury room from where the green jury was deliberating to begin its deliberations.

On the morning of the sixth, Judge Pastor addressed the Weaver jury: "We got a call from Red Juror Number Two. He is ill, so we are going to excuse you for the day. I heard that the storm of the decade is coming in. Three inches of rain expected in Los Angeles, so take that into account. See you tomorrow at nine A.M."

There was a nasty storm rolling in. Tomorrow, December 7, was the sixty-sixth anniversary of the attack on Pearl Harbor. It probably should have been evident that there was a bad moon on the rise.

Friday, December 7, was as miserable as Judge Pastor had predicted. Torrential rains pounded the L.A. area. Since both juries were in deliberations, I had time to pick up my sister Kathy at her friend's house in Chatsworth. We were in the cafeteria around 1:20 P.M., when Detective Fleming called my cell phone. He asked us to come up to Department 107. He sounded troubled.

Stephanie was waiting at the door to the courtroom. Her face was ashen. "There's a problem with the Steinberg jury," she said. "Please have a seat in the courtroom."

"Oh, God, please, no," I said to myself.

Kathy sensed something was afoot, but had no idea what was happening. We took our seats. The green jury was nowhere to be seen. My whole world was about to come crashing down.

"At the end of the morning session today, the jury buzzed and sent the following note," Judge Pastor announced to the mostly deserted courtroom.

"Dear Judge Pastor, after four and a half days of deliberation, I feel we are hopelessly deadlocked. Eleven jurors unanimously agree on seven of eight counts. One juror holds a completely opposite point of view. We feel that further deliberations will not change the votes. Count two is an eight/four split. We need your guidance on how to proceed," Judge Pastor read aloud.

I could barely focus on the fact that the jury had disregarded specific instructions not to mention the details of the split in the event of a deadlock. Instead, the irony that it was four and a half years since Christopher's body had been discovered, and now, after "four and a half days," the jury was hopelessly deadlocked, struck me as some sort of cruel, metaphysical hoax.

Judge Pastor had a brief discussion with the attorneys and then called in the green jury.

"I know that this trial took several months and that it is Friday afternoon. The weather outside is frightful. I think it best that we excuse you for the weekend. We ask you to simply forget about this case over the weekend, each of you. Come back Monday morning to resume your deliberations," the judge instructed.

As I rose to leave, I noticed Steinberg out of the corner of my eye. He had been waiting to get my attention. I made the mistake of turning my head in his direction. He smiled, ever so slightly, gloating over his good luck. I imagined him similarly grinning as he watched Christopher struggle to live, but didn't have the strength to leap over the railing to make him eat that evil smile.

We walked to the elevators with Stephanie and Detective Fleming in complete silence. We were all shaken to the core.

"Well, at least it's not over yet. The jury still has to come back on Monday," Stephanie quietly said without a trace of conviction.

I drove Kathy to her friend's house without saying a word. That night I sat in the dark with Johnny Rio and Frank the Cat, drinking Jameson until I passed out. I spent the rest of the weekend in a catatonic state, nursing a hellacious hangover, trying to watch football and Turner Classic Movies, one after another. The image of Steinberg's smirking face damn near ate me alive. I later learned that Stephanie Sparagna had spent her weekend in similar fashion, minus the Jameson Irish.

The brick foundation of the prosecution's case now appeared to support nothing but a house of cards, all aces and eights.

On Monday, the green jury resumed its deliberations. I was convinced we were facing a mistrial. In the meantime, Weaver's jury was unable to resume deliberations due to the absence of Red Juror No. 8.

Around 11 A.M. the judge announced that deputies had crashed down the door to Red Juror No. 8's house and found him comatose in the bathtub. The juror had suffered a stroke. The deputies' swift action had saved his life. Every day it was something new in this trial.

Mrs. Benson randomly selected Alternate Juror No. 3 to become Red Juror No. 8. The red jury was instructed to begin the process of deliberation all over, including picking a foreman.

In the meantime, after deliberating all morning, the green jury broke for lunch, giving all of us the slightest glimmer of hope. At the end of the day, they were excused without any mention of being deadlocked. Detective Fleming, Stephanie, Ann Ambrose, and I were exhilarated.

"It ain't over until it's over, Detective," I told Detective Fleming in the hallway.

The next morning, both juries continued to deliberate. Kathy had returned to Vegas for work. Both juries had been calling for read-backs of selected testimony. Once again the green jury broke for lunch without having announced a deadlock, another good sign.

My brother Dan had a birthday coming up on the 14th, Steinberg's was on the 17th, mine was on the 18th, and Weaver would be turning thirty-eight on the 20th. It remained to be seen who would have cause to celebrate.

A little after 2:30 P.M. I was sitting in the cafeteria doing the crossword puzzle when Detective Fleming called.

"Get up here right away," he said. "Steinberg's jury has a verdict."

I had been waiting an eternity for this moment. It seemed like forever before the light above one door in the bank of elevators finally lit up. I jumped in and punched the button for the ninth floor. The ride up was excruciating as the car stopped at just about every floor. I sailed through the metal detector on the ninth floor and into the hallway. Detective

Fleming stood in front of Department 107, motioning to me to hurry. In the anteroom between the hallway and the courtroom, he paused to clasp his hands in prayer. I was touched by the gesture. I took a deep breath and grabbed a seat in the courtroom as the green jurors entered the jury box.

After a few preliminary remarks, Judge Pastor read from the jury verdict form.

"People of the State of California, Plaintiff, versus David Michael Steinberg, Case PA046378, Los Angeles Superior Court, Department 107, Verdict Count One. We, the jury in the above-entitled action find the defendant, David Michael Steinberg, guilty of the crime of Murder in the First Degree in violation of California Penal Code Section 187 subdivision A, alleged date on and between June 24, 2003, and June 26, 2003, alleged victim Christopher Walsh as charged in Count One of the Information."

I was overcome with a wave of emotion, and struggled not to break down. The system had worked. David Steinberg was going to spend the rest of his life in a cage for murdering my brother. Most of the weight I had been carrying for years disappeared with Judge Pastor's pronouncement. The reading of the verdicts in the other seven counts was just a blur. Stephanie would relate them to me later.

Steinberg clenched his jaw and stared straight ahead. He was not about to give me the same satisfaction that I had given him. The judge discharged the jury and informed them that they were welcome to speak with the attorneys in the hallway. Sentencing was set for February 5, 2008. I hugged Stephanie and Ann and shook hands with Detective Fleming, thanking them as best I could. I wiped the tears from my eyes and walked into the corridor.

One juror, an African American woman in tears, ran up and embraced me. "Dennis, I prayed all weekend for you and your family that the hold-out juror would come around," she said.

Another juror, an Asian man, grabbed my hand with both hands. "I wish I had a brother like you," he said.

A couple of the younger guys just shook my hand and nodded. Yeah, they had gotten it, all right. Another juror explained that the holdout juror had been reluctant to convict Steinberg on the basis of the testimony of jailbirds, felons, thieves, and dopers. The other jurors led him through the many items of physical evidence, showing him how the words of those nefarious witnesses were corroborated by the evidence. Like Ann Ambrose had told them, "because they were there."

The DA's office had made the right call. Had they sought the death penalty, that holdout juror might never have come around.

I couldn't thank the jurors enough. Mrs. Benson came into the hallway and announced that the jurors needed to go to the jury assembly room to check out. I continued to talk with them as we walked to the elevators.

"How's your sister?" one woman asked. "I hope your family can find some peace now."

"Thank you, thank you, thank you," I told them all as we watched them cram into the elevator.

The door slid shut. Suddenly these people, who had been such a huge part of my life for the last few months, disappeared. It was as surreal as the scene I had come upon that first day at the Erwin Street storage facility.

"That's one down. Now let's get Jeffrey Weaver," Stephanie remarked.

The next morning a headline in the Los Angeles *Daily News* read, JURY CONVICTS IN CASE OF BODY KEPT IN STORAGE. The green jury had also found Steinberg guilty of the special circumstance allegation of lying in wait, but deadlocked 8–4 on the other special circumstance allegation of killing a witness. He was acquitted of making a terrorist threat against Carolyn Vasquez, but was convicted of two counts of attempted murder and assault with a semiautomatic firearm against Deputy Dixon and one count of assault with a semiautomatic firearm against Moises "Joey" Tovar. He was found guilty of possession of a firearm by a convicted felon. Steinberg was looking at two terms of life without parole, plus "a gang of time," as Don Mercatoris might say.

I spent most of the day in the courthouse cafeteria waiting for any word from the red jury. They deliberated all day with no results. The following day, December 13, Kathy joined me at the courthouse. Around 11:15, DDA Sparagna came into the hallway.

"The red jury has reached a verdict," she said somewhat somberly.

We were prepared for the possibility of a finding of not guilty on the first-degree murder charge. When the judge read the not guilty verdict, Kathy and I sat in anticipation of the finding in the lesser included charge.

Dear God, please don't let this fat bastard walk, I said to myself.

Seconds ticked by like days before Judge Pastor's words, "Guilty of the crime of Murder in the Second Degree," provided a welcome relief. Weaver's head slumped forward, perhaps like Christopher's head had reacted when Weaver pumped the .22-caliber slug into his brain.

Judge Pastor set Weaver's sentencing hearing for January 7, 2008. Weaver looked my way as he rose from the counsel table. I grinned and nodded.

Who's stupid now, Fat Boy, I thought.

Before the door to the lockup closed, Weaver flipped me the bird over his shoulder. We quickly adjourned to the hallway to speak with the red jurors. The scene was similar as with the green jurors.

It was finally over, although it would never really be over.

I enjoyed one of the best birthdays and most relaxing Christmas holidays in years. Nobody had beaten this case as the result of anything I had said or done. I was looking forward to the sentencing hearings, where my family and I would have the opportunity to address the murderers.

After the convictions, I received a call from Detective Fleming. "Fleming here," he said as usual. "I'm just calling to thank you, Dennis."

"Thank me? For what, Detective?" I asked him.

"I know Stephanie was on your back all this time," he replied, pausing to chuckle, "but if you didn't do what you did, we wouldn't have been able to make this case."

I had already felt vindicated by the guilty verdicts, but Detective

Fleming's comment meant the world to me. Not too many cops would be willing to share the glory with a civilian. This veteran detective had literally spent thousands of hours tracking down leads, interviewing witnesses, and shepherding wayward witnesses to and from the courthouse, all the while maintaining a cheerful and professional attitude. Detective John William Fleming is not only a kind and extremely modest man; he is also one the most decent individuals I have ever met.

The morning of Weaver's sentencing was dark and stormy. I was just about to put on a suit and tie.

"Fuck him," I said to myself.

I left the house dressed in jeans, boots, a cowboy hat, and a long black duster. As I strode down the hallway of the CCB ninth floor, I saw my mother in front of Department 107, squinting in my direction.

She finally recognized me as I approached. "Dennis, I didn't know that was you. I thought it was Wyatt Earp," she said as I kissed her on the cheek.

I wished I was Wyatt Earp. He had the satisfaction of killing the guys who murdered his brother.

The rest of the family and various friends were present as well. There were four or five extra deputies assigned to the courtroom. Inside the packed courtroom, my mother was permitted to speak. She thanked the court, the prosecutors, and the police for all they had done. She rebuked Weaver for killing her boy. I was barely able to listen, and was thankful that her remarks were brief. Christopher's daughter, Ashley, tried to speak, but was too distraught. The female bailiff and the court reporter had tears in their eyes. Stephanie said a few words on Ashley's behalf. Then it was my turn.

The fury that consumed me for four and a half years turned up a notch. I approached the lectern and slammed my cowboy hat down on one of the jury chairs. I made some comments to the court and then addressed Weaver directly.

"Remember when I told you to talk to the police or ride a murder beef for the rest of your life, and you told me, 'Don't get stupid'? Well, who's stupid now?" I asked.

"You need to get on your knees and thank God that when Tim beat the hell out of you on Kimmi Balmes's front lawn, we did not know that you were a shooter. Make no mistake about it, my brother Tim would have split your head wide open on the curb like a ripe melon," I said.

When I mentioned that he had his attorney smear me and my family at trial, Seymour Amster jumped up to protest. "I'm sick and tired of this, Your Honor," he complained. "Dennis Walsh threatened me during the trial."

Judge Pastor told him to sit down or he would have him handcuffed. At a hearing prior to trial, I had playfully put my arm around Amster and made a remark in jest to Stephanie's law clerk, Patrick Ball.

"Patrick, I can't wait until the trial is over so I can kick the shit out of Seymour," I said.

"Thanks a lot, Dennis," Seymour said. "I'm glad you feel you can kid around with me."

He clearly knew there was no threat intended. I finished delivering my statement through gritted teeth.

My brother Tim took the podium and delivered a short but not easily forgotten statement.

"First of all, Weaver, when my brother Dennis was talking, you were smirking. Take that smirk off your face, or I'll come over there and take it off for you. What my brother Dennis said about smashing your head open on the curb is true. Your Honor, I don't think I should say anything else," Tim fumed.

"Yes, Tim, we get your point," Judge Pastor managed to reply, causing some laughter from the spectators.

Weaver addressed my mother, my sisters, and Christopher's daughter, specifically omitting me and my brothers. He admitted that he should have called paramedics after Christopher had been shot, but denied having fired the final shot.

Judge Pastor sentenced Weaver to forty years to life. At his sentencing hearing on March 7, 2008, he was sentenced to an additional fifteen years, consecutive to the murder sentence, for the robbery of the adult entertainment business. He won't be eligible for parole until 2052. He'll be eighty-six years old, if he lives that long.

At Steinberg's sentencing hearing on February 5, 2008, the courtroom was once again filled to capacity. I took the podium to deliver my Victim Impact Statement, more or less the same statement I had made to Weaver, but specifically tailored for Steinberg. The text of that statement is as follows:

"I'd like to thank you for the Court's indulgence, Your Honor. It's been a long five years. A very painful, traumatic event for my family. My brother, Christopher Walsh, was murdered by this gutless coward who sits before us. He was shot in the back of the head by this gutless coward who sits before us. His body was stuffed in a trash can by this gutless coward who sits before us.

"Your Honor, there is no way to prepare for the gut-wrenching agony that follows when a family member is murdered. There are no words to adequately explain the pain and the sorrow. I will tell you that for the first few months, every morning when you wake up you think it is a nightmare, a terrible nightmare. Then you lay there and realize, no, it's the truth. You get up and do what you have to do. Finally you are able to go out, able to go back to work, able to deal with people. But it is never far from your mind. It is always there. It is like a cancer that eats away at you. It may have been almost five years ago, but to my family, it is like yesterday.

"My brother had a mother, a father, two children, two sisters, and three other brothers. Our family and friends have been here throughout this ordeal. I've been coming. I haven't seen anybody show up for David Michael Steinberg, except for a couple of hoodlums. That should give you some idea of the person we are dealing with.

"David Michael Steinberg, being unable to cope with life and the consequences of his own actions, decided to play God and take my brother's life in a cowardly, callous manner. He has no remorse for his actions, only remorse that he was caught. He actually thought he could get away with it, and if he had gotten rid of the body, maybe he would have. He caught a bad break there, then caught a few more bad breaks when this case was assigned to two very tenacious LAPD detectives, Detective John Fleming and Detective Brad Cochran. Then it got even worse for Mr. Steinberg when the District Attorney assigned Stephanie Sparagna and Ann Ambrose to this case.

"Your Honor, these people were a godsend to my family. On behalf of my brothers, myself, and my family, I'd like to thank these detectives and these prosecutors for their dedication in the pursuit of justice in their investigation and prosecuting this case so zealously. We will always be grateful for their effort and their commitment.

"Now, Your Honor, David Michael Steinberg, a career criminal, stands before you for sentencing after having been convicted of first-degree murder with special circumstances. You know what a murdering, lying coward David Michael Steinberg is, Your Honor. You saw him take the stand, and you heard him blatantly lie as if those twelve jurors were as stupid as the thieves, the dopers, and the morons that he normally associates himself with.

"Your Honor, I know that you have seen a lot of bad people come in and out of your court, but I don't know how many truly evil and conniving people as evil and conniving as Mr. Steinberg that you have seen, but I think you understand the depth of his depravity. So I would ask, Your Honor, that you sentence Mr. Steinberg to the maximum sentence for murdering my brother, life without parole, and that you run that sentence consecutive to any other sentence that you may dole out in this case.

"He can't even look at me. He couldn't look at my brother when he shot him in the back of the head. Look at me. Look at me, Silent Thunder. Do you realize how ridiculous that sounds now, how grandiose, and what a little man you actually are, Silent Thunder?"

Steinberg turned in his seat and flashed an evil, malicious grin. Had I taken one step forward, there would have been eighteen people flying across the railing and all hell would have broken loose. I held my temper.

"Sit there and grin," I continued.

"Do you remember when I spoke to you in San Fernando Court, and

I told you that you were in my ballpark now? You probably thought I meant the judicial system. Well, it was more than that, because I meant intellectually. From day one, I've been hearing about the genius David Steinberg, and for five years I haven't seen one iota, any indicia of genius. You were matched up with a couple of DAs that you couldn't compete with. You didn't go to college because you couldn't. You put yourself in the midst of people where you could appear to be someone smart and someone intelligent. And you really weren't, were you?

"It was my brother Christopher who first realized that. After listening to your self-aggrandizement, then living with you, he realized you were just nothing, the Emperor who had no clothes. He saw you as just a pathetic little man. You didn't like that. You craved respect from all those people, all those dopers, all those thieves, and there was nothing to respect. You were just a scared little man with a gun. When you saw how my brother treated you in front of these people, you were deathly afraid they were going to learn the truth about you. So you took matters into your own hands and eliminated your problem as well as a witness to the shooting at the Deputy Sheriff.

"Tell us again how smart you are, Mr. Steinberg. The shots to the back of the head, the storage facility, the refrigerator, the gloves, the storage key around your neck, your own incredible testimony, and the watch. You just had to take the stand, like we all knew you would, genius sociopath that you are. You had to talk about what a knockoff it was. Well, how smart are you now, Silent Thunder?

"I think this fine judge should order you to wear a dunce cap in prison for the rest of your life to give people a heads-up when you start telling them how smart you are."

At this point, the entire courtroom burst out in laughter. A few deputies tried not to laugh out loud.

"Let's hold it down, please, in the audience," Judge Pastor ordered.

I had not meant to draw that type of reaction, but was glad to see that my comment had humiliated the murderer. He glared straight ahead while I continued.

"You complained that I was in court tapping my wrist. You shoot my brother in the back of the head and stuff his body in a trash can, and you complain about me tapping my wrist?

"Well, I'm tapping on my wrist now. Tap. Tap. Tap. Your time is up. Level four time. That's where you're going. You're going to a life of misery. The rest of your life, you can think about this every single day.

"Some people would say that locking you up for the rest of your miserable life is justice. Well, true justice would allow you to be put in a room with me and my three brothers. I can assure you, you would die a slow and painful death. The last sensation you would have would be my teeth ripping out your jugular vein and spitting it in your face and watching you die like you watched my brother die.

"You need to get down on your knees and pray to whatever god or Satan that you answer to. Thank him that you got arrested immediately because as sure as I'm standing here now, you wouldn't have seen a courtroom. Instead, my family and I have to accept the fact that you will live like an animal in a cage for the rest of your life.

"Up until now, you have been in high-power lockup in county jail. I know how miserable that is, but it gets even better. Level four time. Be advised that whatever prison you go to, they will be made aware that you are not a big-time murderer. You're someone who shot his friend in the back of the head while he slept. See how much respect you get.

"Now, here's something I told your crime partner, Weaver. I want you to think about it. Think about the last cold beer you had, because you are never going to have another. Think about the last steak dinner you had, because you are never going to have another. Think about the last woman you were with, because you will never be with another. Every day my family will take comfort in the fact that you are doing hard, miserable level four time. Every time I grill up a couple porterhouse steaks and feed one to my dog, I'll know he's eating better than David Michael Steinberg, Silent Thunder.

"And know this. I'll be thinking about your private hell every day of my life. Every time something bad happens to you, every time you have to think about where you are, every time you close your eyes and think about the endless days and nights of hell that is your future, I'll be there. You're going to die in prison, old and alone.

"In the meantime, this is my promise to you. Take a good look at my face, Silent Thunder, because anytime you appear in court, you are going to see me. You should have picked someone else's brother to kill, but I guess you know that now.

"Like I told your crime partner, *'Coimhead fearg fhear na foighde,'* which in Gaelic means, 'Beware the anger of a patient man.'

"Your real hell is going to begin soon. You will be catching the chain anytime now, and I hope you can ride it without slitting your own throat like the pathetic little coward that you are. Thank you, Your Honor."

Judge Pastor imposed a sentence of fifty-nine years followed by two consecutive sentences of life without parole followed by twenty-five years to life. David Michael Steinberg will never see the light of day.

So that is my story of how I helped to avenge the murder of my brother, Christopher John Walsh, born September 17, 1965, died between June 24 and June 26, 2003.

EPILOGUE

D AVID MICHAEL STEINBERG AND JEFFREY Lawrence Weaver appealed their convictions on various grounds, with strong emphasis on my involvement in the case. In the State's opposition to their appeal, Mary Sanchez, Supervising Attorney General for the State of California wrote:

> Granted, Dennis Walsh is a street-wise criminal defense lawyer who could talk tough to the drug addicts, porno queens, and street criminals who were his brother's friends. Indeed, it took tough talk to get these "friends" to go to the police. But appellant Steinberg's attempts to color Dennis Walsh on appeal as a dangerous mob-connected avenger are not just over the top, they are irrelevant to the analysis of this claim: The jury was the sole judge of the credibility of the witnesses and it was solely the province of the jury to resolve any inconsistencies in their testimony.

> This case was not "created" by the Walsh brothers. It was appellant Steinberg who "created" this case out of his own fevered imagination: an evil stew of metamphetamine-induced paranoia, Sopranos-style gangster-mentality, and prison racism, culminating in the murder of Chris Walsh.

The California Court of Appeals, Second District, denied their appeals. The California Supreme Court denied their petitions for review. During the trial, David Steinberg was caught passing kite notes for members of the Mexican Mafia. As a result, the California Department of Corrections designated him as a validated gang member and transferred him to Pelican Bay State Prison, where only the worst of the worst are housed. He was subsequently transferred to High Desert State Prison. He then served time in the SHU, Security Housing Unit, at Corcoran State Prison, and was transferred to the Substance Abuse Treatment Facility at Corcoran. Jeffrey Weaver is currently serving his time at California State Prison in Lancaster. I drive by that facility a few times each month. I honk the horn every single time.

In 2009, Tony Shane Wilson, the ex–Shankster Gangster, caught yet another case and spent two years in jail and prison. When I visited him in Orange County jail, he hung his head as I told him that had he summoned paramedics, my brother may have survived. I contacted Detective Fleming to see that he was placed in protective custody and to speak with the DA in his behalf. He may be a despicable coward, but I don't believe he should get stabbed again for testifying. He was released from custody in September 2011.

Peter Kinsler, Debbie Wilcox, Indian Gary Balmes, Gary Schimmel, Scott Ryan, and the sweet Talking Tina Arnone are all dead. That particular lifestyle does not favor longevity.

The "lackey" George Jassick—who supplied the Shop-Vac, rented the U-Haul truck, and took possession of the bloodstained couch—returned to work for the studios, denying that he had any knowledge of being an accessory after the fact to murder.

Troy Wilcox, who had actively tried to dissuade witnesses from cooperating with authorities, finally understood the meaning of "Nobody walks." When his neighbor called me while the LAPD was raiding Wilcox's house, I called Detective Fleming. Coincidentally, he was standing in the middle of Wilcox's living room. They weren't having any luck finding any meth. I conference-called a confidential informant who suggested they check the crown molding. Wilcox wound up going to prison.

Don Mercatoris was released from prison in July 2009, after serving five years for the motel bust. He violated the terms of his parole and was returned to state prison. After his release in December 2011 he was arrested again and sentenced to 486 days in county jail. His sentence was no doubt enhanced due to his conviction on the motel bust. It's the gift that just keeps on giving.

Deputy Sheriff Alex Dixon retired from the sheriff's department shortly after the shoot-out with Steinberg and followed his legendary grandfather, Willie Dixon, into the field of music.

Detective Brad Cochran retired from the LAPD in 2005. It turns out that I represented his father-in-law in a civil matter in the 1980s. Detective John Fleming was nominated for the 2008 Top Cops Award for his outstanding work on the case. He received an honorable mention and accepted his commendation in Washington, D.C. I attended his retirement party in October 2010. He may be retired, but to me, he will always be Detective Fleming.

Detective David Holmes works out of the Robbery Homicide Division. Someday I expect to see him promoted to captain, and eventually maybe chief of police.

Judge Michael Pastor, who so expertly presided over the pretrial proceedings and the trial, exhibiting great care to be fair to both defendants, still sits in Department 107 of the Criminal Courts Building. He recently presided over the manslaughter trial of Dr. Conrad Murray for the death of music star Michael Jackson.

Deputy DA Ann Ambrose left the Los Angeles District Attorney's Office and moved out of state with her family. She has since had another child. In 2008, DDA Stephanie Sparagna was honored by the Association of District Attorneys for her exceptional efforts in obtaining the convictions of David Steinberg and Jeffrey Weaver. I still speak with her from time to time.

My "shooter," Barry White, who always had my back, works for the studios and remains on call. I hope I have no further need of his services.

My eyes and ears, Pat Murphy and Jim Cavanaugh, were finally able to get back to their own lives. I have no doubt they would be at the ready if the need arose. Cavanaugh proudly sports the T-shirt I gave him bearing the phrase HONORARY WALSH BROTHER on the front and NO, I AM NOT A WALSH BROTHER on the back.

Christopher's son, Shane, graduated from high school in 2011. My niece, Ashley, will soon graduate as well. My mother just celebrated her eighty-fourth birthday and vows to dance on my grave. My brothers Tim, Dan, and Bobby continue to toe the straight and narrow line. Kathy and Laura bravely shoulder the burden of being the sisters of the notorious Walsh brothers.

Frank the Cat passed away at age eighteen in 2008. My devoted wolf-dog, Johnny Rio, developed bone cancer. In 2009, after a year of chemotherapy, the vet came to the house and put him to rest. They're both buried on my property. Two more trusted companions a man never had.

Although I've managed to put the tragedy of my brother's death behind me, the murder of a family member has such a profound impact that it can never be too far from your thoughts. Participating in obtaining justice in behalf of my brother offers some small measure of satisfaction. Writing this story forced me to relive a very painful period of my life. Whether it proves to be cathartic remains to be seen. I manage to stay busy with my practice, my Border collie, Dusty, and my trusted paint, Rowdy, who turned eight in April 2012.

Oh, by the way, David Steinberg and Jeffrey Weaver, know this: If you ever escape from prison, you can count on running into at least one of the Walsh brothers.